George Balanchine

Don McDonagh

Photographs by Costas

Twayne Publishers

Twayne's Dance Series

Don McDonagh, Editor

Choreographer and Composer:
Theatrical Dance and Music
in Western Culture by Baird Hastings

Denishawn: the enduring influence
by Jane Sherman

George Balanchine
by Don McDonagh

George Balanchine

Don McDonagh

Twayne Publishers

George Balanchine

Don McDonagh

Published in 1983
by Twayne Publishers
A Division of G. K. Hall & Company
70 Lincoln Street, Boston, Massachusetts 02111

Printed on permanent/durable
acid-free paper and bound in
the United States of America.

This book was designed by
Barbara Anderson and typeset
in Garamond by Compset, Inc.
with Snell roundhand display type supplied
by Typographic House.

0-8057-9601-0
0-8057-9607-X (pbk.)

To
Georgi Melitonovitch Balanchivadze
Georges Balanchine
"Mr. B"

Contents

Preface

Writing about the work of George Balanchine involves dealing with over four hundred ballets, opera ballets, dance sequences for musicals, revues, dramatic productions, movies, cabaret specialties, television productions, and a circus parade for elephants and their riders. Just assembling an accurate chronicle of this enormous body of work, produced over sixty years, demands a large volume of its own.

The writer of a monograph is faced with the necessity of choosing those works from the total oeuvre that will represent the choreographer's enduring concerns. In a handful of cases there are obvious choices such as *Apollo, Serenade, Agon, The Nutcracker, Concerto Barocco,* and *Symphony in C.* A half-dozen others fall just a hair's breadth outside this group. Beyond them the writer must determine those ballets that complete the artistic profile.

In making my own selections I have been guided by two considerations, the first of which is excellence and the second thematic necessity. Given a choice between discussing *Chaconne* and *Symphony in Three Movements* or *Stars and Stripes* and *Western Symphony* the logical choice would be the first two. Yet they are part of a constellation of other ballets having similar concerns, whereas the *Stars-Western* duo is needed to balance *Ivesiana* in the canon of works using music by American composers. That is why they were included. Similar decisions governed the selection of all the works dealt with at some length in the text.

Since Balanchine is obviously destined to become a scholarly industry like Beethoven, Shakespeare, and Rembrandt, we can look forward eventually to discriminating discussions of all of his works.

Don McDonagh

Acknowledgments

Once again I am indebted to the Dance Collection, Performing Arts Research Center, New York Public Library at Lincoln Center; Astor, Lenox, and Tilden Foundations, its director Genevieve Oswald, and her considerate, professional staff. I am also indebted to Sarah Jefferies for her close reading of the text and helpful queries.

Chronology

1904   Georgi Melitonovitch Balanchivadze born in Saint Petersburg on January 22.

1914   Enters the Imperial School of Theater and Ballet.

1915   Appears on the stage of the Maryinsky Theater for the first time as a student dancer in *The Sleeping Beauty*.

1917   Bolshevik Revolution causes closing of the imperial schools and theaters.

1918   Schools and theaters reopened as state institutions and Balanchine resumes studies.

1920   First ballet, *Night,* presented, a duet for himself and Olga Mungalova (possibly Lydia Ivanova).

1921   Accepted into the Maryinsky company after graduation.

1923   First performance by the Young Ballet, with the bulk of the program choreographed by Balanchine, including *Marche Funebre*.

1924   Second and last performance by the Young Ballet. Departure from Russia with the Soviet State Dancers and decision to remain in Western Europe.

1925   Joins Les Ballets Russes de Serge Diaghilev as soloist and is appointed resident choreographer.

1928   Choreographs *Apollon Musagéte,* a ballet he recalls as being the turning point in his creative life.

1930–1931   Choreographs for the popular theater in London and Paris.

1932   Appointed the resident choreographer of the newly formed Ballet Russe De Monte Carlo and creates *Cotillon*.

1933   Edward James produces Les Ballets 1933 with Balanchine as chief choreographer. During its London season Balanchine meets Lincoln Kirstein, who invites him to found a school and company in the United States.

1934   Balanchine choreographs *Serenade*, his first ballet in the United States for the American Ballet.

1935   American Ballet resident at the Metropolitan Opera House, appearing in opera ballets devised by Balanchine and presenting isolated evenings devoted to ballet.

1936   Balanchine choreographs the first of eighteen Broadway musicals and revues. Establishes the title of choreographer in production credits for *On Your Toes* and designs danced sequences as integral plot elements for the first time.

1937   The first Stravinsky Festival comprising *Apollo, The Card Game,* and *Le Baiser de la Fée,* presented for two evenings at the Metropolitan Opera House.

1938   Severs connections with the Metropolitan Opera. Invited to Hollywood by MGM to choreograph *The Goldwyn Follies,* the first of four films he works on for as many studios.

1941   American Ballet Caravan undertakes a four-month tour of Central and South America, for which Balanchine choreographs *Ballet Imperial* and *Concerto Barocco*.

1946   Ballet Society is formed after World War II by Kirstein, with Balanchine as artistic director.

1948   At the invitation of Morton Baum, Ballet Society becomes the resident ballet company of the New York City Center for Music and Drama and changes its name to New York City Ballet.

1950   The company undertakes its first foreign tour, an eight-week engagement, six at the Royal Opera House Covent Garden.

1954   Balanchine choreographs his first evening-length ballet, *The Nutcracker,* and also the first ballet using the music of the then ignored Charles Ives, *Ivesiana.*

1956   Third European tour of New York City Ballet.

1957   Premier of *Agon,* the definitive junction of twentieth-century rhythms and the classical vocabulary.

1962   The second full-evening ballet, *A Midsummer Night's Dream,* and the company's first tour of the USSR. It marked Balanchine's first return to his native land since 1924.

1963   Precedent-setting grant by the Ford Foundation to establish national professional ballet instruction centered on the School of American Ballet.

1964   New York City Ballet moves to become resident of the New York State Theater at Lincoln Center.

1965   *Harlequinade,* the third full-evening ballet and the first to be choreographed for the new expanded facility. It was followed by *Don Quixote* with an original score by Nicholas Nabokov.

1967   *Jewels* acclaimed as the "first full evening 'plotless' ballet." The company appeared in its first annual summer season at the Saratoga Performing Arts Center, Saratoga Springs, New York.

1972   Second, "the great" Stravinsky Festival, during which Balanchine presents *Symphony in Three Movements, Violin Concerto,* and *Duo Concertant.*

1974   The full-evening *Coppélia* is given world premier at Saratoga Performing Arts Center.

1975   *Hommage à Ravel* festival on the occasion of the centennial of his birth, during which Balanchine presents *Tombeau de Couperin.*

1977   Premier of *Vienna Waltzes,* one of the most popular productions in the company's history.

1978   The first of a continuing series of telecasts of ballets adapted for Channel 13's (New York) *Dance in America.*

1981   A Tchaikovsky Festival, during which Balanchine presented his setting of the *Garland Dance,* a waltz from Act I of *The Sleeping Beauty.*

1982   The third "retrospective" Stravinsky Festival, which celebrated the enduring collaboration between composer and choreographer. It concluded on June 18, the correct centennial anniversary date of the composer's birth.

1983   Dies in New York April 30.

Chapter 1

The Choreographer's Concerns

George Balanchine is unquestionably the single most powerful artistic force in twentieth-century ballet, yet the exact nature of his contribution remains somewhat elusive even in the minds of many of his admirers. His ballets have entered into the repertories of companies throughout the world where the art of classical dancing is practiced, and of course they comprise the creative backbone of his own New York City Ballet.

He is widely known as the architect of "abstract" ballet, a term he himself disdains, and has influenced the work of virtually all contemporary choreographers. If anything could be designated as the international style it would be the abstract or plotless (Balanchine's preferred term) ballet to which he has dedicated his protean talent. In questioning the designation, he has asked how ballets with people in them can be considered abstract; yet the term persists because it contains a germ of truth.

His ballets have disengaged themselves from overt story telling in the great nineteenth-century narrative tradition, but significantly, have not abandoned the presentation of human relations by their interpreters. Casual inspection of his non-narrative ballets reveals works of great structural harmony and vigorous rhythmic impulse that on first glance may seem to be pleasing abstract designs with little emotional warmth. Similarly, the smooth execution of their intricacies is accomplished by his own company with such apparent ease that their physical virtuosity is often unremarked on. To the eye accustomed to observing nineteenth-century classics with stated plots and characters performed by dancers trained to move with the deliberate expansiveness of the declamatory style, Balanchine's masterpieces do appear to lack dramatic incident and often, virtuosic interpretation.

The appearance is deceiving, since his works require training of the highest order and they are saturated with human incident. Their form derives from the music to which they are set and their characterizations from the dancers' personalities as expressed through the steps of the classic vocabulary. The ballets are symphonic rather than operatic in shaping, and reveal very human and at times painfully exposed relationships in response to the musical demands.

Music and its interpretation lie at the heart of Balanchine's contribution to the ballet stage. For him creative activity stems first from the rhythmic structure of music and second from its allied attributes of melody, harmonic development, and other elements. If composers are the masters of time, then Balanchine is the master of visual realization of that time in human terms. He does not devote his energies to music visualization by assigning so many dancers to represent strings, so many the brass, and others woodwinds or percussion, but by creating a visual analogy in space that restates the musical structure with the trained dancer's body. In this effort he is guided by the music he has selected or commissioned, and the techniques and personalities of the dancers available to him. He familiarizes himself with the music to discover the composer's intent and then chooses a theme that agrees with it. Like his long-time friend and artistic collaborator the late Igor Stravinsky, he never sets out to fashion a masterpiece, but works with the materials available to make the best possible work. This requires the greatest sensitivity to both the score and the dancers who realize it, and accounts for the enormous variety contained in his body of work.

The importance of music cannot be overemphasized, as a simple glance at the titles of his ballets shows. To an extraordinary degree the titles of his works derive from the names of the musical compositions or their composers. His early *Theme and Variations* was set to the final movement (thema con variatione) of Tchaikovsky's third Suite in G Major for orchestra. When he decided to choreograph the entire work, the resulting ballet was named *Suite Number 3,* and presently is more precisely designated as *Tchaikovsky Suite Number 3.* When in 1947 he was invited by the Paris Opera Ballet to be its guest choreographer, he remounted several of his older ballets and created a new one to a little-known composition by Georges Bizet. It was given the name *Le Palais de Cristal.* A year later when he remounted it for his own company it was entitled *Symphony in C,* as was the music to which it was set. Throughout his career he has always tended to name his ballets after their musical antecedents and three-quarters of his ballets are so designated; those that are not are the exceptions. He has always asserted that his choreographic starting point is the music, and has been at pains to make this obvious to those who view his works.

Balanchine respects music and understands it as no other choreographer does. He is a trained musician, having attended the Conservatory in Petrograd (formerly Saint Petersburg, now Leningrad) as a student of piano and composition. This study was in addition to his regular training as a dancer at the Maryinsky School from which he also graduated. One of his earliest ballets during his first years as a choreographer was set to a waltz of his own composition. A regular feature of his visits to the parents of his first wife Tamara Geva (formerly Gevergeyeva) was an interlude at the piano, playing compositions that appealed to her father. While he was still a student in the Maryinsky School he was asked by fellow students to play for their dance recitals, and when the school was temporarily closed after the revolution in 1917, one of his temporary jobs was as a piano accompanist to silent films. Stravinsky thought enough of his ability to remark that he would have made a good concert pianist, but quickly added that he had a much greater gift, and that was as a choreographer. When Balanchine designed ballets to some of Stravinsky's spare, late scores the composer noted that these works revealed aspects of his own music to him.[1] Surely a rare tribute from one creative artist to another.

Balanchine came to his musical sensitivity quite naturally. His father, Meliton Antonovitch Balanchivadze was a composer and was called "the Georgian Glinka," his mother was musically educated and taught her children how to play the piano, and his brother Andrei is a composer who lives in the family's native Georgia. Music was a part of his life from the beginning and has remained so throughout his career. In a humorous aside describing his alertness to musical values he remarked, "I get killed through my ears."

He is justifiably proud of the quality of the New York City Ballet orchestra, whose playing has been compared favorably by Leonard Bernstein to that of virtuoso symphonic ensembles. This orchestra has had only two musical directors in its history, the talented conductors Leon Barzin and presently, Robert Irving. Balanchine has remarked that if people don't like to look at his ballets they can close their eyes and listen to the impeccable playing.

His selection of musical compositions has been adventurous, and in one notable instance the ballet orchestra presented the first New York performance of any kind for Iannis Xenakis's *Metastaseis and Pithoprakta* when Balanchine choreographed a ballet to the music.[2] The name of the ballet, it goes without saying, was *Metastaseis and Pithoprakta,* and music critics from the local press found themselves attending a ballet performance to review the composition, which was not programmed that season by any other performing group, musical or otherwise.

On selected occasions Balanchine has even conducted the orchestra for performances of his ballets, and he routinely makes his own piano reductions of scores if these are not already available. In the case of Bizet's long-lost Symphony in C it was an absolute necessity. The work had been composed when Bizet was seventeen and then put away when the composer reportedly feared that it would show too directly the influence of his teacher Gounod. It was uncovered in 1935, and Balanchine, who had been told of the score's existence by Stravinsky, decided that it would make a most suitable ballet to present to his French hosts. When he came to Paris to choreograph the work, however, no piano reduction had yet been made.

The business of making a piano reduction is an exercise of skilled musicianship and demands total familiarity with the composition as well as comprehensive knowledge of the coloristic capacity of the piano. These reductions are integrally important in creating a ballet, since choreographers work in the restricted space of a practice studio where there is no room for a full orchestra; of course the expense of one would be prohibitive. Each working hour produces perhaps a minute or two of finished choreography and the cost of an orchestra for a twenty-five-minute composition would seriously tax the budget of any organization, not to mention the patience of the musicians working in such fits and starts.

Thus by training, inclination, heritage, and conviction Balanchine came to regard music as the floor on which ballet rests. He has stated that the choreographer can't invent rhythms but can improvise for only a few minutes, and therefore needs a composer to provide the larger time structure required for sustained creative movement. It is this time aspect of music that engages his attention first and foremost when he considers a score for his own use. As a young choreographer, Balanchine worked with a wide variety of scores, and in one instance, to rhythmic declamation of poetry, but he has subsequently confined himself to music as the accompaniment for his dances.

Although he has choreographed ballets according to the framework of librettos, he really has a profound mistrust of words as the basis for danced incident. During the years that he was chief choreographer for the Ballets Russes of Serge Diaghilev, he had little choice but to work with librettos given to him. Similarly, he had little choice as to the music he would use, since Diaghilev selected the compositions and composers, and presented

Balanchine with the finished score. Fortunately, Diaghilev had adventurous and excellent musical taste and at times allowed Balanchine to work without a libretto, using the score alone as the subject of the ballet. Most fortuitously, one of these ballets was Stravinsky's *Apollo* (originally, *Apollon Musagète*), which Balanchine flatly stated changed his artistic life. For Balanchine the score is the plot of the ballet, supplying the mood and dramatic structure of what he creates within its framework. This structure is not literal, since Balanchine has created entirely different ballets to the same piece of music, most notably in the case of Stravinsky's "Variations in Memory of Aldous Huxley 1965," to which he made three different ballets to be presented as a unit. The first time the short eight-minute piece is played through it is performed by twelve women, the second time by six men, and the third time by a solo woman. The theme is stated in twelve tones and there are twelve variations, so characteristically, Balanchine selected twelve dancers for his first ballet, half as many for his second, and concluded with a solo "theme" woman performing the entire chromatic scale and variations on which the ballet is based. Just as characteristically, he called it *Variations.* Thus in addition to supplying the plot of the work, the music suggested its casting in terms of numbers.

The most important ballet of the ten Balanchine created for Diaghilev was *Apollo,* in which he first used the mature working methods that were to characterize his approach to all subsequent ballets. Considering its large emotional impact, the ballet is miniscule in numbers. It is cast for seven dancers, three of whom are only seen briefly at the beginning and at the end of the ballet; the development basically comprises the actions of one male dancer and three women. Whatever program provided the basis for the composition was Stravinsky's own and was incorporated into the music, which consists of two scenes. The first is the birth of Apollo and involves his mother Leto and two attendant nymphs; the second concerns the maturing of the young god and his relationship with the three Muses, Calliope (poetry), Polyhymnia (mime), and Terpsichore (dance as well as song). These three were selected by Stravinsky from among the nine Muses as being the most pertinent to the presentation of a ballet that was to celebrate the harmonious union of rhythmic movement and music.

Stravinsky composed the work for string ensemble, so that it has a singing quality throughout. It was originally commissioned by the Elizabeth Sprague Coolidge Foundation and was first performed at the Library of Congress in Washington, D.C., with choreography by Adolph Bolm who also danced the lead role. After this performance Stravinsky was free to offer the music elsewhere, and Diaghilev chose to mount his own production with Balanchine as choreographer. In a tribute to the composer in *Dance Index* in 1947, Balanchine wrote, "*Apollon* I look back on as the turning point of my life. In its discipline and restraint in its sustained one-ness of tone and feeling the score was a revelation. It seemed to tell me that I could dare not to use everything, that I, too, could eliminate. . . . I began to see how I could clarify, by limiting, by reducing what seemed to be multiple possibilities to the one that is inevitable. . . . It was in studying *Apollon* that I came first to understand how gestures, like tones in music and shades in painting, have certain family relations. As groups they impose their own laws. The more conscious an artist is the more he comes to understand these laws and to respond to them. Since this work, I have developed my choreography inside the framework such relations suggest."[3] Balanchine characterized the time patterns as being "uncomplicated, traditional," and choreographed the ballet using the traditional vocabulary but expanding it with novel lifts, poses and balances. Diaghilev, who observed the process, commented enthusiastically, "What he is doing is magnificent. It is pure classicism such as we have not seen since Petipa." Unfortunately, Diaghilev chose a French primitive painter to design the costumes and decor, which the composer felt were totally out of sympathy with the mood of the ballet. Over the course of the years, several changes have been made in these designs until at present, the Muses wear plain white tunics and the man a simple triangular white shirt and tights.

To the ancient Greeks, Apollo was the god of light, the arts, and prophesy, and the passage of the sun through the sky was associated with him. Poetic allusions were made to his chariot drawing the sun in its course, and images of his doing so were featured in Greek painting and pottery. In the ballet, his role as inspirer of the Muses became the central aspect, although at one point the three Muses line up beside him and each extends one leg outward to suggest rays of the sun emanating from him.[4]

The darkened stage is illuminated by a shaft of overhead light that picks out the figure of his mother Leto, seated above the level of the stage, stretching her arms outward and upward in distress. After this brief mime passage she bows forward and the young god emerges from the area beneath her, hopping forward with his torso wrapped in swaddling birth cloths. The two attendant nymphs move to him and support him as he leans stiffly back with his mouth open in a silent cry for assistance. They each grasp ends of the cloths and circle about him as they unwind the confining strips. He becomes impatient and whirls his body to spin free. It

Peter Martins in "Apollo"

is his first demonstration of independence, but after a few coltish leaps he stops, apparently bewildered. The two nymphs return bringing him a long-necked lute. Standing behind him they show him how to hold it and place his fingers on the strings. After he plucks them the stage is darkened. He has shown the mixture of dependence and fierce independence that will characterize his development throughout the ballet, as he realizes his mission as instructor of the Muses.

In the second scene he stands proudly in the center of the stage holding the lute authoritatively. With large circling sweeps of his arm he strums the instrument, but he is not yet its master. He reaches heavenward, with the fingers of his hand splayed out as if to grasp inspiration. He carefully places the lute down and begins his first solo dance, reaching out toward it then picking it up and holding it at arms length in front of him while he turns slowly. The Muses now enter from different corners and walk respectfully to him. He raises his arm to greet them and they acknowledge him with a bow. He kneels, holding the lute aloft and they form a three-pronged cluster around him as they extend one leg upward with an arm resting lightly on his shoulders. Their destinies are entwined in the service of art and he is the center of that process.

He rises and they follow him to the center of the stage where they stand side by side. With a slicing gesture of his arm he separates Terpsichore from the other two and stands behind her. She leans back and he gently lowers her to kneel on the stage. The other two come to him and he powerfully grasps each around the waist and lowers them to the floor. He shows his partiality to the Muse of dance early, and develops this predilection as the ballet proceeds. The other two Muses are his charges as well, but he doesn't dance singly with them as he does with Terpsichore.

She rises and joins hands with her still kneeling sisters and Apollo, and circles them. They stand together as Apollo leaps around the stage in a large circle, after which he returns to them. They cluster tightly and shuffle about on their heels taking little babylike steps as they are linked with him in this initial stage of their involvement. Without them he has no vessel to embody his creative energy and in turn they depend on his animating force for their fulfillment. Their close attachment in this passage and elsewhere in the ballet stresses their mutual dependence. Now, however, their relationships have not yet been fully developed, so they link themselves to one another with simple hand-holds. The Muses come to rest in a line and Apollo gently elevates them on point with a push that sends them into a short walk taking tiny steps in unison, this time elegantly on pointed toes rather than earth-bound heels.

Now Apollo stands, and with a firm, commanding thump of one raised and lowered heel summons them to receive the symbols of their respective arts. Terpsichore is first, again a sign of favor, and receives a lyre. Polyhymnia receives a mask and Calliope a scroll. Apollo sits grandly on a low stool down at the front of the stage to the right and observes how well each of them is versed in her art. The first to dance for him is Calliope, who clasps her scroll to her heart and then places it down. She puffs up her chest and shoots one arm tautly and dramatically in a curve up across the torso and extends it palm outward from the mouth. She is emotionally expressive and continues to use this gesture as she circles the stage with large swings of one leg. She pauses and points her forefinger and then repeats the emotional gesture. Finally she makes hasty little scribbling gestures on her palm as if she were still working on her verse. At the end of her variation she kneels momentarily at Apollo's side. He averts his gaze and places his hand as a shield over his face to show his disapproval. Admonished, she darts quickly off, hiding her own face in shame since her unfinished, word-based art did not find favor with him.

Polyhymnia enters with her mask and places it down but places her forefinger across her lips to emphasize the silent nature of traditional mime artists. The spritely nature of her dance expresses her bubbling good spirits and exuberance, however, this is her undoing as she suddenly bursts out of her traditional silence and makes a silent shout. Appalled at her error she quickly claps her hands over her mouth, but the damage has been done. She has violated the rules of her art form and Apollo raises his arms angrily to send her away.

Terpsichore enters holding her lyre aloft and dances with her body in profile. Her movements are balanced and harmonious, undistorted by the dramatic exclamation of Calliope or the unwarranted play-acting outburst of Polyhymnia. She embodies the balance that is restrained and yet expressive, and which is designated apollonian in its classic blend of form and content. She finds favor and Apollo rises to salute her. She is the mistress of her art and has demonstrated it in the pleasing control of her dancing.

Alone now, Apollo dances his second solo, which relates to the first one but is more accomplished and complete. He starts with arms stretched upward with palms bent out, suggesting the shape of a lyre, Terpsichore's symbol, and reemphasizes his pleasure with her art above all the others. The pleading gesture of the outstretched arm with splayed fingers is now completed with the second splayed hand just visible at his waist. As the overhead hand clenches the other one opens, almost as if he gathers energy with the one hand, passes it through his body, and dispenses it with the other. His own dancing is grand and vigorous but as he has done in the past, he tires himself with the discharge of energy put into his exuberant dancing and he sinks to the floor, momentarily exhausted.

One arm is held out with a forefinger extended and sweetly Terpsichore returns to touch it with her own, which revivifies him. The image is reminiscent of the Michaelangelo fresco in which the vibrant hand of God reaches for the weak hand of Adam who also is reclining. It is a curious reversal; the god of this ballet is now being revived by one of his subject Muses. It underlines the interdependent relationships of the God-subject, teacher-pupil, choreographer-dancer that is shown by the ebb and flood of energy between the two. They are linked in their dependence on one another: without her the art would lack form and without him it would lack energizing force.

They begin their climactic duet with him still on the ground. Throughout, their mutual dependence is reiterated in a variety of ways. Drawing up his knees he offers her a "seat," which she occupies fleetingly. He holds her in a supported arabesque over himself, displaying her as he would a wonderfully wrought object. He rises and they dance gracefully and then suddenly kneel facing one another. He offers her his palms and she places her elbows on them opening her own palms to him and he blissfully rests his own head on them momentarily. Refreshed, he offers her support on his back while still kneeling, and she gracefully balances on it. Both softly sweep their arms as if swimming in a striking image of balance and grace. As he eases her to the ground he rises and she remains curved to his back. They have been united in a dance of serene order and control.

They separate as Calliope and Polyhymnia return to canter with pulsing grace. Terpsichore joins them and does a brief solo just before Apollo returns, dashing on with a vigorous leap that makes the kneeling Muses almost appear timorous. While in the air he half turns his body, lands triumphantly, and lunges forward. The mood of joyful fulfillment accelerates as Apollo stands and flexes his muscles, bringing his clenched fists to his shoulders. Calliope and Polyhymnia swing from his arms, demonstrating both his strength and their dependence. He joins all three Muses in a team, the traditional Russian troika, and holds them in control while exhorting them. He reins in the team and pirouettes as they watch. They clap their hands and extend their palms, on which Apollo suddenly slumps his head. Again we have a momentary pause as he gathers his strength. He raises his head and strides around as if listening, then returns to the Muses who have patiently seated themselves to wait for him. He extends his palm over them and one by one each raises a leg to touch the palm with the tip of her toe to confirm their unity with them.

He makes a large circle of his arms and they in turn circle one of their own arms around his. Now the four interlocking arms confirm their total involvement and they turn in an intricate meshing of bodies and arms that are always linked, shuffling along on their heels with the tiny steps they used when they first encountered one another. Then they held hands but now they are fully committed to one another. The formation breaks and Apollo takes them by one hand and this time draws them along behind him. It is the last time that they will lead him, he has established his priority of place. They follow him in a single line with Terpsichore closest to him as he ascends a ramp leading upward to Olympus. The end of the procession is joined by his mother Leto and the two attendant nymphs. Leto sinks backward, as her son has now demonstrated his maturity. Her outstretched arm suggests a combination of farewell and respectful celebration of his new state.

Thematically, the ballet strives for balance and order against dionysian excess. Expressiveness has to live within the rules of art, not exceed its boundries. These are the rules both for the Muses and Apollo. Polyhymnia broke her silence and was rebuked by Apollo, while they in turn had to call him to order with a hand-clap when his exuberance threatened the order they sought. Balanchine wrote that "he [Apollo] is the wild half-human youth who acquires nobility through art." In another light he might also be the indiscriminately inventive choreographer taming and shaping his creative gifts for greater expressiveness through restraint. The image of Terpsichore balanced on his back in the "swimming lesson" remains a most vivid demonstration of such measured order.

The use of the extended forefinger is a subtle and telling bit of gestural economy. Calliope points and "scribbles" in her palm with it, breaking the rules of her art of declamation. Polyhymnia holds her forefinger in front of her lips to remind herself to keep still, but she breaks her silence and loses favor. By contrast, Terpsichore uses her forefinger to revitalize the momentarily exhausted god.

Although Balanchine had always worked sensitively with music, this collaboration with Stravinsky set the course of his future creative life. Henceforth, his most fully realized ballets took their plot lines from the score to which they were mounted. The ballet was first presented in 1928, and while Balanchine remained in Europe with Diaghilev until 1929 and then with the Ballet Russe de Monte Carlo (1932) and his own Les Ballets

1933, he still prepared ballets using librettos. He took his choreographic inspiration, however, from the music, which was commissioned or arranged by himself. A brilliant example of the latter was *Cotillon,* with notes by Boris Kochno who also had been a collaborator of Diaghilev's. Balanchine decided that the eight sections of the ballet would be best served with music composed by Chabrier. Accordingly, he selected six of the "Dix Pièces Pittoresques," rearranged their order, repeated one, and included the third of the composer's "Trois Valses Romantiques" to complete the score. Ordinarily this work would be done by a company's musical director, but an accomplished musician such as Balanchine naturally did it himself.

In effect he was writing the libretto by arranging the order of the musical selections. Subsequently he would do the same for a variety of ballets including *Serenade, La Valse, Jewels, Who Cares, Glinkiana, Stars and Stripes, Union Jack, A Midsummer Night's Dream, Vienna Waltzes,* and *Western Symphony.* In these ballets his musical intervention was major and elsewhere minor such as the inclusion of two selections from Delibes's Sylvia Pas De Deux in the Act III duet for the principals in his *Coppélia.* What was constant, however was Balanchine's extreme attentiveness to musical values.

The use of music to supply the atmosphere and indicate the action of a ballet did not originate with Balanchine. Choreographers have created dances to reflect the mood of music from the start of ballet history, but the main thread of its artistic development wound around a stated libretto with identifiable characterizations for its dancers. In the case of the brilliant Jean-Georges Noverre, these librettos reached pamphlet thickness. Narrative and dramatic complexity were the tradition of Russian ballet as well, and it was this ordered world that Balanchine entered to take his training. He rebelled against it and found a secure base for his own choreography in the balance and structure of music. As a trained musician he penetrated to the heart of the music he had selected, in the way that a conductor or a trained pianist will study a score analytically to be able to interpret it to an audience. This interpretation means respecting the composer's time and expressive markings to make the overall shape of the composition comprehensible to an audience. This shape conveys the intent and presents the thoughts and feelings of the composer as embodied in the particular sequence of notes and pauses through whatever scoring he has chosen. The difference, of course, is that in addition to being a trained musician Balanchine is a choreographer, so that his interpretations take visible shape. His performance of a given score takes place through the bodies of specially trained dancers in whatever numbers he feels appropriate. Also, among his dancers he selects certain ones for certain ballets because they have a quality of movement that is appropriate to the tone of the music. Perhaps it is straightforward vigor, perhaps demure innocence, perhaps a sensuous appeal. Whatever it is, it is right for this ballet.

In effect, the dancers are being cast for roles by virtue of the qualities of movement that derive from their individual characters. It is type-casting, and the dancers are asked to play themselves but to do so with the new series of step combinations that make up the ballet.

At times these are obvious, as in the case of a romantically alluring dancer, but at other times they are quite subtle and require real study to come into focus. In this way Balanchine's ballets make very real demands on audiences.

With stories abandoned, a very convenient handhold has been removed for the audience. What has replaced it is a less literal, nonverbal musical score. Without assigned characters the dancers supply characterization by projecting their personalities through the steps. While the ballets are sumptuously ordered in the placement of dancers on stage and the fluidity of transformations from one grouping to another, they can appear to lack motivation unless the relationships of the dancers to one another are carefully observed. It requires a slightly different way of watching, one that is more alert generally, and that demands listening quite carefully to the music. Whatever happens on stage has already happened first in the music and that is why its visual interpretation takes that special shape. The result has been described as "hearing dancing and seeing music." This is the way that the musically sensitive choreographer has arranged it. He trusts and respects music for its ordering of time. Since dancing is the only art form that expresses its message both in time and in space, Balanchine stripped his ballets to the essence, moving in direct response to a musical pulse without any literary pretext to get in the way.

To achieve this creative juncture, he had to change the technique of classical ballet as it was taught. As any live art form, ballet has evolved its techniques gradually over the years, always being shaped to conform to the needs of great choreographers. Innovations were absorbed in the system of instruction in the schools and passed on to generations of pupils. The schools in and of themselves tend not to change anything, but to respond to the creative needs of dancers and choreographers. What musician-choreographer Balanchine needed was dancers who could move more quickly; not necessarily faster, though this is useful as well, but who could in effect dance more steps in the same amount of time than had previously been done. This was necessary because the plots of the ballets that Balanchine was creating were musically based and were quite dense with musical incident. Thus to be able to present his interpretation of these nonverbal scripts, the dancers' training had to change.

There are shades of differences between various national schools of ballet, but to a great extent they adhere to the broad conventions of dancing time, which to a great extent is not musicians' time. Dancing time is slower, and in fact dancers will never be able to pack as much incident into a given moment as a trained musician can with an instrument. One of the basic reasons for slower performing time has been the accepted practice by dancers of making preparations; those anticipatory stances that are assumed before launching into a virtuosic move. Of necessity the music has to slow down to accommodate the dancers, or the effect of a simultaneous physical display will not coincide with the musical effect it is supposed to match. For Balanchine, such mauling of music was unacceptable. It had to be played as close to the composer's rhythmic pulse as was possible. It became necessary therefore to dance without preparations, which would enable dancers to move within the composer's time scheme and smoothly include all of the movement that Balanchine had choreographed into the musical phrase.

Presently, Balanchine's company, New York City Ballet, dances without preparations and is the only one to do so as a matter of creative necessity. One of the reasons that Balanchine's ballets never look as good when they are presented by other ballet companies is that the dancers cannot keep both to the musical time indicated by the composer and to the choreography, thus they distort the shape of the ballets. Also, members of other companies inadvertently reveal the virtuosity necessary to dance these works, for by slowing them, they highlight the intricate difficulties involved in dancing the ballets correctly. At times the ballets look more spectacular when danced in this way, but they don't have the same musicality. It is this musical flow that contributes to the "hidden" virtuosity of New York City Ballet dancers. Unless the music has a pause in it they cannot insert one to take advantage of a particularly difficult feat and in effect, hold it up for a moment to let the audience admire it. The difficult move is incorporated into the overall choreographic design and the ballet moves ever onward.

An audience accustomed to seeing Balanchine's works as presented by New York City Ballet learns to appreciate the technique necessary to perform them, but at first glance one is taken much more by the flow of the entire work rather than by virtuoso incidents. To appreciate the magnitude of this change in traditional balletic pedagogy, a sports analogy may provide a useful frame of reference. Football is a game of exciting incidents with "preparations" before each down as players assume prepared stances. Ice hockey, on the other hand, is a game of continuous flow in which the players move steadily but at varying speeds. The important thing is that they are moving all of the time. If one removed the preparations from football while retaining all of the action, it would be comparable to the transformation Balanchine has made in the traditional manner of dancing. His choreography is simply denser and faster, thus music has dictated virtually every aspect of his art: it changed technique itself, it guides the shaping of the ballets, at times it suggests the number of dancers to be used and determines the length of the works, and sets the tone of the ballets, which accounts for their truely astonishing variety. The only thing that music does not do is supply the impetus to create ballets. That derives from Balanchine's adoration of women.

More exactly, it derives from his endless interest in the ways that the classically trained female body can move, which presents a continuous challenge to reshape and present that body in ever new ways. He has made brilliant ballets with wonderful roles for the male dancer, but he maintains the supremacy of the female. "Ballet is woman," he has been quoted as saying. Interviewed during a tour of the Soviet Union in 1962, Balanchine elaborated his basic belief: "I consider that woman is queen of the dance and that man is but her page, her aide. I am always extremely sorry if some beautiful, talented ballerina expresses through her movements only some literary theme. The human body and particularly the feminine body is truly beautiful in itself."

While Balanchine's all-consuming interest in making ballets for female bodies that intrigued him has produced a string of masterful ballets, it has tended to destabilize his relationships with the women themselves. Tamara Geva writes candidly of her marriage to Balanchine when they were both teenagers in Russia in the aftermath of the revolution. Because of the unsettled times, her father abruptly suggested to them that they would be better off married.[5] A bit taken aback, the two agreed and were married in 1923. They managed to leave Russia a year later and were hired by Diaghilev for his company; she as a dancer and he as dancer and choreographer. Diaghilev then proceeded to dictate the ballets and their casting; none of which included Geva in any major way. She left and Balanchine stayed. His attention fell on Alexandra Danilova, who had fled Russia with them and was now one of the reigning ballerinas of the company. Their relationship lasted until he chose not to include her in a new company that was being formed in 1932. After his emigration to the United States he met and married Vera Zorina in 1939. Their marriage foundered after he choreographed a couple of unsuccessful Broadway musicals, one of which starred Zorina. In 1946 he marred Maria Tallchief, but the marriage was annulled six years later. He married another ballerina from the company, Tanaquil LeClercq, in 1952 but her career was ended by a polio attack in 1956 and Balanchine abandoned dance to stay with her. Eventually, however, the pull of ballet brought him back and they were quietly divorced years later. He never married again but continued to have various Muses to inspire him, most notable among whom have been Suzanne Farrell and then the youthful Darci Kistler, promoted to principal dancer at age 18.

Balanchine has always been attracted by youth, since for him creatively, it represents the largest number of yet untried possibilities. This has been true throughout his entire career. It was the presence of the famed "baby" ballerinas Irina Baronova, Tatiana Riabouchinska, and Tamara Toumanova, all of whom were in their middle teens, that caused him to tell Danilova, age 28, that she was too old for his new company. For Diaghilev she had been the extremely valuable successor to the legendary Karsavina. The result of his creative fixations has been a string of new ballets for the public and wonderful roles for the women who inspired them; their special individual qualities have been brought out as no other choreographer could have done or has done. Despite deteriorated personal relationships, they have retained professional contact, and Balanchine continues to create ballets being guided by his twin stars, fine music and exceptionally gifted ballerinas. It is what he does best. "Nobody asks a horse what he does all day. A horse lives as a horse," he has commented when asked about his work. He himself moves people to music.

Chapter 2

Beginnings

Georgi Melitonovitch Balanchivadze was born in Saint Petersburg on January 22, 1904, the second of three children.[1] He was preceded by an older sister Tamara and followed by his younger brother Andrei. Saint Petersburg then was both the cultural and political center of Russia and the residence of Czar Nicholas II. It was a cosmopolitan city and Russia's chief contact point with the West by virtue of its access to the Baltic Sea. The arts flourished under the personal patronage of the czar, and none more glitteringly than ballet.

Balanchine's mother encouraged her children to play the piano by example and urging. All of them did, and Andrei later pursued a career as a composer. When she reached the official age for admittance to the Maryinsky School, Tamara was taken by her mother for an audition. The ten-year-old Georgi was taken along as well, but without any intention of having him perform; it was thought that he should pursue a naval career. While waiting, however, an acquaintance of the family suggested it would not do any harm if Georgi auditioned as long as he was there. He was accepted and Tamara was not.

As a student at the Imperial School for Theater and Ballet he was officially a member of the czar's household. The financing of the theaters in Saint Petersburg and Moscow, their schools, and performing companies were all paid for from the ruler's private purse, not from the government treasury. This gave the performers access to the highest authority in the land on an informal basis. The czar and czarina customarily attended performances of opera and ballet in the royal box of the Maryinsky Theater, where they would receive visits from artists whom they wished to praise

17

and distribute gifts. They also visited the school for the young aspirants to the ballet company and had dinner with the students on selected ceremonial occasions.

The very day that Georgi was accepted he was enrolled and delivered to the Imperial School. It was a boarding school and his mother left him and returned with Tamara to their home in the suburbs. Completely upset at the sudden change in his life for which he had in no way been prepared, Georgi ran away. He was taken in by an aunt who was sympathetic but who firmly brought him back to the school. It was August 1914 and his career got off to a somewhat hesitant start.

The life of the school was strictly but not harshly regimented. Both boys and girls wore uniforms and lived in supervised dormitories. Family visits were permitted once a week and the children returned home during summer recess. Otherwise their lives were spent in classrooms or at the Maryinsky Theater. Since the stage was their ultimate destination, they were introduced to performance early. After the first miserable year in training, Georgi's life was brightened when he was taken to the theater in his second year to appear as a cupid in *The Sleeping Beauty.* The splendor of the production entranced him, and the regimen of the school became for him a means of gaining entry to this most wonderful of worlds.

The lavishness of these productions was made possible by the completely noncommercial nature of the imperial theater system. It was maintained for the pleasure of the court and did not in any manner have to pay its way. Theatrical designers and stage engineers were encouraged to present spectacles without any thought to cost or efficiency. With such encouragement it is not surprising that stage effects were truly spectacular. A ship under sail would founder, if this was needed, a house would be consumed in flames, an entire palace would become overgrown with vegetation on cue. There seemed no limit to what was possible. In one memorable instance when the effect of a heaving sea was desired, a detachment from a nearby military regiment was dispatched to crawl beneath a cloth covering the stage to imitate the motion of the waves. Having performed their function, they marched back to their barracks. Nothing like the imperial theater system existed anywhere else in the twentieth century and Georgi was eager to become a part of it. It had the splendor of ritual, the beauty of disciplined movement, and in *The Sleeping Beauty,* the finest ballet score Tchaikovsky ever wrote.

The turmoil of the outside world only lightly touched the children of Theater Street, the broad cul de sac outside their dormitory. As a gesture to show solidarity with the soldiers at the front they gave up the use of sugar one day a week, but opera and ballet continued to be performed at the Maryinsky Theater and dramatic productions continued at the Alexandrinsky Theater down the street from the school. The country was suffering a series of defeats that imperiled its entire fighting capability. The internal dissent that had plagued Russia from the turn of the century still existed but was controllable by the authorities; however, the worsening situation of the army and navy contributed to continuing unrest. It was obvious that the war was being mismanaged by an incompetent imperial government. Agitation grew bolder and the arrival of Lenin from exile increased the level of revolutionary activity.

The harsh realities of political contention reached the children of Theater Street in 1917 when the final wave of revolutionary activity deposed the czar. It was an unthinkable situation. The children had been brought up to believe life was impossible without the presence of the czar, the "little father" they addressed familiarly when he visited. But the unthinkable was to become a way of life for all the residents of Petrograd, as Saint Petersburg was renamed at the outbreak of war.

Anything to do with the imperial system was suspect in the eyes of the revolutionaries. The school was closed, the children sent home, and it appeared that ballet would be permanently undermined. Life for Georgi became a race for survival. Food was scarce and he, like virtually everyone else, spent his days in a desperate search for daily nourishment. Currency was worthless, the city was ruled by martial law, and chaos replaced the ordered world he had so recently occupied. As his future friend Stravinsky accurately observed, "I was born into a world of cause and effect and grew up in a world of chance."

The world of chance decided to give ballet another opportunity to prove itself. The school was reopened by order of the Minister of Education, Anatole Lunacharsky, a devoted follower of ballet. This time no regiment of soldiers would be dispatched to make waves in a production. There would not even be enough fuel to heat classrooms, studio, or theater. Food would be scarce, but the staff reassembled and started to pick up the pieces. The only sure and unchanging order in this chaotic world would be the regular discipline of daily dance class and its techniques of classical ballet.

During this time Georgi lived with the aunt who had sent him back to school when he had run away. His parents had moved to Georgia, where it was hoped life would be somewhat easier, but Georgi had been left behind to await reopening of the school. Georgi developed a reputation for his skill at the piano and was in constant demand as an accompanist.[2] The theater had also been reopened, and the students were called on to perform at irregular intervals. It was a far cry from the imperial days, however. Now their performances were preceded by political meetings and the audiences remained wrapped in their outer clothing because of the cold. But this was the theater that had housed the tradition of ballet, and the students were able to perform so that their lives had some focus in their new, uncertain world.

Toward the end of his formal schooling Georgi designed his first ballet, *Night,* for fellow student Olga Mungalova and himself to a score by Anton Rubinstein. It was an adagio, and did not follow the usual form of the pas de deux with its opening, individual variations, and closing coda, but was more loosely structured, in one movement. It was presented in the little theater in the school and was well received by the students, though faculty opinon tended to be disapproving. (One member wanted to dismiss him from the school but the director wouldn't go so far.) The principal violation was having the female dance on point while costumed in a tunic, which broke the rule (i.e., custom and usage) that point work was reserved for dancers wearing the classical tutu. Another ballet, *A Poem,* featured Danilova and himself and was even more daring. He entered with Danilova lying across his shoulders and arms. This was thought to be going too far altogether. Overstepping the bounds of costuming could be tolerated, but the voluptuousness of draping a girl across the body was beyond the permissible. In the tradition of the imperial ballet contact between male and female was confined to the waist, when the male would support his partner in turns, to one hand when he would lead her around in a promenade, or to the man's shoulder where she might pose her hands while lightly maintaining balance. It was unheard of to hang a woman over your shoulders. It wasn't done, it wasn't proper, in fact it was obscene and shocking. So from the beginning, Balanchine succeeded in disturbing an audience. His fellow students, however, clamored to be allowed to perform his little ballets.

In 1921 Balanchine's class graduated and he was taken into the corps de ballet of the Maryinsky Company. His training had prepared him to become part of the tradition that had managed to survive the revolution. Unfortunately, he did not enter into the secure world of regular pay, guaranteed pensions, and a stable society. Instead, the salary was meager and sporadic, and everything in society was open to question. Lunacharsky had only been able to reopen the school and theater by making a case for the propagandistic value of the art form. This political orientation would soon enough dominate ballet in Russia, but for the moment the world of ballet was open to change.

The entire society had been stood on its ear, the "little father" and his family had been murdered, sheer survival became a triumph, commerce was chaotic, a new political system was engaged in a civil war for survival, in the border provinces foreign expeditionary forces were striving to unseat the new government, the ports had been closed to trade, and the aristocratic customs of the imperial days seemed totally out of date. In the arts a period of experimentation began that saw an enormous fertility of plastic, visual, musical, and literary imagination. The period ceased abruptly in 1929 when Stalin emerged as the clear victor in the struggle for Lenin's mantle, but the decade after the revolution was the most brilliant creative period in Russia's modern history. Later, the socialist realism of picture postcard art was officially imposed and the works of Malevitch, Tatlin, Kliun, Popova, and a score of others driven underground. Composers Shostakovitch and Prokofiev managed to survive, though they were somewhat chastened. Poets Anna Akmatova and Ossip Mandelstam were out of favor and Mandelstam ended up in the gulag. Experimenters Fyodor Lopukhov, Nikolai Foregger, and Kasyan Goleizovsky were discouraged from their attempts to change traditional ballet. Full-evening ballets with morally uplifting tone (i.e., prorevolution) were demanded. Lopukhov ended up restaging the classics, which were "safe," Foregger became a regisseur in provincial companies, and Goleizovsky retired to a shadowy world of semiretirement out of the mainstream. For the moment, however, their experimentation was approved, and it affected the young Balanchine.

Painters make pictures, writers complete manuscripts, and choreographers design ballets out of an inner compulsion. While Balanchine enjoyed performing well enough, he positively delighted in the exercise of the choreographer's art. While still a member of the Maryinsky Company he began a series of presentations called Evenings of the Young Ballet. The Young Ballet was not a company in the ordinary sense of a regular performing ensemble with regular seasons and a stable personnel roster. It was an informal group, constantly changing and performing when and wherever the opportunity arose. It existed as an outlet for Balanchine, whose quiet determination won the respect of artists of his own age and earned him the disapproval of the directors of the Maryinsky Company.

Ultimately, the latter made it evident to members of the company that their careers would be blighted if they continued to appear with Balanchine on his evenings.

One of the characteristics of the artists operating during the free period before Stalin's heavy hand descended was an implicit belief that all of recorded history was but a prelude leading up to the millennium that was the revolution. Accordingly, Balanchine's first program June 1, 1923, was billed as *The Evolution of Ballet: From Petipa through Fokine to Balanchivadze.* It sounds unbearably pretentious to contemporary ears, but such proclamations were routinely made and understood in the context of the time. Balanchine was consciously moving away from the classicism of Petipa and modifying it as Fokine had done previously; and as Fokine came to reassert Petipa's values, so too would Balanchine. For the moment, however, Balanchine looked for new sources of movement to extend the expressive range of classical dance.

He found them in the work of acrobats and the popular art of variety entertainment, and he drew them out of his own body. In an interview given in the 1960s he commented, "I was a hippy," and he looked the part, with a thick rebellious lock of dark hair draped over the left side of his face. He created an adagio for himself and Geva that was danced barefoot and costumed in short tunics. To appreciate the break with precedent it has to be remembered that not only did male and female dancers wear ballet slippers, but that when Fokine wished to present a ballet in the Grecian style and have his male dancers appear bare-legged, he was forbidden to do so. First of all they could not appear bare-legged on the imperial stage; they would have to wear tights for decency, and then they could paint toenails on the tights and slip sandals over these. Well, here was Balanchine—bare-legged, bare-footed, hair poetically dangling in his face, wearing a short tunic—with a bare-legged, bare-footed be-tuniced woman slung over one shoulder, on that very same stage dancing an erotic adagio of his called *Enigma.* The costuming was provocative enough, but at the climatic moment, when Geva was doing a backbend on stage, Balanchine performed a darting jump across her body. It was the first time that anyone had ever seen anything so "explicit," and even a sympathetic observer such as choreographer Fyodor Lopukhov thought it was obscene (although a similar moment turned up later in one of his own ballets).

Balanchine's performance in traditional works was noticed and praised. His dancing at the Maryinsky was characterized by an athletic vigor and he was particularly cited for his acrobatic agility in the Buffoon's variation in the company's production of *The Nutcracker*.[3] While he was still in school, it was acknowledged that he had an extremely keen sense for characterization. Accordingly, he was often asked to take the roles of older characters in plays as well as ballets because he was the only one of his age who could portray them convincingly. It is relatively easy for an older performer to play a youthful character because he has had the experience of youth, but the reverse is not true, and it takes a very keen observer to make such a portrayal believable. Such a talent indicates an analytical sensibility, and Balanchine's direct unblinking gaze had something of x-ray penetration about it. He was not a danseur noble and was not cast in such roles by the directors of the Maryinsky, who selected his parts to match his gift for characterization.

In 1921, the year he graduated, he danced Jean, the male lead in *Javotte*, a pastoral romance with young lovers and furious parents that was thoroughly traditional. That same summer he saw a concert by Goleizovsky's Chamber Ballet that was thoroughly unconventional and profoundly provocative.

Goleizovsky himself had graduated from the Imperial School in 1909 and subsequently became a first dancer in Moscow as a member of the Bolshoi. He, like so many others, had become dissatisfied with the restrictions placed on choreographers and dancers under the imperial system. (Fokine had joined Diaghilev in the West in 1909 to escape from the stifling regulations, as had Nijinsky, Nijinska, Karsavina, Pavlova and later Massine to name only the best known.) The restrictions were the most severe in Saint Petersburg since it was Nicholas II's residence, but the interfering hand could be felt in distant Moscow as well.

Goleizovsky resigned from the Bolshoi without waiting around to collect his pension, and opened his own studio in 1919. He was profoundly dissatisfied with the predictable thumpty-tum monotony of the standard ballet score and wanted to present his dancers unfettered by elaborate costumes. His ideal presentation was to musically complex and emotional compositions, with dancers in scanty costumes and bare feet. He felt that this was the only way to avoid the overdecorated, overly technical, overly refined, and to his eye, trivialized presentations of the imperial theaters. The art form had lost expressiveness and was maintaining itself on sheer technique and sumptuousness. He and the others did have a point about the rigidity of the system, but it did produce *Swan Lake* and *The Sleeping Beauty*, and kept the art of ballet alive after it had declined elsewhere in Europe. At this point in his life, however, Goleizovsky wasn't taking the long view—he was too frustrated. After he had prepared his first compositions he decided to visit Petrograd to show the public there his radical new work.

Naturally, he was not able to put it on at the Maryinsky, now the state theater, and so he had to seek an alternate performing space, the Hall of the Nobles (anyway, it probably pleased him to appear in an unusual setting.) Balanchine was among the spectators, and he was ecstatic at the daring and the invention of the work. Among the older, more conservative members of the audience there was a substantial level of disapproval: where Balanchine saw the liberated human body they saw seminudity; where he saw fresh, inventive movement they saw distortion and ugliness. Goleizovsky's presentation was the embodiment of the two wellsprings of Balanchine's choreographic impetus: good music, and the human form reshaped in a new gymnastic or acrobatic manner and lightly clad. Goleizovsky's artistic sermon had been preached to the already converted in Balanchine. [4]

Balanchine immediately wanted to open a studio in collaboration with Goleizovsky that would teach the new dance. Artistically, the sight of these novel works made him bolder. He had already begun to choreograph and now he could be even more daring. The feeling was heady but this generation of artists felt that the possibilities of their individual arts were unlimited—after all, it was the millennium. Lurking in the background, moreover, as an influence on all of the choreographers was the example of Isadora Duncan.

She had visited Saint Petersburg in 1904 and had made a profound impression on dancers, artists, and the choreographer Fokine, who immediately thereafter submitted a libretto for approval on the story of Daphnis and Chloë. In his presentation he made two points: (1) there was a need for greater realism in ballets and that all of the elements should be meshed—choreography, design, and story should be consistent with one another and should have the same historical outlook; and (2) that the whole dancer's body should be a mimetic instrument rather than just the stylized gestures of the arms and hands currently in practice. By the time Duncan had appeared for her second visit in 1905, the work had still not been approved, although Fokine was allowed to put on a ballet for a student performance. Duncan's artistry was expressive in exactly the way that Fokine had imagined, although he himself would never abandon classical ballet for the free style she favored. What he would do was modify the existing, formalized vocabulary with new movement.

The artistic freedom that Fokine had enjoyed for the first several seasons with Diaghilev ended when Nijinsky started to choreograph, at which time Diaghilev's interest was centered wholly on these efforts. Fokine made his peace with the imperial theaters and returned in 1914 just after the outbreak of war to resume his career. He mounted several of his older productions including *Chopiniana,* which in the West is known as *Les Sylphides,* and is the Fokine ballet most admired by Balanchine. (*Chopiniana* had been re-choreographed by Fokine at Diaghilev's insistance and renamed for the Paris season of 1909.) Among the new ballets were *Eros,* using Tchaikovsky's Serenade in C for strings and *Jota Aragonesa* to Glinka's music. Years later Balanchine choreographed ballets to the same scores, and before he left Russia he restaged Fokine's *The Dying Swan.* Shortly after the revolution and the start of the civil war Fokine left, but he had been an influential presence during the four years of Balanchine's young life in which he was a pupil at the Imperial School and regularly attended performances.

Another experimental choreographer, also Moscow-based, like Goleizovsky was Nicholai Foregger, who felt that the dynamic movement of the new society that was being born should take its clue from the brusk, blunt, and powerful motions of everyday life. His *Dance of Machines* caused quite a stir, and Foregger denounced classical dance as being completely outmoded. He felt that significant dance in the new society that was being formed should take pedestrian movement as its point of departure, and praised the motions of crowds, the speed of automobiles, and of course, the articulation of industrial machines. Like the others, he contributed to the seething creative energy of the time.

Mikhail Mikhailov, a fellow student of Balanchine's in school, wrote years later of the intense urge that he and all of the other young students around Balanchine had to create and stage something new. Balanchine had been choreographing solos and adagios as well as incidental variety pieces, but Vladimir Dimitriev, ex-soldier and friend of Mikhailov, thought something more organized was needed and suggested to the young students that they form a group around Balanchine. Mikhailov joined, as did the critic Yuri Slonimsky, Leonid Lavrovsky, later the balletmaster of the Bolshoi, Olga Mungalova, Nina Mlodzinska, Pyotr Gusev, Alexandra Danilova, and Lydia Ivanova, Balanchine's frequent partner in school productions, were among the first group of a dozen. Balanchine became chief choreographer by virtue of his intense proficiency and prolificacy— he no sooner completed one ballet than he was preparing to work on another.

Formation of the Young Ballet provided an occasion for the dissatisfied dancers to contribute to the formation of a new development in ballet artistry. There was, of course, no pay, and rehearsal time had to be found outside of the schedule of the Maryinsky Company. The first concert was given in an alternate space, the city council building. Its central meeting hall was a steeply banked amphitheater that was full for the occasion. As Goleizovsky's concert had divided generations, so too, did the Young Ballet's. Older spectators were disapproving and the younger ones were exhilerated. Mikhailovitch recalled that the works on the program bore some resembalnce to those of Goleizovsky, though no imitation had been intended, and all were firmly designed not to have any connection with the works regularly presented at the Maryinsky. The concert collected some favorable reviews and Balanchine began to be talked about outside of the confines of the Maryinsky School as being a choreographer of promise. In the eyes of the establishment he was a suspect personnage, which perhaps added to this interest.

Right from the beginning, however, he attracted the unfavorable notice of a major critic. In this case, Akim Volynsky, who had previously had some favorable things to say about Balanchine as a dancer and budding choreographer, was sarcastic. He referred to the "quaintly licentious" ballets and summarily dismissed Balanchine as an innovative talent. Uncharacteristically, Balanchine responded to the goad with a printed attack of his own in *Theater* magazine. The article concentrated on the studio school that Volynsky was backing with Nicholas Legat as its head. Legat had been a leading dancer of the Maryinsky and was an excellent teacher, but only possessed modest choreographic gifts. He really was a poor choice to set up as the new standard-bearer for the future of ballet. The furor added to Balanchine's notoriety.

One of the most successful pieces on the first program had been *Funeral March*. The music was the familiar Chopin composition, and the title of the ballet, as it almost always would, derived from the score. It was set for three men and eight women. The costuming was simple, as it was for most of the dances of the time. The women's heads were covered with little caps and they wore tunic-length sleeveless dresses with small sashes.

Six of the women on point step slowly onto the stage with their heads bowed and their arms stiffly extended and crossed in front of them. When all reach the center of the stage they gravely raise their arms and move out to the periphery of the circular performing space, where they kneel facing outward with heads bowed. The three men enter carying a woman (Mungalova) lying on her back face up. She is motionless and the three men cross to the center of the stage, lower her, and assume the kneeling posture of the six women. A solo woman (Danilova) now enters with youthful grace. She goes from one kneeling figure to the other touching them lightly to rouse them from their grief. As they slowly rise she does a solo variation and as she leaves they all follow her, the three men first, carrying the motionless woman, and then the six women who first entered.

Because of the nontheatrical nature of the performing space, the cast entered and left through the audience, adding another antitraditional element to the production. It was without overt story but mirrored the mood of the music and was named after it. Costuming was simple and the only virtuoso dancing was confined to Danilova's solo revivifying the ground. It was a "no frills production" that suggested the passing of the older ballet and the hope of the new. The vocabulary of movement included backbends, kneeling, and dancing on point, again with the women not wearing tutus, and in general flouted the customs of the Maryinsky.

In addition to the influence of Goleizovsky, some also detected a trace of Lopukhov. One might also cite the influence of Fokine and Duncan-through-Fokine, although Balanchine's own viewing of Duncan's performance in 1922 produced something akin to loathing. She was at the time over forty, overweight, and past her dancing prime. Balanchine saw nothing of her greatness, not even a trace. He saw a fat overage woman rolling on the floor "like a pig." Nevertheless, she had spoken to Fokine directly and artistically by her concerts in 1904 and 1905, and the experience had liberated Fokine whose work in turn had an effect on Balanchine. With all of these influences there was also the obvious new artistic sensibility of Balanchine himself, who began to be in demand in theaters other than the Maryinsky. At the Maryinsky he got on reasonably well as a performer but not as a choreographer. He was chosen to partner Olga Preobrajenska at a benefit concert, and reigning ballerina Yelisaveta Gerdt selected him on short notice for an out-of-season performance when her regular partner was unavailable because of a last-minute injury.[5] The administration would not have made that choice because they were conservative, and they had Balanchine marked as a character dancer and that precluded partnering first dancers.

It didn't really matter to Balanchine because his interest in performing was rapidly waning before his passionate preference for choreography. The Mikhailovsky (now Maly) theater wanted his services, as did the Alexandrinsky (now Pushkin), and in addition to ballets they wanted him to arrange dance sequences in opera and dramatic productions. The year he was accepted into the Maryinsky Company he also enrolled at the Conservatory to further his musical education. He was unquestionably a young man of talent and ambition. He was also burning the candle at both ends.

Regular class is necessary for any dancer who wishes to maintain a high level of performance; this requires at least the better part of two hours each morning. In addition, rehearsals were necessary for each ballet that was presented in the regular Maryinsky repertory. Classes at the Conservatory demanded attendance as well as practice time of their own. Choreographing a new ballet ordinarily requires an hour of rehearsal time for each finished minute. On top of that, additional rehearsal is required to polish each ballet before a concert. In addition, there was a persistent need to secure outside income to buy food, as hunger was the companion of every resident of Petrograd and a great deal of energy was required to scrape together enough to eat.

Since a large number of variety clubs and outdoor entertainments sprang up in the summer months, there was a demand for performers. Dancers regularly appeared on these variety bills and Balanchine accompanied on the piano at times and at times he also put together little dance routines for them. He and Geva quickly had a success in these clubs and she was aided by a good voice for singing popular songs. Danilova and Ivanova confined themselves to danced presentations, and Balanchine would accompany all of them. At the Conservatory he was also composing music as part of his instruction, and eventually he set ballets to two of these works. Favorable comment was made particularly about a waltz. Balanchine seemed to care little for these compositions and they appear to have been lost, along with the ballets he was busily choreographing. Slonimsky noted years later that Balanchine's interest was obviously drawing away from performing and focusing more on choreographing. In her memoirs Geva was much blunter, stating that he "hated to dance."[6] She also commented that he was very good at it, being "agile and wirey." One critic of the time commented, "Second only to the ballet's heroine, one must single out G. M. Balanchivadze who performed the Danse de Bouffons' [*The Nutcracker*]. With his technical virtuosity and beautiful performance the young artist raised a storm of applause from the audience." Balanchine, however, was like a painter who had spent his time dutifully copying the works of the old masters and was eager to get on doing his own work. The dancing experience is of course absolutely necessary to the choreographer, but it is demanding and does take time away from the business of designing new ballets. As it was, Balanchine was stealing time from the rest of his life to support his creative work.

Lopukhov had become the director of the Maryinsky Company in 1922, the year before the first performance of the Young Ballet, and while he was not as revolutionary in his approach as was Balanchine, he did present an "abstract" ballet at the Maryinsky in which Balanchine danced and danced well. *Dance Symphony* was only performed once in 1923, but it made a very strong impression on Balanchine, who responded to its imaginative handling of Beethoven's Fourth Symphony. It was danced within the broad frame of classical ballet, was costumed modestly and not radically, and above all, drew its inspiration from the music. Its handling of choreographic materials was sustained at a high level and there was no story to get in the way. Lopukhov was an unusual mixture of experimenter and conservator. He believed that ballets with plots could exist with abstract ballets in the same repertoire. He had a profound respect for the tradition of Petipa and mounted careful productions of his most famous ballets, always being guided by the music in their restaging. Balanchine too, was to show his respect for Petipa by returning to the classical tradition after a period of experimentation, but for the moment he was obsessed with the new and newer.

The second and final Evening of the Young Ballet on June 15, 1924, was even more radical than the first. For the first, Balanchine had presented works with musical accompaniment. For the second, his ballets were backed by chanted recitation of poetry. The administration at the Maryinsky considered this beyond the realm of the faintly acceptable.

In addition to the full evenings presented by the Young Ballet, individual artists associated with Balanchine and the group presented his ballets on other programs. Indeed, these radical works seemed to turn up everywhere. To the traditionalists of the Maryinsky, Balanchine must have seemed like a metastasizing cancer. They had routinely turned down his request to mount a work for the company, and now they threatened the dancers to frighten them away from appearing in any of his productions. Some stayed away and some didn't, but Balanchine continued to work steadily during the few hours he had regained in his busy day since graduating from the Conservatory in 1923. His ballets were popular with the young dancers who presented them in the many variety halls that provided some diversion from the grey life of the city.

The dancers moved from day to day without any special plans beyond getting through the difficulties of each twenty-four-hour span. One man on the fringe of Balanchine's world, however, did have a long-range plan. Vladimir Dimitriev was arranging to leave the Soviet Union. Employed at the Maryinsky Opera and an admirer of Balanchine's work, he formulated a plan to leave by the front door, with government approval. Now that the port had been reopened it was possible. He was resourceful and had acquired enough money to present sufficient bribes to the officials, but he had to make his scheme plausible. He proposed that a group of singers and dancers assembled by him would tour abroad during the summer recess of the Maryinsky Theater as good-will missionaries for the vigorous new culture of the Soviet Union. In years past Diaghilev had presented the best of Russian opera, ballet, and painting to the West, and here was an opportunity to demonstrate that the lyric theater was still in splendid shape despite the slanders being whispered abroad. The company would tour under the name of the Soviet State Dancers. The proposal was reasonable and would stand up to scrutiny; it sounded reassuringly patriotic and it wouldn't cost the state anything since Dimitriev would fund it from profits made acting as a croupier in a gambling casino. The dancers and singers had had no brushes with the law and were politically clean, with the exception perhaps of Lydia Ivanova, who had begun to keep company with several of the local communist officials. They would all be drawn from the Young Ballet and included, besides Balanchine, his wife Geva, Danilova, Ivanova, and Boris Efimov. In 1924 the project was approved and exit visas were granted.[7] Before they could leave, though, Ivanova was drowned in a boating accident that appeared suspicious; no official explanation or examination of the occurence was ever made. The small company departed on the designated day from their home city, now renamed Leningrad. It was impossible to get clearance for another dancer at such a late date so they made do with the two couples, the three singers, and the conductor-accompanist. They traveled to the German port of Stettin aboard a German liner and ate luxuriously, that is, adequately, for the first time in years. They reached Berlin by railroad trip, but once there, they found that no real tour had been set up properly. Then came a telegram ordering them to return to Russia immediately. The conductor and the singers returned. Dimitriev and the dancers stayed. They had little money, no tour, an uncertain future, and only Geva among the group spoke German. The present did not look particularly good, but it did look better than the past.

Chapter 3

Finishing School

During the summer, Rhineland spas are crowded with patrons taking their vacations and enjoying the restorative waters and thermal baths. Having a great deal of time on their hands, the tourists are the natural audience for variety entertainment. With some help from the Russian emigré colony of Berlin, Dimitriev and the young dancers were put in touch with the producer of such shows who hired them for the summer season. Conditions were not ideal. They danced indoors and outdoors on reasonable to bad stages and in one instance, before the inmates of a mental hospital. Ironically, among the inmates was Ernst Toller,[1] whose play *Eugene the Unlucky* had been presented at the Mikhailovsky Theater two years previously. At that time Balanchine had been asked to design various crowd scenes that needed choreographic shaping. Now the author was temporarily institutionalized and withdrawn. Even if Toller were not in the grips of depression, the two could not have spoken, since neither knew the other's language. Such incongruities seemed typical of the unsettled times.

The variety format had proved workable for the small company with its program of duets designed by Balanchine, and Dimitriev sought out similar engagements. He succeeded in securing a two-week engagement in London at the Empire Theater. Two variety houses, the Empire and the slightly older Alhambra, had a tradition of presenting ballet as part of their bills of fare. Katti Lanner, former dancer and daughter of the composer, had been in charge of choreographing ballets at the Empire and set the pattern by successfully engaging the Danish ballerina Adeline Genée. Two of the first dancers from the Imperial Theaters ever seen in

31

London, Lydia Kyasht and Adolph Bolm, appeared there in 1908, the year before Diaghilev astounded Paris with his first presentation of ballet.

The young Soviet State Dancers, now billed as Principal Dancers of the Russian State Ballet, were definitely not a success in the Empire tradition. As a matter of fact they were fired after the first week of their engagement, but they were paid for the full two weeks. The chief difficulty arose from the swift pacing of the shows. The dancers were not prepared for it and could not make necessary costume changes. The conductor of the orchestra covered for them by repeating introductions but the restless music hall audience would only tolerate so much interlude music. It has been estimated by veterans of the halls that the audience's attention had to be caught in the first half-minute or it would not be caught at all. The game and able young dancers simply did not have the timing for the halls.

They also did not have passports that were welcome in the British isles now that they were without employment. France was more hospitable to travelers from the Soviet Union, and the group headed for Paris. They had no engagement there either, however, and their money dwindled rapidly despite careful economies. Geva had already sold her ash blond hair to a wig maker in Berlin when they were low on funds, and their present land of refuge appeared rather bleak. They had heard of the Diaghilev company but it seemed a remote possibility. What they did not know was that Diaghilev was actively seeking them.

He finally located them in their rooming house and asked them to audition for him at the home of Misia Sert, his one, true, female friend whose patronage and taste he relied on. After the audition, during which Balanchine and Geva performed their duet *Enigma,* all of the dancers were engaged. They were paid according to their balletic ranking and in terms of their usefulness to Diaghilev. Danilova, as a soloist at the Maryinsky, received the highest pay as a dancer, Efimov the next highest, and Geva, who had not been a member of the Maryinsky, earned the least of the three. Balanchine was handled differently. At the Maryinsky he was a coryphée, just one step above the entering level of corps de ballet, and would have been paid less than Danilova; but as a choreographer he received additional pay that placed him above the others. The choreographic skills that had held him back in the Soviet Union provided him with a step up in the Western world. It was a small thing at first, but a pattern had been set. The Diaghilev company featured creativity and had done so from its very beginning; here Balanchine would be encouraged, not discouraged.

At this point in his career Serge Diaghilev was the most potent artistic force in ballet. He was fifty-two and had been presenting ballet for fifteen years, and without him this art would not even have been taken seriously. During the nineteenth century it had withered in France and England, hibernated in Denmark and was losing its popularity to opera in Italy. In Russia, however, it flourished in the hothouse atmosphere of the imperial theater system. Diaghilev had worked briefly within the system, producing an annual report on the year's productions, but his sights were set on the more active role of directing new productions. This ambition was thwarted by some intrigue that even today remains obscure, and Diaghilev's energies were wholly turned to Paris, which he considered the artistic center of Europe. He first showed Russian art, which was respectfully received. He next presented Russian opera and revealed the magnificent Chaliapin to the West. Finally he presented Russian ballet to the astonished audiences of 1909. Its sensational reception encouraged him to continue annual presentations.[2]

Their success was dependent on two factors, the undoubted talent of his choreographers and their ballets, and the astounding technique of the dancers, especially the men. Dancing, such as it was in the West, was pallid, and the Russians were as vivid as the colors of the decors that surrounded their dances. In addition, Diaghilev's restless spirit kept him constantly on the alert for new expressiveness in choreography, music, and design. He presented Fokine's revolutionary ballets when the imperial theaters would not. He commissioned Stravinsky's early scores and dazzled the eyes of his audiences with the barbaric color and daring of Léon Bakst's costumes and decors. He did not compose, choreograph, or paint, but he was at the creative heart of the ballets he presented. On one occasion King Alphonso of Spain jokingly asked him what he did. "Like your majesty, I do nothing but am essential," he replied.

He had a real need to be an animating force, a role he was not able to play fully with Fokine, who had made a declaration of his own creative intentions and needed only the opportunity to put them to the test. Despite this desire to be at the center, Diaghilev provided five glorious seasons for Fokine to show his revolutionary new ballets with their unified theme, music, choreography, and design elements, and they were a triumph for all concerned. Diaghilev, who wished to remain at the leading edge of artistic expression, however, felt that Fokine had done his best work and there was need for a fresh artistic approach. In Nijinsky he saw a talented dancer whom he wished to develop into a talented choreographer thus, in effect, creating him artistically. For Diaghilev this would be a more satisfying arrangement than the producer-choreographer relationship between himself and Fokine. (After Fokine departed, Diaghilev had snorted that he could make a choreographer out of his inkwell!) Nijinsky choreographed three ballets, all of which were controversial because of theme or form. Before he could expand in this role he was dismissed from the company by Diaghilev for a personal breech in their relationship (Nijinsky had chosen to marry), but he returned to lead the company on an American tour and to create another ballet before his deteriorating mental state forced him into a hospital.

Diaghilev summarily replaced Nijinsky with Leonid Massine, a dancer from the Bolshoi in Moscow, introducing the young man to advanced music and painting and encouraging him to create adventurous new ballets. They worked harmoniously for a while but then separated to work independently. Massine was replaced as choreographer by Bronislava Nijinska, Nijinsky's sister, who had previously appeared as a dancer with the company. She too created several wonderful ballets for Diaghilev before they had a falling out. It was at this period of strained relations with Nijinska that Balanchine happened along.

Diaghilev was actively seeking a choreographer. His first question to Balanchine after seeing his work was, "Can you work quickly?" It was a most significant query, since the home of the company had become Monte Carlo, and part of the agreement reached with the principality was that in addition to performing programs of its own ballets, the company would create and appear in opera productions requiring ballets. These productions were directed by the opera house staff who did not want to engage another choreographer when the Diaghilev Company was already in residence. It was another burden on Diaghilev's choreographer and one Balanchine assumed without complaint.

Balanchine was twenty, energetic, provincial, and awesomely gifted. He could easily answer in the affirmative when asked if he were quick. Between 1920 and 1924 he had created thirty ballets, designed movement sequences in three plays and one opera, and had tossed off a handful of piéces d'occasion for cabaret presentation. All that while he was performing regularly at the Maryinsky and studying at the Conservatory. He was just starting his first year with Diaghilev, and before it was over he would create one ballet, a dozen opera ballets, and four occasional concert pieces. Yes, indeed, he could work quickly.

His talent both delighted and distressed Diaghilev. He was obviously good, but creatively Balanchine was essentially formed. He did not need the talents of the older man to mold him; instead, like Fokine, he needed the opportunity to work. Unlike Fokine he was not sensitive to painting and sculpture, and the contributions of the talented artists in the Diaghilev collaborations always remained somewhat alien to him. Diaghilev set him to work on a production of Stravinsky's *The Song of the Nightingale,* with decor and costumes by Matisse. Balanchine didn't know who Matisse was. The most important thing, however, was that he was inventive, imaginative, and quick.

While appearing in London, Balanchine had auditioned a young English dancer Alicia Marks, and decided that she would be perfect for the part of the bird. She was only fourteen, but was obviously talented, and she was taken into the company. (Her name was changed to Alicia Markova to trade on the popularity of Russian dancers—a practice common to non-Russian members of the company. Balanchine himself had his name changed from Georgi Balanchivadze, which Diaghilev considered unpronounceable for anyone other than a native speaking Russian, to Georges Balanchine; the s was dropped when Balanchine emigrated to the United States.)

Balanchine was clearly still finding his way as a choreographer. He had emerged from the traditional schooling of the Maryinsky only to turn his back on it. The Russian school of ballet had developed under the guiding hand of Petipa (French) Christian Johansson (Swedish), and Enrico Cecchetti (Italian). The comtribution of these foreign teachers was to bring together the precision and finish of the French school with the exuberant athleticism and virtuosity of the Italian. Their students absorbed the technical instruction and brought to it the national temperament. The result was a style of dance that fulfilled Pushkin's prophetic phrase describing Russian ballet as "soul inspired flight." Balanchine had been thoroughly steeped in this tradition, but as a choreographer had found that the Maryinsky was stifling creatively.

There was no room for the passionate expressiveness he felt was necessary. Romantic excess in choreography as well as in the music of composers such as Chopin, Scriabin, and Rubinstein attracted him. The degree to which his instincts were truly reflective of his time is demonstrated by the readiness of dancers and choreographers to adapt his new acrobatic innovations to their own. One of the most striking of these moves was the overhead lift of the female at full arm's length. It was a brazenly daring move that seemed to imperil what had been upheld as the "chasteness" of the female. In another ballet, to express anguish a woman opened her mouth in a silent scream. Then too, there was the notorious leap across the female's torso arching upward from the stage. He also included splits and gestural innovations, loosely called "duncanesque," for the arms, sinuously liberated from the classically determined positions. Within two or three years these startling changes became accepted as part of the dance vocabulary, so much so in fact, that it hardly seems possible that they were introduced so recently. The big overhead lift is practically a trademark of contemporary Russian companies.

Balanchine was guided by rude vigor. He was an expressive force bursting out of the confines of classical dance. Diaghilev was aware that while Balanchine's talent was of gemstone quality, it needed a setting to be seen to best advantage. In addition, he himself had found the restraints of the imperial ballet too confining and was innately sympathetic to Balanchine's need to expand his art. After *The Song of the Nightingale,* Diaghilev assigned Balanchine the score of *Barabau* with a libretto by the composer Vittorio Rieti; it developed as a knockabout farce. *Jack in the Box* and *The Triumph of Neptune* were similarly broad in their approach. *La Chatte* and *La Pastorale* both had librettos by Boris Kochno, who was Diaghilev's secretary. Both were extreme in their individual ways: *La Chatte* used heavy-gauge cellophane overlays on the costumes, among other scenic innovations, and *La Pastorale* purported to be the love story of a movie star and telegraph messenger.[3] They were typical examples of the chic shock ballets that Diaghilev regularly delivered to his Parisian audiences.

It was a coterie audience, dominated by post-World War I disillusionment and a resultant search for easy, immediate pleasures, eager to be in on the last word in the arts, fashion, or anything that did not involve the mundane. Diaghilev was a master at catering to this taste, though he was not imprisoned by it. In the face of such novelty-seeking he had remounted *The Sleeping Beauty* for performances in London three years before Balanchine's arrival. Despite the excellent work of his collaborators and an outstanding number of first dancers, the production was unable to run profitably. At the time one could not attract enough of a London audience for a solid month to make such an ambitious series of performances possible. Today there would be no such difficulty; but as Balanchine noted in a later reminiscence, "Diaghilev was always twenty-five years ahead of his time." In 1911, however, his third season in the West, Diaghilev presented *Giselle* and shortly afterward, *Swan Lake,* both of which found greater favor among London audiences than among his beloved Paris followers.

Diaghilev presented these classic works at carefully spaced intervals as a way of maintaining contact with the ballet's roots that led back to Petipa, who had been the shaper of the style from which they sprang. He might have had his arguments with the restrictions that had been placed on ballet, but he knew that the strength of the art came from the school of Petipa. The great French master had produced dancers who were fluently articulate in the language of classical dance. Clarity, virtuoso energy, and precision marked the graduates of the Maryinsky School. Refined balance and harmonious development characterized the ballets that Petipa devised to set off such dancers to best advantage.

Stravinsky, with his great sympathy for ballet and its guiding principle of aristocratic refinement, had been thinking of some music that would reflect the essence of this classic art. For him the ballet blanc, typically characterized by uncluttered white costuming, was the pinnacle of academic dance. In such ballets the sheer technique of form and the dancers' artistry carried the choreographer's thoughts without distortions of character or nationalistic references. It presented the core of the art in its most expressive manner. It may have been this quality that attracted Diaghilev to the score for *Apollon Musagète* when Stravinsky played it for him before its premier in Washington, and made him mount it despite his annoyance that a production had been staged elsewhere. It was not a revival in the way that *Giselle, Swan Lake,* or *The Sleeping Beauty* was, but it could be the basis for classical dancing such as he, Stravinsky and Balanchine knew firsthand. He offered the score to Balanchine without a libretto; the choreographer could make of it what he would. To Balanchine, the mood of the music was white, and in places, white on white. He was enchanted with it, partly because there were no words to come between himself and the score. It was the most significant commission by Diaghilev from Balanchine, since it altered the latter's life and allowed the former to present contemporary classicism to audiences who had treated *Giselle, Swan Lake,* and *The Sleeping Beauty* coolly.

Stylistically, it was dubbed neoclassicism, and to this day it remains the favored style for Balanchine. After the triumph of *Apollon Musagète,* Balanchine arranged three more ballets for Diaghilev, all with librettos by Kochno: *The Gods Go A-Begging, Le Bal,* and *The Prodigal Son.* The last was based on a series of etchings described by Pushkin in a short story "The Stationmaster," that portrayed the biblical story. It was the third ballet score that Prokofiev created for Diaghilev, but the only one by the composer that Balanchine worked on.

Balanchine chose to choreograph the ballet with a range of acrobatic gestures grafted onto classical dance. Methodically, he played and replayed the score until he felt that he had understood its structure and mood, and then he began to work with the dancers. After the choreography had been completed and the premiere date set, Prokofiev arrived to conduct the first performance. What he saw did not please him. He wanted much more in the way of naturalism and less stylized movement. It was too late to change a whole ballet, but up until a few hours before the premiere Balanchine was still rearranging portions.

Even for a Diaghilev production with its usual tensions, *The Prodigal Son* had a special air of hysteria about it. Balanchine was being as sexually explicit as he had ever been choreographically and it made Felia Dubrovska, who was to play the Siren, nervous and embarrassed. Serge Lifar, who was to play the Prodigal, couldn't seem to grasp the character and was highly distraught. The ballet's protagonists were significant departures from the lighthearted or reserved characters they had danced most recently. Diaghilev encouraged the dancers to invest the ballet with dramatic energy, however, and to portray their characters vividly. Everyone was feeling the pressure.[4] Then there was the incomplete state of the ballet as the premiere performance moved closer. On opening night all of the pieces fell into place and the work was generously and warmly received by the audience. The libretto that Kochno produced completely ignored the reproof of the younger brother who had stayed at home with the father, but concentrated on the willfulness of the Prodigal, his rioting in a far land squandering his inheritance money, the unfaithfulness of his own servants, thieving companions, and of course, the seductiveness of the Siren who besotted the young man's senses with unleashed passion. All of this concluded with a display of deep regret by the Prodigal.

The scenery and costumes designed by the contemporary religious painter Rouault were primitive. They consisted of bright daubs of color surrounded and shaped by bands of black. The opening scene showed a broad plain with a couple of domed huts and a curve of shore with a bright sun, with a cloth entranceway at the right of the stage.

The prodigal bursts out of the doorway and goes to converse with two servants preparing for his voyage. He hefts one jug and tosses it playfully to them. Two sisters emerge and the bearded father enters to observe his young son dashing and leaping about within the family enclosure (indicated by a low fence at the left). The Prodigal releases some of his pent-up energy in a soaring leap with the front leg fully extended.

Mikhail Baryshnikov in "The Prodigal Son"

The father kneels and summons the two daughters and the son to him. He places their hands on his outstretched palm one after the other and caps the cluster with his right hand. The attempt to strengthen family cohesion lasts only for a moment, as the Prodigal pulls his hand away, jumps to his feet, and pounds his clenched fists on his thighs. He is too committed to his departure to respond to this parental appeal. With a beckoning sweep of his arm he motions his two servants to follow him. They gather up the urns and gold implements that comprise his inheritance and bustle out through the gate in the low fence. The Prodigal ignores the gate and leaps dramatically across it with a mighty liberating bound. He pauses for a moment thrusts his arm forward and dashes off toward his longed-for adventure.

The second scene is a large banqueting hall. The backcloth shows the draped opening of a tent furnished with a long table. A raucous blare announces the entrance of a snakey line of men with sinister shaved heads, identically dressed in short tunics. As they wend their way around the room in a half-crouch they alternately thrust their arms out to the sides and place them on the hips of the man in front. The centipede-like procession is mechanically practiced and quite menacing. These are obviously adept debauchees stamping along, awaiting their next visitor. There is an air of sensual energy to their cavortings. They break formation, pick up the low fence of the first scene, and invert it to transform it into a table near the rear of the stage.

Their antics continue as they leap energetically to and away from one another maintaining the bent-legged stance they had in the centipede formation. Their arms joggle clownishly up and down. Four of them lie on their backs with their outstretched legs touching to form a four-pointed star. A fifth member of the group reclines like an acrobat in a backbend on the outstretched legs while the other four grasp the hands of those lying down and circle to make the whole formation revolve like a wheel of fortune. Like the other caperings, it is an exercise of predatory anticipation. There is no immediate object of their attention and they rise to rehearse yet another of their malevolent gymnastics.

They cease as the Prodigal enters with his servants. There is a moment of hesitancy and tension between the two groups. The revelers retreat to the opposite side of the stage to form a three-tiered formation with their arms at their sides. The closely packed rows are as calculating as the keys of an adding machine. The Prodigal approaches and cautiously extends a greeting hand toward one of the men. An answering hand darts out and is quickly withdrawn by another member of the compact group. The Prodigal thrusts his hand toward that spot but is answered with another elusive hand coming from a different member of the blank-faced ensemble. These comical yet menacing attempts at greeting continue for a moment more until the formation moves greedily forward to touch the young man's garments. Their puzzling greeting followed by obvious envy causes the Prodigal to withdraw, but his servants push him forward. After all, their urging gesture implies, they have traveled a long way and this seems to be what they have been looking for, so it is foolish to be timid now.

Having failed to establish friendly contact with a handshake, the Prodigal offers the men a jug of wine, and the mood is transformed completely—now they are all companions in pleasure. The servants hoist him to their shoulders, and as he is borne about, the revelers hoist their own members to his level to shake his hand. On the ground they were wary of one another, but at this heady, wine-inspired level they become friends in pursuit of the good life. The Prodigal is tossed from side to side as the mood of celebration increases. Lowered to the floor he dances between his servants as the revelers watch approvingly. Enthusiastically, he grasps the servants' hands as if to say, "You were right, this is what we have been seeking." The revelers cluster on either side of him and reach for his hands. In a grotesque parody of a friendly handshake he finds himself pumping two giant bundles of hands up and down. Now completely a part of the group he dances with them and bounds exuberantly over the table as he had hurdled the restraining fence of his father's estate. The section closes with the revelers and servants all clustered about the Prodigal.

The Siren enters, precisely picking her way across the stage on point, in complete contrast to the earthy stomping of the revelers. They all stare at her, no one more than the Prodigal. Her tall headdress is like that of a princess and a broad wine-red cape trails along behind her. She beats her breast with a combination of torment and ecstasy. She is exotically beautiful as she parades in front of them. Slowly she winds the cape around her body as she twists, and then just as smoothly unwinds it. She straddles it and draws it tightly around her thighs in a figure eight, draping the tail across her forearm in a parody of a server's napkin. She continues to dance slowly and enticingly. She unwinds the cape and spreads it full length behind her. With her torso provocatively horizontal she "walks" on her hands and points, to stop in front of the table before the dazzled Prodigal. Crouching on her knees she draws the cape over her. Completely covered, she waits.

She doesn't have to wait long, as the Prodigal leaps forward to her, extends his hand over the cloth, hesitates for a moment, and snatches it off, tossing it away behind him. She rises to display herself to him. He stares fascinated as she extends her arms enticingly in a gesture that is more welcoming than a mere handshake, and moves close to him. Cautiously, he places his hands on her waist as if she were a volatile substance, and follows her as she moves. It is clear that it is she who is the leader. The revelers cluster about the two as she pushes the Prodigal against the table. Swiftly, a few revelers toss her up to others who support her in a seated position high above the Prodigal, who is stretched out on the table where he appears to be the object of the coming feast.

The first flush of passion is allowed to subside momentarily as all watch the two servants dance in front of the table, on which the Siren and the Prodigal sit side by side. Grabbing and roistering around one another, the servants dance a grotesquely coarse translation of the Siren's smooth, brutal solo. She now touches the Prodigal's arm and sensually fondles the jeweled medallion he wears around his neck, and the intensity of the seduction moves forward another notch. It remains only for the couple to consumate the climactic union of greed and desire.

Having cleared the air, the servants return to the table and the foreplay recommences. The Siren and the Prodigal come forward watching one another. He approaches her cautiously and she leans back voluptuously anticipating his support. He approaches her again warily but she avoids his attempted caress. Abjectly, he drops to one knee before her and she confidently straddles his neck. He rises with her astride his shoulders, and then serpentlike she slides down his back. Arrogantly, she rises on point and hooks her leg around his waist, fastening herself to him and is revolved on her pivot foot as he makes a circle of tiny sidesteps. She releases him and he draws her onto his back. Now she grasps both of her feet circling his body like a cinched belt. As he inches his widespread feet together she slides down the length of his legs to rest in a circle on the ground. He rights her, placing her knees on his feet in this coiled position. As he steps backward with his hands under her arms she "walks" on her knees in perfect concert with him. Emboldened he caresses her, but then abashed, he sits and draws his knees up almost as if he were trying to disappear after being so blatantly rash. She comes to him and stands on his inclined shins as he clasps her feet, while she triumphantly settles on his head. As an expression of dominance, it blatantly establishes her power. In a moment she rises confidently to her full height with his hands still grasping her feet. He lies back as she steps away. She returns to lie across his body, and sensually their legs entangle. The seduction is complete. The forgotten familial embrace of the loving parent has been replaced by the calculating clutch of the Siren.

Exhausted, they are pulled apart and the Prodigal is tossed violently from one group of revelers to the other. The servants wholeheartedly join the drunken crowd. The Siren watches calculatingly and pours wine down his throat as he implores her help. The two are carried about by the riotous celebrants. For one hurried moment they embrace and are separated. Standing confused and intoxicated he staggers to the table looking for a friendly face, but finds none. Desperately he runs up the table, which the revelers tilt so that he slides back defeated. His arm stretched pleadingly straight out ironically recalls the similar defiant gesture he made after clearing the fence to seek this adventure. The Siren pins him with her pointed foot.

The stage darkens and the table is stood upright like a pillar, against which the Prodigal is placed. Hideously, the acquisitive hands of the revelers appear around the edges of the table to run their flickering fingers up and down his body. He is held upsidedown and shaken to dislodge his money. Then one by one his clothes are stripped from him, including his shoes, until he is left nearly nude and utterly powerless. The Siren surveys her conquest from the shoulders of the revelers; there is only one thing left to take, and she steals up to him and snatches the medallion from his neck. The drama of debauch has been played out and the revelers leave in a fittingly grotesque manner. They hook arms back-to-back, and in a half-seated crouch, scuttle off looking like partly human crabs. Still dazed, the Prodigal slumps to the ground against the pillar. He has nothing. His money, his clothes, his servants, who have joined the revelers, and his home have been lost through his own foolishness. He sees a puddle of water, crawls to it and drinks. He crouches and then exits on his knees in despair, thoroughly beaten and humbled.

The thieves return to the scene of their crime carrying all of the Prodigal's goods. The Siren strides behind them wearing her cape, ready for the next adventure. The column is placed horizontally again, and the thieves enter it. The Siren hangs on to the front of it and bows her body outward like a figurehead on a ship. They stretch her cloak out like a sail and make rowing motions with their arms. The stage darkens on their triumph.

The final scene is the same as the first, with the gate and the entranceway to the father's house. The Prodigal slowly enters wearing a miserable cloak and worn shoes, crawling and supporting himself with a staff. He collapses at the gate unable to enter. He left flying grandly over it with an impetuous leap and now he cannot even drag himself through it on his hands and knees. His sisters emerge and see him, and tell the father, who enters to stand near the doorway. He looks at his chastened son who struggles to him, crawling, falling, and finally clawing suppliantly at the father's long cloak. The compassionate father opens his cloak and cradles his returned son in his arms like a baby, then protectively closes the folds of the garment around him.

Balanchine's gestural invention for *The Prodigal Son* was brilliantly imaginative, daring, and controlled. The chaste restraint of *Apollon Musagète* was not suitable to the theme of this ballet, but its economy certainly was. Thematically, hands and arms are consistently exploited for maximum expressiveness. The openhanded concern of the father is first shown in his tender drawing together of his children's hands as they are grouped in the first scene. The Prodigal's defiance and wrongheaded resolve is expressed vibrantly as he jerks his hand violently away to pound his clenched fists on his thighs. Meeting the revelers, he is given a warning of their duplicity through the deliberately tricky offer and withdrawal of their supposedly friendly handshakes.

The Siren's open embrace is betrayed for the ploy it is in the avaricious dandling of his medallion. His misguided caresses lead to ruin, and the flesh-crawling patter of the revelers' hands over his body clearly reveals their interest in gain. After looting his treasure those same hands became the blades of oarlike arm-sweeps taking them away from their crime. Extending a sinuous arm over her head with spread fingers is the siren's way of expressing initial triumph. The final, exhausted yet hopeful clawing gesture at his father's garment shows how much the proud young Prodigal's life has been changed by his experience. The ballet closes with the father's gentle embrace, full of forgiveness.

The eroticism of the ballet is developed in a series of fresh acrobatic gestures that alternate with the steps of the standard classical vocabulary. The characteristic stance assigned to the revelers is the crouch. They are hunched over when they first appear in their centipede formation, and when they separate they continue to move with the bent-kneed walk of primitives. Their characters are base with no redeeming qualities, and when they leave hooked back-to-back, they are once again down close to the earth looking like things that might emerge from under a flat rock. The Prodigal's servants are a step above this in their carriage, and their balletic vocabulary suggests character dance combining classical steps with grotesque fervor.

As the principals of this drama, the Prodigal and the Siren must display some nobility of character to be worthy of their dramatic encounter. They are clearly set off from the others by their execution of classical steps; they are not simply slugs bent on mindless coupling. The Siren is an expert seduction machine as she enters walking on point, which elevates her from the flat-footed stomping of her cohorts. She expresses some ambiguity of purpose by her breast beating, but this is the life she has chosen and she will carry through the seduction with professional hauteur. Whatever second thoughts she may have are brushed aside by greed.

In a similar fashion, the Prodigal's better nature is shown in his execution of classic leaps and by his upright bearing. He is in the grips of a passionate compulsion, however, that causes him to clench his fists, pound his thighs, contort his body, and shake hands with people to whom he would not ordinarily give a second glance. He too is greedy, greedy for experience that appears far more attractive to him than the calm order of his father's home. He is looking for dionysian pleasure and under this pressure distorts himself into gymnastic postures, as does the Siren. With these two it is a deformation of their normal bearing and not their habitual stance, as it is with the revelers.

This was the last ballet that Balanchine did for Diaghilev, and in fact it was the last new ballet that Diaghilev's company ever produced. Three months after its first performance Diaghilev was dead and his ballet company scattered to the winds.

The company was unquestionably Russian in origin and in its esthetic. Through Diaghilev's efforts over the twenty-year span of his company the short one-act ballet came to prominence. Composers, choreographers, and painters of the first rank had combined their talents to create its repertory and ballet had moved from a position of obscurity to one of prominence in the artistic vangard. Audiences had been developed in Paris and London, and emigré teachers had settled in both to prepare students for performing careers. When Diaghilev died in 1929, however, his dancers were on their summer break. Balanchine was in London with Lydia Lopokova (as Fyodor Lopukhov's sister spelled the name) and Anton Dolin, both members of the company, choreographing a ballet for a film in which the three would appear. They all knew that without Diaghilev there was no company.

There were, however, various state companies still extant that needed the services of choreographers. Balanchine was approached by the director of the Paris Opera and asked to mount a major production of *The Creatures of Prometheus*. Shortly after he began, he caught penumonia and was hospitalized. His health deteriorated to the point where he had to spend a prolonged period in a sanatorium regaining his strength. He suggested that Serge Lifar, a fellow member of the company, replace him as choreographer. Lifar eventually replaced him to the extent that he became the company's resident balletmaster for the next three decades.

Balanchine had developed enormously since he left Russia, but for the moment he was a choreographer without a company for which to choreograph. The years with Diaghilev had been of great use to him in a number of ways. Although he was not vitally interested in performing, he had appeared in a wide variety of ballets and grew to know the work of Fokine, Massine, and Nijinska intimately. He received a compact education in twentieth-century ballet in a brief five years. Fokine made the deepest impression on him and later on he commented, "Fokine emphasized the evolution of masses whereas prior to Fokine the ballets were essentially linear. Orchestration of the mass is the quintessence of modern choreographers. It is the co-ordination of choreographic arrangements in spatial positions."[5]

Petipa had framed his principal dancers with lines and arcs of extreme grace but the members of the corps de ballet did not interact as "characters" with the principals; rather, their function was to provide a setting for the actions of the lead performers. Their formations were limited to a fairly small number of set groupings that were imaginatively alternated, but remained the same from ballet to ballet. Fokine had enlarged upon the essentially passive role of the corps to make its members part of an active ensemble.

For him the essence of Fokine's contribution was to be found in *Les Sylphides*. There the corps de ballet was not a decorative fringe around the principal dancers, but a sensitive group that reshaped itself in response to the movements of the principals, so that it too became a contributing "character" to the development of the ballet. The brilliant handling of groups of dancers was to emerge as one of the dominant traits of Balanchine's style.

By being a member of the Diaghilev company that considered France its home, Balanchine came in direct contact with French culture. This included its literature, art, and music. To a great extent he remained aloof or disinterested in the literature and the art, but worked happily with French composers then and subsequently. One of his special discoveries was the music of Chabrier. He had known the music of Milhaud, Saint-Saens, and Ravel in Russia, and had designed ballets using works by all three. With Diaghilev, in Monte Carlo, he was able to undertake a setting of the premiere of Ravel's *L'enfant et les Sortileges*. The music continued to exert its attraction for him and he remounted it three more times, the last being a production specially conceived for television in 1981. He worked with scores by Satie, Auric, and Sauguet as well, He continued to work with Chabrier and Ravel's music for the next five decades and undertook to mount a centennial celebration of Ravel's birth in 1975. Selections from the scores of Fauré, Ravel's teacher, provided the music for the first portion of the full-evening ballet *Jewels,* choreographed in 1967.

Since he disliked literary themes as the pretexts for dancing, he was little affected by French literature. He endured those librettos that were thrust upon him, but ceased to use them almost entirely during the bulk of his career. The trained human body shaped according to the impulse of music was all the libretto he needed. Similarly, he found little satisfaction in the work of painters designing elaborate costumes and decors for his ballets. Again he endured it, but clearly preferred simple uncluttered costuming that did not draw attention to itself, and dispensed almost entirely with elaborate decor.

France, in the magnifying glass world of Diaghilev's company, became his finishing school. He had emerged from a society in Russia continuously bordering on anarchy and almost immediately began to feel the polishing effects of the most refining cultural buffing wheel that the century has known. That world was not without its problems, however, and one of the first that he faced was the awkwardness of being placed in a supervisory position to dancers who, for the most part, were his seniors. These dancers were artistically formed and he was the outsider. He endured their resentment and steadily worked under Diaghilev's encouragement. Choreographic talent was his chief weapon in the struggle, together with Diaghilev's authority. The resistance of the older dancers left its impression on him, however, and he began to look for less formed talents with whom to cast his new ballets. Markova at age fourteen became the first of his choreographic "babies" when he persuaded Diaghilev to assign her the role of the Nightingale in his first ballet for the company.

Diaghilev had seen Markova audition twice previously at the urging of her teacher and former company member, Serafina Astafieva, and company member Anton Dolin, but it was only after an audition under Balanchine's direction that the decision was made to hire her. During that difficult audition Balanchine had asked the prodigiously gifted child to perform varieties of complicated phrases, which she was able to accomplish. She performed impressively, and besides, since his student days in Russia, Balanchine was predisposed to young dancers. In his homeland he had worked with fellow students who were enthusiastically cooperative, and it was to such eager dancers that he gravitated throughout his career. For the duration of his time with Diaghilev, however, Balanchine worked with the dancers Diaghilev chose, as he did with the music Diaghilev commissioned and the librettos he passed along. Despite such difficulties, the opportunities were vast. Balanchine was working steadily with intelligent encouragement and his work was being made known throughout Europe. Until he came to Diaghilev no one knew who he was. By the time he was cast adrift everyone in the world of ballet knew him, as did several discerning members of the world of variety entertainment. He had a reputation, and though he had choreographed thirty ballets in Russia, with *Apollon Musagète* he found his own true artistic identity. Diaghilev had served him well, as he had Diaghilev.

Opinions about his work among the public and critics were characterized by extreme approval or disapproval. While Diaghilev had brought Balanchine to general attention, the director's predilection for narrative ballet ran strongly against the choreographer's natural bent. Since the company's repertoire had presented story ballets for the most part, audiences had become habituated to literary plots interpreted through dancing. If Diaghilev, the acknowledged revolutionary, had found narrative ballet most congenial, then this must certainly be the wave of the future. The critic of the literary journal *La Nouvelle Revue Française* commented, "I never admired Massine greatly (except for *Rite* [*The Rite of Spring*]) but Balanchine's productions have made us grieve the departure of his predecessor very much"[6] (translation mine). The reviewer went on to excoriate the grotesqueness of the ballets, which he thought brutal and at times almost obscene. Similar terms of disapproval had been expressed by critics in Russia only a few years previously. On the other hand, a critic writing in *Dancing Times* could state, ". . . it is probably not an idle prophesy to say that in his hands lies the form of the ballet of the future."[7] Balanchine remained controversial, as revolutionaries do.

The question of obscenity dogged his steps as it had those of Diaghilev. In an age of sexual liberation it is difficult to appreciate the attitude of the 1912 public that found the erotic reverie of Nijinsky's *The Afternoon of a Faun* violently objectionable, and well nigh impossible to grasp the shock produced by dancers appearing bare-legged. In prerevolutionary Russia the czars' administrators could forbid such display in the imperial theaters. Yet these very same administrators, along with the dancers, flocked to see the uncorseted and bare-legged Isadora Duncan appear triumphantly on the stage of the Maryinsky the year of Balanchine's birth, and invite her back for a second appearance a year later in 1905. The conflict between private and public morality was intense.

When the social system was overthrown the repressive lid was off, and while day-to-day living was hard, artistic expression flourished. Women's beauty and physical attractiveness had always been a core element of nineteenth-century ballet, but was treated as the reason for a chivalrous display of honor on the part of men or as the basis for pastoral comedy. Balanchine, like Goleizovsky, saw that the solutions of courtly honor didn't apply when the court (i.e., the state) itself had been swept away. The reason for the old behavior no longer existed, but to assert new behavior caused shock. Dancing like a machine, as Foregger did, in response to an increasingly mechanized society was shocking. Dancing in direct response to symphonic music without a story, as Lopukhov did, was shocking, and dancing out nonidealized relations between men and women was scandalizing. Who knows whether Balanchine would have accommodated himself to creating ballets about female tractor drivers had he remained in Russia, or have been banished to a remote provincial ballet company. Fortunately, he was encouraged by Diaghilev to develop his creative ideas in a supportive atmosphere.

During the Diaghilev years Balanchine, himself another sort of prodigal, went through an artistic transformation. To free himself of the restrictive regulations of the imperial theaters he had systematically sought movement and gestures that went deliberately against the grace and style of Petipa's dancers. His training in the Maryinsky School had impressed itself thoroughly on him, however, and when the time came he knew the classical vocabulary intimately. He returned to Petipa as to his own inheritance. The tradition of the imperial schools was a living thing that could adapt to the changing esthetic climate. He did not want to imitate the style of the older productions, but to extend and modify tradition so that it spoke directly to a newer generation. He had no desire to be a choreographic curator of museum pieces endlessly repeating past successes.

He has consistently referred to his ballets as flowers or butterflies, and casually added that no one wants to see last year's butterflies. A ballet is created for specific dancers at a specific artistic moment, and that moment has to be seized—and also firmly released when its time is past. This attitude has made him artistically ruthless in terms of preservation, but continually drives him on to make new ballets. The present contains all of the time that he is concerned with. The past interests him only as a connection with serious artistic tradition and a base from which to step forward. He has little interest in the future, believing as he does that people will dance differently in response to different esthetic concerns and the enhanced possibilities of the trained human body.

As he found in Stravinsky the rhythms appropriate to the mood of the twentieth century, he looked for dancers who were capable of responding fully to them. He turned his back on the technical proficiency of older dancers to look for a newer, leaner, musically expressive dancer. As a traditionalist in the profoundest sense, he sought to develop the essence of the system and not just preserve its current manifestations, although his new classicism was considered profoundly radical by those wedded to past triumphs. For Balanchine, his work is the logical development of the tradition he loves and naturally returns to. He is indeed Petipa's heir.

Chapter 4

On His Own

The next four years of Balanchine's life were spent exercising his choreographic talent under diverse circumstances, and marked his withdrawal from the stage as a dancer. His previous failure in English variety entertainment was replaced by success in London as a choreographer for showmen Charles Cochran and Oswald Stoll. He also was invited to Copenhagen where he staged ballets for the Royal Danish Ballet, and created *Aubade* for Vera Nemchinova's short-lived ballet company in Paris. A White Russian, Vassili de Basil, and René Blum, an enthusiastic follower of Diaghilev's company, organized the Ballet Russe de Monte Carlo in 1932 and invited Balanchine to be its resident choreographer.

It was a fresh start, and he selected three young dancers, Irina Baronova, Tatiana Riabouchinska, and Tamara Toumanova, to be the company's stars. They had all been taught by prerevolutionary imperial dancers who had settled in Paris. They had all also previously appeared as novelty dancers in cabaret acts and were exceptionally accomplished despite their youth. Because of their prodigious abilities, they presented Balanchine the opportunity to expand his own creative development. In a later interview he commented, "Choreography, the formulated design of dance pattern, has developed so enormously over the last fifteen years that perfected mechanical repetition, a hallmark of pre-war [WW I] ballet, has now become a hindrance. It is the choreographer's duty and responsibility to amplify the language of ballet by his inventiveness. If dancers only performed compositions created two or ten decades ago, they would make no technical, to say nothing of esthetic advance."[1] The world of ballet was dazzled by the innocent glamor of the "baby ballerinas."

Behind that public glamor Balanchine saw the great uncertainty of the world they were living in. They, as he, were exiles, fifteen years his junior and embarked in the same hazardous career. In truth the only "country" they owed allegiance to was the ballet company they were associated with. Its business was dancing and the formal ball was a fitting metaphor for their condition. Accordingly he began framing a ballet to express his feelings about the glamorously hectic nature of that world. Attracted to the music of Chabrier he selected seven piano pieces to be the framework of the ballet. Kochno, who was also engaged by the Ballet Russe de Monte Carlo, prepared elaborate librettos for other ballets Balanchine would devise for the company but for this one contented himself with the briefest sketch. Significantly, it was based on the music of Chabrier and so credited. There was no literal narrative thread running through the ballet but instead brief notes on each of the sections. In the company's souvenir program other ballets' stories are set out in great descriptive detail while *Cotillon* is presented as a ballet without such a verbal pretext. Each of its scenes is listed with a brief statement of its setting. The ballet consists of a series of episodes which occur in the private ballroom of a leisured family. The setting features stage level boxes set into the walls of the room. Their lush dark interiors contrast in a somewhat sinister fashion with the light enchanting colors of the costumes and the rest of the set. Chabrier himself had orchestrated two of the pieces from his "Dix Pieces Pittoresques" and the others were orchestrated for the ballet.[2] The longest of them, the "Pompous Minuet," was used as the overture as well as accompanyment for the first two brief sections of the ballet.

COTILLON

THE TOILET—ballroom in which final preparations are interrupted by the arrival of the guests.

THE INTRODUCTIONS

THE CONDUCTOR OF THE BALL—runs in late.

THE GARDEN OF PLEASURE—the master and mistress of ceremonies indicate the first steps of the first dance which are repeated by the guests.

NEW ENTRANCE AND DANCE OF THE HATS—Harlequins, Jockeys, Spaniards

THE HAND OF FATE—the cavalier approaches a screen to choose one of the hands among those which peep over it but he is stopped by a black gloved hand which appears suddenly.

THE MAGIC LANTERN—young girl foretells guests' future. Appearance of the bat and the glass of champagne.

LARGE CIRCLE AND THE END OF THE BALL

The tone of the overture is amusingly serious. It has an overblown, blusterous stateliness levened with a joyous celebratory air. As the first theme concludes the curtain is raised to reveal the young daughter of the house standing on a low stool preparing herself for the ball. The second theme of the minuet accompanys her as she puts the final few touches on her hair. A female friend stands behind her fluffing and arranging the fall of her light, full, calf-length tutu. The girl raises her hand mirror and sees reflected in it a male guest who has arrived early. He quickly approaches her, places his arm around her, and embraces her as she leans backward. It is a fleeting moment and he dashes off. "The Toilet" is over.

With the return of the opening theme, other guests begin to arrive before preparations are complete, but courtesy demands they be greeted, and so the female assistant to the Conductor of the Ball begins to make "The Introductions." The dozen men and women are presented to one another graciously, but are unable to begin without the Conductor of the Ball. To the rapid cadences of "Whirlwind," he arrives breathless and flustered. He is late and dashes rapidly around the circle of guests, fluttering and bowing. Exhausted, he sits as one of the guests deftly slips a chair under him. He bounces up again, and again relapses into the chair. The pause is momentary but necessary for him to regain his composure.

Once again poised, he is joined by his assistant for "The Pleasure Garden." They are accompanied by the selection "Mauresque" as they demonstrate the first figure of the ball to the attentive guests. These in turn pick up the measure of the dance, and at its conclusion they are presented with party favors for the next selection. The ball has been launched and picks up briskly.

The "Scherzo-Waltz" sets the pace for "The Dance of Hats: Harlequins, Jockeys, and Spaniards." These three variations are characterized by changes of head gear and props. In the first, the young girl with the young man who embraced her are joined by her companion of "Dressing." The women wear spangled dome-shaped caps, while his is pointed front and back. The dance is spritely and has something of the mood of the traditional commedia dell'arte. It is followed by a vigorous "Jockey" divertissement in which the young man is joined by two companions who gambol in and out of the stage-level boxes. The final variation, "Spaniards," finds the original trio wearing matador's hats, with the young girl playing a guitar. She holds it aloft while hopping on point as if to place it protectively out of reach of anyone who might wish to take it from her. She is alone with her instrument as the other two dance together.

The whole has a robust vitality, and concludes as figures from the hunt sweep across the stage.

Despite the vivacity of these divertissements, they have a sophisticated elegance, as does the entire ballet, due to the basically formal attire of the guests. The women all wear the calf-length tutus and the men have short jackets and black knee breeches with black hose. All wear white gloves, women's stretching over the elbows.

As the men pass across the stage, they unfold a large, four-paneled screen toward the rear at the right-hand side. The silhouette of a hand with fingers spread is in the center of a circle on each panel. The second panel from the right can open like a door, though it is closed at the start of the pas de deux, the mood of which is set by the strains of the lilting "Idyll." A man approaches the screen to choose a partner from among the gloved hands extending over the top. Before he has a chance to make his selection he is stopped by a black-gloved hand, that appears suddenly to claim him. The gloved women emerges dressed in black and wearing a black mask, and she has most definitely reversed the rules of the game. The cavalier does not get to make the choice of the woman, instead, he is chosen. Throughout their variation she seems quite clearly in charge as they face one another in the common social dancing posture. It appears to be an arrested moment in time as the hurley-burley of the ball has subsided and these two are utterly alone. She subtly emphasizes her control over him by placing her hand on his cheek to adjust his gaze firmly onto her. They obviously do not know one another, yet remain linked by some mysterious bond.

At the somewhat menacing conclusion of the pas de deux, a "Rustic Dance" brings the guests back to the floor. The young girl passes among them examining their palms and telling fortunes of various women during the following "Romantic Waltz." Glances suggest romantic attachments between some of the guests as she drifts through them seeking a sympathetic hand. For a moment it appears that the assistant to the Conductor of the Dance is that person as they rest hands on one another's shoulders. The instant passes, and the young girl runs in front of the guests and then enters one of the stage-level boxes without finding what she sought. During her search, the black-gloved woman appears and removes her mask, revealing her identity as a vampire. Her terrified partner flees. The man who embraced the young girl in "The Toilet" appears with a champagne glass in his hand, obviously drunk, staggers, and falls behind the screen. When it is removed he is not there.

The return of the "Rustic Dance" announces the end of the ball. The guests look for the drunken man and then form a large circle around the girl. As she turns, they file off, hands on one another's shoulders. They return to circle her with heads down once again as she does whipping leg turns in the center. The curtain descends on the animated scene.

The action of the ballet emphasizes the improvised nature of relations among the ball's participants. The self-absorbed girl has her toilet preparations interrupted when the image of the ardent young man is reflected in her mirror as he steals in on her. His swift, transitory embrace takes her by surprise, as does the unexpectedly early arrival of the guests. At no time do her parents appear; she is alone from the very onset, almost like an orphan, however, it is obvious that she did not summon the guests who are members of an adult world. That world is the one of her unseen parents, but she is suddenly thrust into it, to make her way as best she can.

The Conductor of the Ball, the surrogate host, is not even present, he has been unexplainedly delayed so his assistant has to make the needed introductions of the male and female guests. The young woman certainly cannot do it since, she herself is being introduced to their society. The assistant acts as hostess, aiding the young woman across an awkward moment. The action creates some small bond between them but later when the young girl reads palms, she fails to find the sympathy she expected from her erstwhile mentor.

The playful atmosphere of the ball has an enchanting glitter, but conveys an understated atmosphere of illusiveness. Despite its festive air, darker forces intrude upon the glamorous setting. Roles are assumed and furtive glances exchanged mid the revelry, only to evaporate almost as quickly as they appear. The glitter both delights and leaves one uneasy. Everyone except the young girl knows the rules of the social game, the seriousness of which flares out momentarily as the man flees his fate and the transitory suitor seeks release in champagne as demonstration of their participation in that darker world.

The metaphor of a ball as a microcosm of the larger society was a theme that attracted many choreographers in the past and continues to do so. Balanchine himself, with Kochno as librettist, had prepared *Le Bal* for Diaghilev's Ballets Russes only three years prior to the presentation of *Cotillon*. There were some obvious correspondences between the two versions. Both had Spanish and Italian divertissements and a dramatic unmasking episode and were conceived as suites of interlocking dances. The differences though, were far greater. The scenery of *Le Bal* was created by de Chirico on a large heroic scale and tended to dominate the incidents of the ballet. Christian Bérard's intimate designs for *Cotillon* had a sophisticated elegance underlined by a sombre undercurrent most explicitly revealed in the dark interiors of the stage-level boxes that surrounded the action of the ballroom floor. What was more important, however, was that the score consisted of selections chosen by Balanchine from Chabrier's music.

Central to the action of *Cotillon* is the character of the innocent girl on the verge of womanhood, placed in the midst of an adult social situation that is quite new to her. Her very inexperience makes her especially attractive to the attentive man who first extends a gloved hand to her as she is readying herself for the ball. The press of the society is expressed in the early arrival of the guests. With the arrival of the Conductor of the Ball, some order is restored and the regulated steps of the ball impose formal constraints.

A persistent leitmotiv running through the work concerns the formal movements of the hands. They are for the most part used in an acquisitive or possessive manner by the guests toward one another or toward the girl, from the entrance of the attentive man to the delicately malevolent grip of the black-gloved woman seizing a preselected guest out of the crowd. The girl's gestures are exploratory or protective. In the fortune-telling episode she seeks someone whose sympathetic character will be revealed in her palm, but she is disappointed. In the Spanish variation she grasps her instrument, and fervently extends it aloft to keep it above the reach of those around her.

On a larger scale, in the finale, the girl is clearly isolated in the midst of society. She turns, brilliantly demonstrating her clear mastery of virtuoso dancing, and the guests circle her as a pack of predators might prowl around their trapped quarry. Whether or not their seige is successful is a question left unanswered, as the ballet ends with her figure still turning in the center of the menacing circle. In a way her energy serves to keep her intact as well as to impart impetus to their potential to harm her. None of them is supportive, even the man who embraced her later turns up disappointingly drunk. There seems to be no one with whom she can have a dependable relationship. She is clearly isolated, but just as clearly destined by the nature of things to be part of their world. Society consumes youth as a matter of course and this is her first experience of the process. She lacks the wisdom of maturity and so relies on her most obvious weapon, virtuoso display, which may be her salvation, or may not. Tragedy lurks in the ranks of the glittering ensemble and gives *Cotillon* its special piquancy. It is a ballet of provocative questions without any clear answers. It is glitteringly sophisticated, but veined with real feeling, which accounts for its fascination. Ballet critic Edwin Denby commented, "This piece profoundly affected the imagination of the young people of my generation. It expresses in a curiously fugitive and juvenile movement the intimacy, the desolation, the heart's tenderness and savagery which gave a brilliant unevenness to our beautifully mannered charm."[3]

The theme of fate selecting an individual out of the crowd was one Balanchine returned to later on in *Serenade, La Valse,* and *La Sonnambula,* and in each case the selection was marked by tragedy. Similarly the ball as a mirror of society reappeared in *La Valse, Tchaikovsky Piano Concerto No. 2, Vienna Waltzes,* and *Liebeslieder Waltzer.* In the latter three cases stability was emphasized but in *La Valse* society's menacing aspect predominated and claimed its victim. In *Cotillon* the menace is present as well as the formal order but no firm resolution is indicated.

Under one management or another, a Ballet Russe Company dominated the ballet scene throughout the world for the next decade, however, Balanchine very briefly had charge of his own company, Les Ballets 1933, through the patronage of Edward James. The group was organized around the talents of Tilly Losch, James's wife, and Balanchine was the chief choreographer. He prepared a half-dozen new ballets, including *Errante* and *The Seven Deadly Sins,* which strikingly displayed the theatrical talents of Losch who had appeared in Max Reinhardt's spectacle *A Midsummer Night's Dream.* The company name accurately reflected Balanchine's feelings about the here and now—it was named after the year in which it flourished. Unfortunately for its collaborators, it flourished very briefly, having only one short season in Paris followed by an equally brief appearance in London before it foundered. The collapse marked the end of Balanchine's residence in Europe.

While in London, he was introduced to Lincoln Kirstein, who proposed forming a school and company in the United States. Kirstein was a talented writer and editor with a keen interest in fine art, who had followed the latter years of Diaghilev's company. He was convinced that ballet could take root in the United States as it had in the various countries of Europe, and that Balanchine was the creative talent to make it succeed. Unlike others who wished to found companies, Kirstein felt that the necessary first step was to establish a firm teaching tradition based on the model of the imperial academy. He foresaw a school that would train and graduate students into a company and thus would establish a firm base for any performing ensemble.

As Balanchine well knew, it was a risk-filled proposition, but then so had been his whole life since the revolution had toppled the security of the imperial tradition. He accepted Kirstein's offer to head the school, but insisted that Dimitriev, who had arranged for his escape from Russia, and Pierre Vladimirov be included. The latter would be a teacher for the school and Dimitriev would be an administrator. Risky though it was, the step made sense. As Balanchine commented bluntly later on, "I left Russia and they didn't want me in France or England." There was one substantial attraction, however, and that was the possibility of working with talented, young, athletic women of the Ginger Rogers mold, a dancer Balanchine had admired in the movies.

Kirstein planned to house the school in Hartford, Connecticut, under the sponsoring shelter of the Wadsworth Atheneum, whose director A. Everett Austin offered them an artistic base. Balanchine tried but couldn't work satisfactorily outside New York without the possibility of an adult company, and plans were rearranged to make that the home of the school. Classes began with a handful of students, none of whom looked like Ginger Rogers; for the most part, they were as sturdily built as channel swimmers. Balanchine began to teach, and in a few months started working on a new ballet as if he had the most wonderful dancers in the world.

It was not only the first new ballet that he made in the United States for American dancers, it was a laboratory in which the increasing physical skills of the dancers were demonstrated to an expanding public. Like his friend Stravinsky, he never consciously set out to make a masterpiece, but only to make the best possible ballet with the dancers available.

To begin, he selected three movements of Tchaikovsky's Serenade in C for String Orchestra. As was the case with Stravinsky's *Apollon,* he was working with a score that had a pronounced lyrical quality. Balanchine was familiar with the music and with the ballet *Eros* that Fokine had set to it in 1915. For his own purposes, he chose to use only the first three movements; only seven years later in 1941 did he add the final movement, which was made third in the sequence of the ballet. For the next three and a half decades he altered and touched up various aspects of the work before he was ready to consider it finished in 1970. To a great extent he has treated the ballet as one of continuous process. Its persistent existence as part of the repertoire of New York City Ballet and performing companies that preceded its founding in 1948 testifies to the ballet's special position in Balanchine's mind.

Because of his known and frequently expressed disinterest in yesterday's ballets, Balanchine's sustained involvement with *Serenade* is unique. Its survival, albeit in altered states, results from its adaptability. Originally, it was not made for the virtuoso talents of any of his dancers because, with a few exceptions, there were no outstanding technicians among the first group of students. Moreover, those few with virtuoso skills had little theatrical experience, they were in the process of formation. Also, this was no company of established stars into which he could insert a relative newcomer and have her framed by an experienced ensemble. Therefore the ballet would in effect create the ensemble, so it was designed for the corps de ballet and not principal dancers. Balanchine had asserted that the business of the modern choreographer was to orchestrate the "masses," and *Serenade* became his first effort in his newly adopted country to do just that.

While the principal dancer will demonstrate the choreographer's intent utilizing the more difficult steps of the ballet vocabulary, the corps is expected to show these intentions through presentation of harmonious patterns. The effectiveness of the corps does not rely on idiosyncratic individual excellence so much as it does on concerted and sympathetic efforts by numbers of dancers. While patterns of unison movement were the special strength of the ballet as it emerged, Balanchine acknowledged some incidents that occurred in its formation and incorporated them into the fabric of the work. The process of making the ballet became a dramatic subtext, while its purpose remained the creation of a professional performing ensemble.

The subtext was determined in part by the numbers of students who appeared for rehearsals. Balanchine set portions of the ballet for those dancers who were available at any given rehearsal and devised imaginative passages for them. For the first rehearsal, seventeen women were available, so the opening formation of the ballet has seventeen dancers. While choreographing this first movement he had to work with sixteen dancers, at other times fifteen, and at still others with fourteen dancers. He proceeded with the diminished number, and it would take a quick eye to notice that the unison corps passages of the ballet are not always danced by the same number who started the movement.

At another rehearsal only five dancers appeared, and Balanchine began the second movement with this number, although he had yet to finish the first. On the first day one of the dancers came late to class, and to conclude the first movement he brought on a "late" single dancer to fill out an empty space in the formation, which then became identical to the opening one. At another rehearsal a dancer tripped and fell down, and Balanchine included the mishap as a moment in the first movement and as the central incident of the final movement. There were few male students in the original classes and there are few in the completed ballet. None of the men had virtuoso skills, so they were used as partners without taxing solo variations, appearing sparingly in the second waltz movement and more dramatically in the final one.

This method of composition is unusual and extraordinarily demanding. A choreographer designing a new ballet generally knows exactly how many dancers he is going to work with and can schedule rehearsals accordingly. To allow chance into the process is to place oneself at risk creatively, but Balanchine continued as if nothing out of the ordinary were taking place; nor would the finished ballet suggest anything of the happenstance that accompanied its formation.

Balanchine's initial approach to a new ballet was one of the reasons for his ability to complete the work. Even now, the most important first step for him is thorough familiarity with the score so that the overall shape of the ballet corresponds to the musical "plot." In this case he intended to display his young dancers in the classical vocabulary as best they could manage it. This dictated corps patterns as the dominant image of the ballet. The shape of the score indicated the logical position of the individual incidents and their place in the overall design. Then as now, the actual movement was only determined when he worked with his dancers in the studio. He did not arrive at a rehearsal with set gestures developed beforehand, but they emerged in creative exchange with the dancers present. It was this freedom from preconceived movement patterns that enabled Balanchine to work with such apparent equanimity in the midst of what others would have regarded as chaos. Since the ballet was conceived without a libretto, Balanchine had greater freedom to shape it than if he had to devise movement for set characters and specific incidents. The ballet grew and changed as a reaction to the numbers and abilities of the dancers. Subsequently, it changed again and again as Balanchine responded to the skills of the interpreters in later companies. No attempt is made here to follow this process, and the ballet as it exists today forms the basis of the description that follows. It is a work that incorporates second, third, fourth, and even fifth thoughts.

In addition to alterations in the choreography, the costuming changed several times. Originally, the corps was dressed in midthigh-length tunics. Four different kinds of costumes were used until Balanchine decided that the flowing midcalf, Taglioni-length tutus in light blue were

"Serenade"
[Top] Opening pose
[Bottom] Corps de ballet first movement

[Top] Merrill Ashley and corps de ballet in second movement.
[Bottom] Opening of third movement, Bonita Borne, Gail Kriza, Karin vonAroldingen, Elise Borne and Delia Peters.

[Top] Maria Calegari (behind), Richard Hoskinson and Karin vonAroldingen in the fourth movement.
[Bottom] Final tableau of fourth movement

exactly what were needed. This design was made by Barbara Karinska in 1952 and has endured. The male costume was an all-over, simple, body-hugging garment in powder blue. In 1982 the men's costumes were changed to a hard finished slightly darker cloth with gold decoration around the neck of the "guided" man and silver for the others.

When the curtain rises, seventeen women stand in a bowtie formation that has eight women in each of the diamond clusters and one in the center connecting them. It is an exceptionally graceful formation of vertical files despite the odd number of dancers (1 2 3 2 1 2 3 2 1). Their right arms are raised with the palms outward. All heads are turned in profile to the audience looking off-stage. The hands are brought in to rest lightly across the brows as the faces are turned to look away in a gesture that suggests farewell. The arms are then rounded into the parenthetical shape in front of the torso that comprises the first position. Suddenly their feet, which have been facing forward in the parallel, everyday "civilian" position, briskly snap open to the sides in the first position with the heels pressed back to back. In a brief moment the young women have been transformed into young ballet dancers assuming the opening stance of the standard ballet class. The change is effected with great economy without anyone moving from place. Martha Graham said that this opening brought tears to her eyes.

The women quickly run through a crisp series of standard exercises that would be performed at the barre in the beginning of class, and close the feet in the fifth and final position to conclude the brief resumé of steps. This "condensed" drill reminds one of the regular morning class each dancer takes. It provides the basic limbering-up exercise necessary to get the muscles warmed for later performance, and here it introduces the rest of the ballet.

The corps dashes upstage to form a square and then deploys into diagonals. The first soloist flashes brightly through and exits. The group returns upstage to assume a triangular shape and the second soloist enters to take her place at the peak of the formation. It is a memorable image of the actual organizational structure of a ballet company, with the principal dancer occupying a position at the apex of the corps, which forms the essential supporting mass; it is from this trained base that principal dancers eventually emerge. They sweep downstage to form a large diamond and then soften into a parallelogram. The third soloist follows the other two with a brief variation, and exits. Then a striking diagonal of all the corps slashes across the length of the stage. The woman closest to the audience arcs her arms in an upward curve and runs off. Each of the corps dancers does exactly the same a fraction of a second later, so that the image retained is like that of a breaking wave.

The third soloist returns to execute a series of languorous leg extensions, after which the the is joined by four corps women. The second solo dancer flashes through doing vertiginous turns, leaves, and returns a moment later still full of energy. She then raises the back of her hand as if she feels faint, and sinks gracefully to the stage. This echoes the farewell gesture of the opening formation, but here suggests the strenuous exertion required of the classical dancer. That is usually carefully hidden from the public, and this incident has a charming frankness to it.

Immediately she is attended by fifteen corps women who sit like five spokes that radiate outward from her. Gracefully and in unison, they perform a series of staccato unfolding arm gestures while in place. They may be momentarily rooted but their arms continue the flowing movement of the dance. Despite the many pictures formed by the corps during the course of the ballet, the momentum of the onrushing score is never lost. At the end of the sequence their arms are folded across their torsos, momentarily recalling the submissive and melancholy pose of the doomed Wilis in *Giselle,* and showing a sympathetic identity with their fallen soloist.

She now rises with renewed energy, leaps, and dashes off. One by one the corps dancers glide into a large circle, pivoting and turning. The beauty and simplicity of it climaxes the emergence of the corps into a fully fledged ensemble. They began with the first position, the most basic stance for the beginning dancer, and perform this spectacularly exciting series of piqué turns before their exit. When they return a moment later it is to the still, opening bowtie formation. As they stand, the first soloist enters "late" from the rear and steps carefully through the standing group until she finds the empty space at the front of the diamond on the left. Conscientiously, she extends her arm in the farewell gesture that they all have again assumed and in effect disappears into the ensemble. The opening measures of the music repeat and they all repeat the gesture of placing the back of the hand across the forehead then step slowly off into the wings, leaving the "late" dancer to await a young man who is walking slowly on as they depart.

The music for the romantic waltz begins as he lightly touches her shoulder to invite her to dance. As is normal in the instruction of young dancers, they are first taught to master the vocabulary of steps alone without attempting to dance with one another. The adagio class for the male and female as partners follows later. In *Serenade,* the adagio class is, in

effect, the second movement coming right after the stunning demonstration of the standard vocabulary of steps in the opening movement. The
cool blue lighting suggests a romantic interlude, and the trellislike
formations of the corps at times hint at shapes that might be encountered
in a formal garden. The couple begin the waltz happily circling within the
gracious frame provided by the corps lining the sides and back of the stage.
As they dance, the corps women bend forward at one point and kick one
leg high behind them, creating the effect of a jet of water with their tutus
cascading.

The man leaves and the woman is joined by the second and third
soloists. The latter continues alone for a moment in the happy, celebratory
dance until she is succeeded by the couple and the corps. The duet
continues and the corps forms a sinuous curve when they exit. After the
rigorous framing lines of the earlier part of the movement, the curve looks
organically vital contrasted to the right angles. They now divide into two
diagonals of eight members each. As they intersect, the second soloist
dashes ahead of the intersection point and moves quickly downstage
toward the audience so that she is at the peak of the V formed by the
meshing corps women. The image lasts only a moment, but in that short
time it echos her capping position of the much less dynamic triangle of the
first movement. At that time the corps formed a static grouping, but this
image emerges suddenly from the highly energetic intersecting of the two
diagonal lines.

The couple returns to lead the entire group in the final measures of the
waltz. The man lifts her in a considerate demonstration of her primacy
among all of the other dancers present. She alone has a partner toward
whom to express romantic feeling in a beautiful waltz. Just before its
conclusion, they leave and all of the corps members begin to walk slowly
off. Coincident with the general exit, five of their number gracefully defect
from the group, stepping in carefully plotted arcs to assemble in a line
upstage as the music concludes. It is as if they have been selected from a
large class to remain behind for further work after the majority of the
group has been dismissed by the balletmaster.

The tema russo accompanies the movement vigorously, though it
begins softly and gently. The five women with hands around one another's
waists perform a slow split to sink to stage level. There the "fatigued"
second soloist in the center of the line offers her hand across the torso to the
woman on her left and does the same to the woman on her right. The
clasping of hands expands outward to the four and the end women offer one
free hand to the empty air beside them as if to include those presently

unseen. They all bend forward over the extended leg in a pose that suggests the patient posture of the spellbound queen of *Swan Lake* as she awaits the appearance of her admirer. The women rise and sinuously wind and unwind holding hands while anchored to the central woman. With the entrance of the lively Russian theme it appears as if their real partner in the dance is the enlivening cadence of Tchaikovsky's music.

The five dance in unison with heads bowed down, kicking the front leg forward. They leave to be followed by four groups of women who continue the vigorous impetus of the music. The first "late" solo woman returns with the man following her ardently. He drops to one knee twice as he pursues her. She appears to step out of his reach in an almost teasing fashion. Briefly alone, she flings one arm and then the other overhead echoing the "Russian" gestures that the second soloist made at the opening of the movement. She is supported by her returning partner who then exits, leaving the corps and soloist deployed over the whole stage. Together they rock back and forth almost like bells tolling softly in their long, full tutus. Again the women perform the farewell gesture of the opening and hold the pose briefly. As the music rushes to its conclusion they all dash into the wings, and when they have gone the "late" soloist is seen immobile on the stage, left behind by her partner and the entire corps. The moment has a poignant feeling of isolation and despair.

The "Elegy" is the final movement, and begins with the entrance of a man, not her former partner, being guided by the third solo woman who walks closely behind him shielding his eyes. It is a curiously ambiguous relationship. He is in front, presumably the lead position, but she is in control of their direction and steers him to where the "late" soloist is lying. When they arrive the guiding dancer removes her covering hand from his eyes and as he bends to assist the "late" soloist up, he is interrupted by his guide, who stands in an imperious attitude on point. Slowly and smoothly as he turns her by grasping her supporting leg, her extended leg sweeps over the prone figure. The two full-circle turns have a fateful, mysterious solemnity, especially since the impetus for the turns is not immediately apparent, as the man is partially concealed by the drape of her long tutu.

He releases her and walks upstage where the two women join him. His guide stands closely behind him and the "late" woman leans back against him dependently. The three form a tight chain with the man as its nexus. He grasps each by one hand, and standing between them, lowers each to the stage where they stretch out as he remains standing. Suddenly a woman appears running toward the man who catches her as she leaps to him and sets her gently down to allow her to continue off. Another woman leaps to be caught and held for a moment before she is allowed to follow the first. The catch of the next woman is even more spectacular. She leaps toward him and then reverses herself in midair so that she is caught facing away from him. He is the center of a cyclone of movement as women literally throw themselves at him.

The two soloists now rise and he partners one then the other briefly before further demands are made of him. Again three women run to him to be caught and set down, and the final catch is on the hip where he holds the "fatigued" woman for a moment before setting her down. The three soloists now engage in a contest for his attention, as first one and then the others throw their arms around him in an embrace. They all exit and are replaced by four men and eight women. The men alternate between the two lines of women supporting and lifting them. Their partnering is straightforward and dignified. There is no attempt at virtuoso display, merely the calm presentation of one group of women and then the other.

This brief episode amplifies the triangular relationship of the man, his guide, and the "late" woman, who now return. The symmetrical movement of the corps men back and forth between the two files of women is a harmonious development of the movement of the man between the two women. After a moment the three separate. The guide stands apart, covering her eyes with the now familiar back-of-hand-to-forehead gesture. The man tries to support the "late" woman whose strength seems to be diminishing. She is almost horizontal to the stage as she rapidly twists over and over with his arms circling her waist. Then she sinks exhausted and he gently lowers her to a reclining position. Gently but firmly the guide returns to flap her arms like summoning wings and shields his eyes once again. The interlude with the "late" woman is over and the guide claims him for her own. The two proceed off as the downed woman weakly extends an arm after them; however, the gesture is in vain.

Six corps women enter in two files and three men stand between them, waiting as the "late" woman is embraced briefly by a seventh woman who takes her into the group. The men lift her so that she stands straight up and slowly carry her to the upper left of the stage where a flood of soft light from the wings pours out like a beacon. As they proceed, the woman opens her arms wide and bends her head backward in an accepting gesture.

Dominant among the many images left by the ballet is the cascade of the corps as it creates the matrix of movement design that provides the constant visual support of the ballet's incidents. The initial farewell of the opening moments has been succeeded by impressive, impetuous formations of great subtlety and variety. At one time in the ballet's history there was only one female soloist who danced all of the solo roles.[5] At other times as many as five women danced them, but the present version has settled on three. To a great extent though, attention is drawn to the first soloist because it is she who is "late," falls in the final movement, and forms the couple with a partner in the middle two movements. She experiences a romantic entanglement and abandonment by two men.

The first is her dancing partner with whom she shares the gaiety of paired dancing. In any ballet company, however, individuals have many partners depending on the dictates of casting schedules, so that his loss could be ascribed to normal circumstances. The loss of the second man is far more profound. From the first time that he appears he brings another female with him, so that he is never entirely hers. The two of them have to watch as other women fly through the air as if magnetically attracted to him. Neither his character nor their relationship is ever clearly defined. In a ballet about dancing, it might be inferred that he is a creative presence around whom interst is likely to center.

The guided man's own attitude is strangely serene and accepting. He never suggests by the least gesture that he resents or questions the authority of the woman guiding him. Far from it. He clasps her to him along with the "late" woman when they perform their brief pas de trois. He detaches himself momentarily from both of them to catch the other women as they sail toward him, but he never makes the least attempt to halt them. He gives them the support they need and allows them to pass off on the trajectory they select. After the embraces initiated by the women, he is tender toward the "late" woman as she slips down, but leaves her without a second thought; he is interested and considerate, but is fatalistically distanced at the same time. He does what is possible given the circumstances, and these dictate that he move on. The imperatives of a larger design command his obedience and the "late" woman is received ceremoniously back into the body of the company. One feels that there will be other encounters, other ballets, and that their transports and disappointments will be similarly enjoyed and endured. At the start of the ballet, the dancers bid farewell to another world to enter that of classical dancing, and within that ordered world there will also be farewells. Sacrifice is presented as a necessary companion to the joy of disciplined movement. The shadow of sadness that haunts the lyrical score finds its correlative in the allied craft of dance.

Classical dancing is a marriage between two types of artists, the creative and the interpretive. The first three movements of the ballet concentrate on the execution of prearranged steps, with little incidents of some dramatic weight studded throughout to provide necessary tension. The attention of the viewer is centered on the corps de ballet and to a lesser extent on individual soloists, the greatest number of whom are women. The men exist as distinctly subordinate characters in whatever capacity they occupy. Considering that there are far larger numbers of virtuoso female dancers than males at any given time in ballet, it is not unusual for Balanchine to have institutionalized the situation into a ballet in which, at least for the first three movements, attention is focused on the female. In the last movement it abruptly switches to the male.

The shift in the emotional center of this final movement is quite deliberate and in keeping with the characterization given to the male. He is not asked to dazzle the spectator or his partners, yet he is special because of the presence of the guiding woman. No one else in the ballet has such a guardian, so he is immediately singled out as being unique. The behavior of the other women toward him is extraordinarily attentive. They contend for his attention with the obvious gesture of throwing their arms around him, and even more spectacularly, of throwing themselves bodily at him. It is a far cry from the male partner pursuing the woman in the waltz movement.

The guiding woman certifies that this man, unlike the others in the ballet, has a mission. In fact, through her control she suggests that it is a fate-ordained mission over which the man has little to say. He is who he is and must act according to his nature. That nature dictates that he dance with the "late" soloist, while his guardian remains literally at his back like his conscience. He never questions why the women rush from the wings, but simply supports them temporarily as needed. He does not attempt to detain them, nor does he tarry when his guide places her shielding hand over his eyes to command him to journey further on. He is like the artist pushed restlessly along from one creative encounter to another. He does not display the virtuoso dancing needed in a first dancer, but instead shows the magnetic presence of one possessing a gift.

The progression of the ballet from the opening gestures of a routine ballet class to the dramatic encounter of dancer and choreographer flows smoothly along. The freshness of the corps patterns is stunning as well as being touched by romantic lyricism. The spikey angularities often seen in Balanchine's previous and later works are nowhere apparent here. The movement vocabulary is rounded, full, and lush, suggesting the contours of the female body as traditionally presented in nineteenth-century ballets. The ballet is a special poem to classical dancing pushing its roots firmly down in the soil of tradition, while announcing the suitability of plotless ballets to extend that tradition in the twentieth century.

If Balanchine looked to Petipa as the source of the tradition, he glanced significantly at Fokine's understanding of that tradition when shaping *Serenade.* As a matter of fact, he opened his ballet with a corps of seventeen women later reduced to sixteen or fifteen, just as Fokine did in *Les Sylphides,* the first plotless ballet. He also made no distinction in costuming between the soloists and corps, again echoing the older ballet. Again, as in *Les Sylphides* the interpenetration of the soloists and corps steadily reemphasized the importance of the latter as a character in its own right.

For all practical purposes, the native American style of movement began to find its form in this ballet. For the first season of the new American Ballet the bulk of the repertoire consisted of works Balanchine had previously mounted for the short-lived Les Ballets 1933. He prepared two other novelties that did not remain long in the repertoire. The first was *Alma Mater,* which presented vignettes from college life, and *Reminiscence.* The latter was set to a selection of ten pieces by Benjamin Godard, a composer whose music was little known in the United States. Balanchine had been familiar with his work since his student days at the Conservatory in Leningrad. Like *Serenade,* it was designed to function as an ensemble ballet with variations for the more technically accomplished dancers in the company. Unlike *Serenade,* it did not engage Balanchine's enduring interest, and shortly passed out of repertoire.

As a choreographer, Balanchine now had at least the beginnings of what he needed—his own company. The five years since Diaghilev had died provided fitful opportunities for him to work. The remainder of the decade, although episodic in terms of performing opportunities, at least left him in charge of the artistic direction of his company. He might not have the chance to work as intensively as he would wish, but he could do the ballets that he felt were needed, and do them on something resembling a sustained basis. The transitory nature of Les Ballets 1933 was not entirely behind him, but he had found his future home.

An unexpected invitation was extended to the American Ballet by the administration of the Metropolitan Opera House in 1935 for the company to take up residence there. Balanchine agreed to prepare opera ballets for the productions that required them, and his company could mount occasional evenings of their own. The situation appeared to be ideal. In a way it replicated Diaghilev's relationship with the Monte Carlo Opera, providing the company with a home and giving it the opportunity to

mount its own productions as well and tour in the summer months when
the opera was closed.

Day-to-day conditions in the opera house were difficult, however.
Rehearsal time and space were limited, dressingrooms were dank, and
all-ballet evenings were not really wanted or encouraged by the management. Balanchine worked diligently, doing more than a dozen opera
ballets and a handful of his own works, but there was persistent muttering
from music critics and the more conservative members of the opera
audience. The seductive ballet in *Aida* drew particular wrath. Simply
stated, it was too sexy. It was not in the tradition of the Metropolitan; the
tension between Balanchine and the administration grew. The American
Ballet did manage to present a danced version of Gluck's *Orpheus and
Eurydice* with the singers heard but not seen, but almost to a man the
music critics condemned the production and after two performances it was
dropped. The next season Balanchine managed to present an all-Stravinsky
evening, his first formal celebration of the twentieth-century composer he
respected above all others. The relationship between the company and the
opera administration worsened, however, and finally ruptured. The
American Ballet departed and the Metropolitan returned to its more
traditional presentations of opera ballets. Uncharacteristically, Balanchine
vented his disappointment to the press, declaring that the Metropolitan
was an impossible place for a talented choreographer because it had a
tradition of "bad ballet."[6]

The American Ballet was homeless once again, with limited performing
opportunities. A handful of the dancers, with Kirstein as director, presented ballets on summer tours under the name Ballet Caravan, rarely
playing New York seasons. Balanchine was invited to work on Broadway
and in Hollywood, and employed many of his dancers in both places. The
school, however, kept on training young pupils for the day when performing opportunities would be available. In 1941 Nelson Rockefeller, then a
State Department official, asked the company to undertake a good-will
tour of South America, and the dancers from Ballet Caravan and the
American Ballet joined under the name American Ballet Caravan for the
six-month trip. In addition to readying repertoire pieces, Balanchine
created two new ballets, *Concerto Barocco* and *Ballet Imperial*.[7]

His reason for designing *Ballet Imperial* was to pay homage to the ballet
tradition in Russia as he had experienced it. It was to be regal and was
costumed accordingly. The braided blue tunics of the men did indeed
suggest cavaliers at court. The tutus of the women eloquently proclaimed
the Maryinsky ballerinas. The backdrop showed a vista of the Neva River

that flowed through Saint Petersburg. Blue draperies and columns framed the view. A large, heraldic, two-headed eagle crowned the scene, a regal setting in an elegant ballroom. Subsequently, Balanchine felt that the imperial image was inappropriate, and simplified both costuming and decor. The tutu was banished in favor of a light shift, the male tunic became a soft large-sleeved shirt, the background became a softly lit plain cloth, and the name of the ballet was changed to *Tchaikovsky Piano Concerto no. 2.* A formal passage of traditional mime between the principals was eliminated from the second movement and replaced by a danced colloquy. Despite the changes, the ballet still has an air of leisure and position, though it is not so clearly set in czarist Russia.

As the ballet opens, a diagonal line of eight men downstage faces a similar group of women upstage. As the men approach, the waiting women open their arms to greet them. The men bow and the women graciously return the greeting before pairing off. They form vertical columns at either side of the stage and four additional women drift through the standing files. A female soloist enters as the piano plays a brilliant passage. The couples have formed themselves into two large crosses like the spokes of wheels, and rotate slowly as she holds center stage.

The men exit and all of the women form behind her and animatedly do unison pirouettes with her as the leader. She leaves and the men return and lift the women one by one to form columns in the center. When the solo dancer and two female companions return down the center column, all of the women form a large circle and walk clockwise, turning and inclining their upper bodies, while the men walk in the opposite direction in a smaller circle inside. It has the formal look of a social round. The men and the soloists leave and four groups of four women each remain.

They form the "sides" of a square canted on its side. Alternately, one group moves toward the center and then back to the starting position. It is almost as if they are preparing the scene for someone who will occupy that strangely empty center space. They dissolve into an arc as the lead couple enter. The woman is quite clearly in possession of the whole situation, and proceeds to perform a dazzling variation, ending with a circle of leaps and swift little turns as she exits. She and her companions return momentarily to lead the corps women in a small reprise of the unison fouettés that were seen at the beginning of the movement. Display is in the air!

The passage of bravura dancing by the lead woman has clearly established her aristocratic character. She is unquestionably first by virtue of her demonstrated skills. While the variation is showy, it is so with purpose.

One must be made aware of the hierarchy of rankings as it existed in the Imperial Ballet, and virtuoso display clearly marked the first dancers of that era—or any other for that matter. Once that is firmly established, the infatuated pursuit by the principal male is clear. He will follow her, not the flirtatious young woman who preceded her. She, too, is part of the social group, but occupies a secondary position in the development of the ballet.

The corps women line up vertically on either side of the stage as the lead male stands pensively in the center. The principal female enters upstage behind him, drifting over to the left and then crossing to the right in front of him. She makes no attempt to stop, but he stretches out a hand to grasp hers. She hasn't sought him out but she does not resist as he draws her to him and enfolds her with one circling arm. Without hesitation she curls into that arm. Proudly taking her hand, he walks her past the four quartets of women who line the stage and welcome the two with a little bow. She is the acknowledged leader of this society. No other individual is singled out for such a reverence, despite the air of polite dignity that permeates the ballet. She executes a series of toe-jabbing turns that are brilliantly crisp, and he follows with a display of clean leg beats that matches her own virtuosity. After a supported pose they dash off.

The duet is marked by passionate but classically expressed involvement between the dancers. It is obvious that the man is the more ardent of the two, and the woman gradually warms. The couple and the corps are replaced by the vivacious younger woman accompanied by two men. She never seems to settle on a single companion, but always turns up with two escorts between whom she can divide her attention, suggesting that she has a certain flightiness. The pas de trois is intricately involved, with the men supporting her elegantly in a variation that is like a miniature version of the duet performed by the lead couple. Since the three are linked closely, there is little occasion for large leaps, so the men restrict themselves to small jumps as they turn her on point. As the music nears its finish, all of the corps men and women return with the lead couple and perform a bright, flashing series of leg beats, and drop to one knee to conclude.

The precision and clarity of the group is a brilliant display of traditional technique. Here the virtues of the imperial tradition are presented most forcefully. Discipline, photographic exactness of the classical vocabulary, and sheer opulent display combine to characterize the whole society. In the midst of that society a love story is played, but it is being done according to the strict rules of behavior set down and adhered to by all.

The second movement finds the lead man standing with face downcast. Five women approach him from either side. The leaders of the two groups are the companions of the soloist, each of whom grasps one hand of the man. The corps women string themselves out so that they are like giant chains stretching out from him, but he scarcely notices them because he is seeking someone else. With an easy forward sweep of his left arm he sends the entire line of women out like a whiplash and just as easily swings them back behind him. He repeats the movement with his right arm and that file of women swings back. Parading the two women closest to him with their arms held high, he forms arches through which all of the other women duck and dash to and fro. The whole scene is just a flurry of women, none of whom is the one for whom he still searches.

The women form two columns reaching vertically upstage and he kneels at the downstage end. Suddenly he sees his previous partner coming down toward him through a forest of swaying arms. He rises to greet her and she retreats up the column as he follows. Playfully, she eludes him by circling outside one of the lines of corps women only to reappear downstage where he just had been. Their duet is full of lifts and gentle partnering, which the two files of women observe from the sides of the stage. To conclude, she embraces him, then backs away upstage as the files close in the center. When they part she is gone and the "chains" of corps women reaffix themselves. After a repeat of the whiplash sequences he walks sadly off. It is the sort of meeting and parting that serves to whet the interest. Obviously, he has been seeking one woman all along and is uninterested in the myriad other women who have presented themselves to him.

The start of the third movement evaporates the "blue" mood of the second movement. Eight men dance a variation flanked by all of the corps women. The men retire in a horizontal line upstage and two groups of four women kneel in front of them facing downstage. The principal male now reappears with his longed-for partner seated on one shoulder and walks briskly between the two horizontal lines of corps dancers. First she dazzles all with her variation, and he follows with one equally brilliant, before exiting. The soloist and her two companions appear briefly and the women form behind them for a sparkling little variation before the reappearance of the lead couple, with her in the same shoulder-sitting posture. Again they perform brilliant solo variations and then lead the entire corps in the finale. The intensity of the music builds to a crashing finish when, with the principals in the center, all of the men hold a woman perched on one shoulder and the remainder of the corps drop dramatically to one knee.

The image is that of a bright, supercharged ensemble crackling with lightning movement. There is a distinguished gravity to the dancing of the men and the women that bespeaks breeding, and the ballet has an innate nobility of carriage that not even the recostuming can entirely do away with. Balanchine has always maintained that all the meaning of a ballet is in the steps, and the metamorphoses of this ballet's costumes proves it, as the patterns of the corps, geometrical and formal, reflect the style of Petipa, after whose work this ballet was fashioned.

For purposes of the good-will tour it was felt that something showing a connection between the new American company and nineteenth-century tradition was needed, but Balanchine rejected the idea of reviving one of the classics like *Swan Lake* in favor of doing this new ballet. Its original title, *Ballet Imperial,* was a clear statement about the shaping of the work, although as usual, Balanchine was guided by the score for its development and balance.

The brilliance of the piano part is made visible in the dancing of the lead ballerina. In a way the piece can be looked at as a concerto for ballerina and company as well as for piano and orchestra. The man selects her to display before the others in the first movement, continues his pursuit of her in the second, and presents her atop his shoulder in the third and final movement. Throughout, the actions of the principals are symmetrically framed by the corps, and the subplot of the solo woman with her attentive male or female attendants. Hers is a soubrette role emphasizing the changing romantic attachments that preceded selection of one person as a companion. Each has an assigned role in this most ordered society, which has the glitter of a brilliantly illuminated chandelier throwing off sparks of light.

By contrast, the second new work that Balanchine designed for the tour was austere. *Concerto Barocco* is set to Bach's Concerto in D Minor for Two Violins, and is one of the most architecturally elegant ballets that he has ever done. It has the merest wisp of a plot, but is visually ravishing. Costuming originally consisted of short skirts for the women. The corps of eight wore simple white headpieces and those of the two solo women were a little more complex. The solo man's costume featured a geometrical overlay on the torso. Subsequently, the costumes were changed to more Grecian-looking tunics for the women and a simple white tee shirt with black tights for the man. At times, the women have worn black tunics, but the ballet seems most effective when they are costumed in white.

The eight women of the corps stand in two vertical files at the opening of the ballet. They form a variety of patterns and then swing into two diagonals that intersect like a large X as the two soloists enter. The two solo women circle inward toward the intersection and then outward toward the tips of the X again until the two lines have passed through one another and the files are completely separate. The entwining musical line of the two violins finds its visual equivalent in the movements of the two women who dance closely with one another and then move away only to return. Toward the end of the first movement the corps again makes the two diagonals like a V with the point chopped off. Each of the soloists stands before one of the files and walks to the woman standing at the rear of the separate lines. One continues off stage at the left and the other exits at the right side. The peppy competitiveness of the movement has been resolved in favor of this latter woman.

As the slow second movement begins, a man lifts the latter woman over a line of the corps and then over the other diagonal. Each successive lift seems a bit higher and grander. Six women stand in two parallel horizontal lines at the right. The man promenades the solo woman so that her leg sweeps over the heads of two other women who kneel at the left. The two soloists and the kneeling women join the other six and link hands to form two closely entwined concentric lines that circle about the standing man. The formation suggests the delicate spiral in a cut-away view of a sea shell. They separate to return to two parallel diagonals as the man supports the woman soloist in a series of pirouettes, after which they exit. The corps women again form the chopped V diagonals and the first entrance of the pas de deux is repeated. Their exit concludes the movement.

The third movement once again features the work of eight corps women and two soloists. The corps formation, while it functions as a unit, is quite clearly split into four pairs of dancers, just as there is a pair of soloists. Rhythmically, the music almost has the feel of jazz syncopation and elicits an exceptionally exciting visual rubato in the movement. The variety of the corps patterns is outstanding, given such spare forces. One of the most striking images occurs toward the end of the movement after the corps has formed and reformed itself into a series of Grecian poses. The women raise and lower their arms from a curved position above their heads while bouncing on point. Pairs alternately dip arms on staggered, slightly off-beats. Four of the corps form a square at the left and four do the same at the right, as the two solo women occupy the space in between. All drop simultaneously to one knee, opening their arms widely to the sides to conclude the ballet.

Poetic geometry dominates the shape of the ballet from the very start. The two violins dictated the casting of two solo females as the leads to Balanchine, and the reduced size of the corps reflected the small size of the orchestral forces employed by Bach. The ballet is about paired symmetry in endless varieties and demonstrations, action and reaction in equal measure characterize its development. Movement of the dancers toward one another is followed by similar movement away. They move to the rear of the stage and then to the front, to the right and just as much to the left. From a spoke formation the corps moves outward and then back to the center. There is a cosmic balance to the work that is exceptionally pleasing.

The second movement is the only time that a man is seen. He replaces one of the soloists, so that in effect one of the violins has been subordinated to the other, and he functions as the "supporting" instrument. All of his actions on stage emphasize this relationship: he lifts the soloist, he leads her in promenade and assists in supported pirouettes, and he forms the pivot for the swirling corps in its circling formation. It is a self-effacing role in every respect, but must be accomplished with true classical finish so as not to spoil the ballet's lyrical architecture. It is almost an exercise in style, but the thread of competition instills a dramatic element into the work that keeps it from being dry and uninteresting. Its enormous vigor conveys a feeling of joyous abandon within precise limits.

Both *Concerto Barocco* and *Ballet Imperial* have made permanent places for themselves in the repertory of New York City Ballet, as has *Serenade*. The American involvement in World War II began a few months after the return of the company from the South American tour and effectively ended its existence until 1946. During the seven years that it was operating though, Balanchine had demonstrated clearly his mastery as a choreographer of genius and as a teacher. The School of American Ballet continued to function and began to provide a new generation of dancers in the postwar years.

Chapter 5

Popular Entertainment

Starting as a young man in Russia, Balanchine had some connection with the world of popular entertainment. That connection was dictated to a great extent by economic necessity and Balanchine showed himself to be adaptable to work both in the intimate Petrograd club and subsequently on a Hollywood sound stage. Except for filmed efforts, nothing of these dances remains apart from their effect on the development of the American musical theater.

While Balanchine did not have the same regard for the works designed for the popular theater as he did for his ballets, he worked very seriously at his assignments and won himself a reputation for being thoroughly professional. During and immediately after the Diaghilev years he created small revue sketches in France and choreographed a production of *Orpheus in the Underworld*. It was in England, however, that he was first able to engage the popular theater under the patronage of a showman with considerable taste.

Precision dancing, that is, groups of highly drilled young women moving in unison, had become the rage in the years between World Wars I and II. Charles B. Cochran, who consistently presented some of the most sophisticated revues seen in London each season, had little liking for such display. Also, he presented his revues in a small theater, The Pavillion, which did not accommodate squads of hefty-limbed young ladies firing out lengths of legs and arms. He had seen Balanchine's ballets for Diaghilev's company and asked him to stage the dances for *Cochran's 1930 Revue* the year after Diaghilev's death. The previous season Balanchine had been entrusted with the dance numbers in *Wake Up and Dream,* staring

79

Tilly Losch, with Jack Buchanan and Jessie Matthews. After a successful
spring in London, the production moved to New York for a winter season.
The Chinese dance for Losch done with hands and arms only was singled
out for praise, as was *Arabesque* and the finale to Act I, which featured
mincing ladies in full crinoline dresses. The revue was in two acts and
twenty-six scenes; included music by Ravel, Bach, Cole Porter, Ivor
Novello, and Arthur Schwartz; and had two men dancing in a horse
costume as well as tap routines, skits and songs. It was cast as a typical
revue, but to a great extent relied more on its dancing than other shows of
its kind. "It is dancing as distinguished from athletics," Brooks Atkinson
commented in the *New York Times* the day after the revue opened in New
York. Richard Watts, Jr., observed in the *New York Herald Tribune* that the
show "is at its best when it dances." Somewhat ungenerously, Balanchine's
name was omitted from the credit listings in New York where Losch,
Buchanan, and local dance arrangers Max Rivere and Sonnie Hale were
listed as being responsible for the dances and ensembles. Whatever the
listing, the important thing was that Balanchine had Cochran's
confidence.

As usual, Cochran's company traveled to Manchester, to shake down the
1930 version of the show before bringing it into London. In its final format
it had seven dance numbers. Balanchine did six of them and Lifar the
seventh. For the most part they were divertissements, but customarily
there was one ballet-length number. For this show it was *Luna Park,* or
The Freaks, and was performed to a score by Lord Berners, who had written
the music for *The Triumph of Neptune,* also choreographed by Balanchine for
Diaghilev. It had a libretto by Kochno, and featured a series of blackout
sketches. In one, Lifar looked like an Indian deity with multiple pairs of
arms casually strumming a banjo with one pair while posing with the
others. Some of the other dances included *The Wind in the Willows,* based
on the popular children's book by Kenneth Grahame, *Picadilly 1830,*
Tennis, and *In a Venetian Theater.* For the last, Balanchine arranged his
twelve female dancers in three rows in a theater box. They were in long
dresses and long white gloves. The entire action of the number was carried
by the hand and arm gestures of the dancers as they indicated a gamut of
behavior such as might be seen in the boxes at a theatrical production. The
dance critic of the *New York Times,* John Martin, saw the revue and wrote
back favorably about it, commenting on Balanchine's "new and authentic
hand;" *In a Venetian Theater* had caught his attention most prominently. A
year later Balanchine was engaged by Oswald Stoll, whose shows at the
large Colisseum Theater reflected traditional music-hall design, including

animal acts, acrobatics, comedians, skits, songs, and of course, dances. It was a less happy time, but since his six-month stint with the Royal Danish Ballet after Cochran's revue closed, no one else had made him an offer. When his engagement at the Colisseum was over he had to return to France, since he couldn't renew his British visa without being employed.

Classical ballet reasserted its claim on him; first the Ballet Russe de Monte Carlo and then Les Ballets 1933. When he emigrated to the United States in 1933 his energies were devoted to the School of American Ballet and the American Ballet in concert with the Metropolitan Opera. When he was offered the opportunity to work on Broadway in the *Ziegfeld Follies,* he accepted. By this time Florenz Ziegfeld had departed this life, but the Shubert Organization continued to produce the *Ziegfeld Follies,* adhering in their fashion to the tradition that had been established. For the 1936 edition, which opened in January, they engaged Balanchine to do the ballets. All the modern dances were staged by Robert Alton. Vernon Duke provided the music and Ira Gershwin the lyrics for the two-act show with fourteen scenes. Vincente Minelli, whose musical films subsequently earned him honors, was the set and costume designer, and veteran John Murray Anderson was in charge of overall staging.

The leading female stars of the show were Fanny Brice, Josephine Baker, and Harriet Hoctor. The last could spin like a top, Baker's tawny epidermis, or as much of it as the censor would allow, was her passport to stardom, and Brice's comedic gifts had been well established for years. Balanchine traded on exoticism in the material he designed for Baker. In *5 A.M.* she found herself confronting African gods in a dream sequence. In the sultry *West Indies* she interpreted a torrid conga, and night horse races in Paris were evoked for her in *Maharanee.* She looked marvelous both in and half out of her clothes, danced up a storm in her own style no matter what the choreographer did for her, and sang badly. Hers was a tiny voice that simply didn't carry in the house. One reviewer noted that she sang "more or less to herself." Although audiences approved her dancing and costuming, it is doubtful that the producers expected anything else from her other than her daring presence. That alone, they hoped, would keep people buying tickets.

Hoctor was expected to dance and dance on point. Balanchine made *Words Without Music,* set in the Metropolitan Museum of Art, into a surrealist fantasy, with Hoctor's costume featuring a third arm clutching her throat as part of the design. In *Night Flight* she was a phantom dancing with three men wearing a dark green outfit. Three other men in black lay on the floor and observed them, stole up, and took Hoctor away, as if the men's own shadows had come to life and taken her off. To a great extent there was puzzlement over the exact meaning of the ballets, but Hoctor herself was admired.

It was Balanchine's first show in the United States and his first chance to work with Vladimir Dukelsky, as he was known when he composed *Zephire et Flore* for Diaghilev. On Broadway, Vladimir Dukelsky became Vernon Duke. Baker left the show to return to Paris where she was unquestioningly adored, and the Shuberts decided to rework the Baker-less show without Balanchine. In the meanwhile, he had been recommended to Richard Rodgers and his librettist Lorenz Hart, who were pulling together *On Your Toes* for that same season.

The plot was improbable, but at least there was one, unlike vaudeville, revue, follies, vanities, or music-hall presentations. Briefly, the hero Ray Bolger is a school teacher, but he is also a third generation song-and-dance man. His father has attempted to break the family tradition by having him pursue an academic career. When first seen, he is hoofing with his parents but soon is directed to be a music teacher well clear of the stage. His girl friend, Doris Carson, writes songs. A touring Russian ballet company visits town and Bolger falls for the star, Tamara Geva, which causes problems with Doris. He resolves to become a member of the ballet (whose Diaghilev-like figure was played by Monty Woolley) and disguises himself to dance as a nubian slave. He appears in a cloak but when it is pulled off he is discovered because he has only applied makeup to face, neck, hands, and legs up to midcalf rather than all over. The company is foundering and he proposes a new ballet based on a composition that one of his students has written about a Tenth Avenue gangster. When it becomes apparent that the leading male dancer of the Russian ballet cannot cope with the jazz accents of the new work, Bolger is asked whether he will do it. Furious at being supplanted, the star, Demetrios Vilan, hires a gangster to shoot Bolger at the end of the *Slaughter on Tenth Avenue* ballet that is the climax of the second act. The plot is discovered by the girl friend who saves Bolger. He consequently forgets his infatuation with Geva and everyone lives happily ever after.

Two big ballets formed the climaxes of Acts I and II. The first was a humorous takeoff on *Scheherazade* called *La Princesse Zenobia,* which spoofed the then rather threadbare version of Fokine's ballet being presented by the various Ballet Russe companies that tromped tirelessly across the country. It was obvious to all that something more up to date was needed, and that was the jazz-inspired *Slaughter on Tenth Avenue.* It saved the company. Bolger contributed enormously to the success of the show and was referred to as a "jazz Nijinsky." Geva with her stunning good looks and Russian accent was just the sort of dancer who could stand up to Bolger. Together they were widely acclaimed.

When Balanchine signed to do the show he stipulated that he be called a choreographer and billed as such in the program and any advertising, including the marquee. Previously, the assigned title had been dance arranger, and the new designation was a first for Broadway. Dwight Deere Wiman, who produced the show after the Shuberts declined, was a tasteful man and little inclined to meddle with composer, lyricist, or choreographer—he just let them get on with what they were doing. It was the first time that a choreographer had been designated as such, and the practice has continued.

The show became the hit musical of the season. What was most appealing to reviewers was its light, easy, informal spirit. It was obvious that this was a fresh approach and that such a production had not been seen before. It was the first time that dancing as such became an integral part of the plot line, so one could not conceive of the show without the presence of the two ballets—it simply would not have made sense. The other dance routines contributed, but the ballets were key to understanding the plot.

At this time, dancing duties were assumed by the chorus girls, whose abilities were adequate to what was asked of them, but not up to the standard Balanchine desired. He put Geva, a trained ballet dancer, in the top female role and slowly over the next decade the versatility of Broadway dancers grew. It was no longer enough to be able to kick and swing arms in unison, the dancing vocabulary was being expanded to accommodate dramatic expression as part of plot development. Thus the unity of dialogue, dance, and song was given its first big push forward. It also helped that Rodgers, Hart, and George Abbot collaborated on the book, which further ensured that the production would hang together.

The wickedly funny takeoff of *La Princess Zenobia* must have given Balanchine a wry sense of satisfaction, since it lumped together the conventions of the old nineteenth-century traditional fairytale classics with the revolutionary, romantic Oriental ballets, and showed both to be outmoded. The ballet that saved the day, however, was his contemporary, jazz-inspired work. It reminds one of the announcement for Evenings of the Young Ballet a dozen years before, when he traced the development of ballet from Petipa, through Fokine to Balanchivadze. At that time the powers that be kept him from presenting his work at the Maryinsky, but in America his show opened at the Shuberts' flagship musical theater, The Imperial. The Ballet Russe de Monte Carlo even took out an ad in the program, congratulating the cast and producers on their success, and suggested that patrons who enjoyed *La Princesse Zenobia* might like to see the original, which was then being presented at the Metropolitan Opera House.

The team of Rodgers, Hart, Balanchine, and Wiman followed up its success with *Babes in Arms, I Married an Angel,* and *The Boys from Syracuse* in the next two years, and Broadway was never quite the same.

Babes was a prototypical production in which kids get together and, starting from scratch, put on a show for some worthy cause. In this case the cause was their own attempt to escape a work farm. The action takes place in Southport, a small town on Long Island where the children of a group of vaudeville parents have been left while the adults are off on the circuit trying to hit it big. To prove that they will not become public charges, the kids start to organize a show but find themselves stymied for want of $42 production money. A local rich kid, played by Alfred Drake, advances the money but then takes it back when two black, tap-dancing kids (the Nicholas Brothers) are added to the roster; so the group is hauled off to the county work farm. Included in the group is Mitzi Green, another young-ster who is just hitchhiking through. Even at the work farm the group continues to organize the show so that they can escape. Their efforts are frustrated until a transatlantic aviator drops from the skies and lands in the back yard to make everything allright. Even friendly audiences found this deus ex machina a little hard to take.

What no one found hard to take was the youthful vitality of the company, the impressively inventive dances staged by Balanchine, and the score by Rodgers, which included "The Lady Is a Tramp," "Funny Valentine," "Johnny One Note," and "Where or When." Also, the note of social protest inserted by Hart about discrimination was ahead of its time. In addition to the regular production numbers, Balanchine did a dream ballet featuring Duke McHale. As with the rest of the numbers in the show, the props for this one were obviously made from materials at hand, and created the world of skyscrapers from cardboard, South Sea palm trees from cellophane, and an ocean from a swirling blue cloth. In his dream, McHale has $500 and humorously moves through various imagined locales that financially were previously out of his reach. Other production numbers were devised using bath towels, lamp shades, clothes hooks, tins of scouring powder, and sheets of newspaper. The theme of an adolescent production was adhered to closely, including the casting of the show.

Mitzi Green had been a child star in movies and was now all of seventeen. Wynne Murray played Baby Rose, a child star whose film career ends at seven. A large girl with an appealing voice, she was referred to as the "hefty Goldilocks" or "adolescent Kate Smith." The whole cast was young and dynamically enthusiastic. One reviewer stated frankly, "There is so much youth hurled at you across the footlights that it might have been more than one could bear were it not so pleasantly presented."

The ingenuity of the dances derived in great part from the unconventional nature of the cast, which was a veritable children's crusade. They were not typical, experienced, professional, show dancers of the time, but Balanchine was able to devise a great deal for them to do in the context of a show within a show. Since it was make-believe, it could be obvious make-believe with props from daily living. It was quite conceivable that they could mount a whole production for $42 using the commonplace objects found in any house. Even the dream sequence could be done with the faux naif props. In addition to production numbers, the Nicholas Brothers did a tap dance routine and Rolly Pickert did a novelty number dancing on stilts. Again the collaborators avoided conventional musical comedy practice and came up with a winner.

I Married an Angel was a dream show in several senses. Vera Zorina became a star through it, there was a dream ballet of special charm, and the dance element came more and more to the central line of story development. The thread of a plot finds Dennis King, a bored Budapest banker, weary of the coarseness of the world. He vows that he will marry an angel, and does. The comic conceit that animates the plot derives from the angel's habitual honesty, lack of tact, and tendency to launch into long philosophical discussions. She nearly ruins his banking business, creates endless social embarrassments for him, and generally disrupts flawed human society with her directness.

The production was sumptuously designed by Jo Mielziner, Rodgers's music was lushly orchestrated, Hart's lyrics had their accustomed sophisticated edge, and Balanchine prepared two show-stopping ballets. In the first act there is a dream sequence in which Zorina and King visit a zoo, where the various animals do specialty dances before she passes on to a snow ballet set in Norway. The dance was designed to show off her special beauty and obviously succeeded in the eyes of the critical press. Her partner Charles Lasky had been part of the American Ballet, and brought a sure sense of classical styling in his partnering to set Zorina off properly.

Act II contained Balanchine's wickedly funny parody of the variety entertainment that was currently being offered at the major downtown movie palaces. It was called *At the Roxy Music Hall,* and contained a chorus line, here reduced to two, the glee club, a symbolic ballet, and Zorina being born out of a sea of green cheesescloth as the pearl in a papiér maché oyster shell. The symbolic ballet had Lasky holding aloft a silver bicycle. Audrey Christy and Vivienne Siegal were the chorus line.

It was Zorina's first big role, and she gave a special glamor to the dancing with her youthful grace and beauty. In the short time that he had been working on Broadway, Balanchine had challenged several hallowed practices by casting ballet-trained dancers in lead roles and also giving them major speaking roles. The traditional Broadway dancer, in his eyes, was too limited, and he was able to design fresh routines for his younger dancers and singers in *Babes in Arms* simply by drawing on their willing enthusiasm. The world of musical theater did not change overnight, but the way was being cleared for its emergence into a golden age in the 1940s and 1950s.

Popular theater had long looked to Shakespeare for material with which to frame humorous skits. Most frequently, these took the form of parody, and were regular features of vaudeville bills and the revues that succeeded them. Now Rodgers and Hart asked Abbott to fashion a libretto out of *The Comedy of Errors*. Abbott promptly eliminated all but a single line of Shakespearian dialogue from his book, *Boys from Syracuse*. When that baroque line appeared in the midst of the colloquial chatter, Jimmy Savo took the audience into his confidence with a knowing, "That's Shakespeare!"

Savo and Eddie Albert were Dromio and Antipholus of Syracuse, respectively, visiting a town in which there were two other gentlemen of the same names but from Ephesus. Teddy Hart was that Dromio and Ronald Graham that Antipholus. The humor arose from the mistaken identities and the fact that one pair of twins was married and the other was not.

Again Balanchine showed his skill at comfortably blending various styles of dancing. There were tap-dancing episodes and ballet sequences. Betty Bruce and Heidi Vosseler as a pair of courtesans were especially effective. Bruce was from the Metropolitan Opera ballet and Vosseler had been in the American Ballet. Balanchine systematically continued to introduce balletically trained dancers into his shows to perform in popular routines. It was an ingenious blend, and Burns Mantle in the *New York Daily News* remarked on it while reviewing *Boys from Syracuse*, "Balanchine has combined art as he knows it from his better ballet training with tap dancing interludes that have a true Broadway swing. He achieves fine effects both with a trio danced as a refrain for one of the popular songs entitled 'Shortest Day of the Year' and a rushing, full ensemble following another well-liked number 'Sing for Your Supper'."

Balanchine's next collaboration came with Irving Berlin, who customarily did both music and lyrics, on *Louisiana Purchase* starring Victor Moore. Moore is an incorruptible, senior senator sent to New Orleans to investigate political corruption. Moore is also a bachelor who neither smokes nor drinks, and William Gaxton, the corrupt politician, tries to tarnish his reputation by strategically planting women in his path. The first is Zorina, who poses prettily in his lap, and the second, Irene Bordoni, turns up in his room. Moore fools Zorina by announcing that she is his fiancée and thwarts Bordoni by calling in a justice of the peace to marry them. "Old Man's Darling, Young Man's Slave" was the music for the dream ballet of Act I in which Zorina does a meditation on her lot in life as a Viennese girl visiting New Orleans, caught between the scheming Gaxton and the fuddy-duddy Moore. The whole complicated tangle is shown in the dream ballet after she and Gaxton sing "Fools Fall in Love." Charles Lasky was again her partner and the ballets were again an integral part of the development of the plot.

A demonstration of Balanchine's impact on the Broadway musical is reflected in Richard Watts, Jr.'s *New York Herald Tribune* review: "Of course all musical comedies *must* [italics mine] have their ballets and since this is the case, it is a comfort to find Miss Zorina in them." When Balanchine had begun working on Broadway four years previously there had been nothing inevitable about dream ballets in any musical, nor was it likely that they would feature classically trained dancers. There were exceptions, such as Harriet Hoctor, but they were exceptions. Balanchine was consciously dissatisfied with two things—the physical skills of the then dominant dancers in the theater who, he felt, were limited by inadequate training, and the subordinate role of dance in the action of the productions. It had been relegated to a position of marginal relevance and served as a diversion from the plot rather than as a contributory element in advancing the story or enhancing the audience's understanding of individual characters. By the time he had finished his fifth show in 1940, he had corrected both deficiencies. Dancers were definitely getting better and ballets were entwined with the central action.

By the end of the year he had choreographed two other productions. The first, *Keep Off the Grass,* was an old-fashioned revue including a monkey act and a pair of duelists. It was fine as summer entertainment and owed its success to the presence of comedian-singer Jimmy Durante, and to a lesser degree, to Bolger. For this show Balanchine was asked to furnish suitable vehicles for Bolger, José Limón (Humphrey-Weidman Company), Sunnie O'Day, Daphne Vane (American Ballet), and Bruce (Metropolitan Opera Ballet.) The corps included a young dancer named Jerome Robbins. There was nothing Balanchine could do to advance the plot since there was none, but he did set off the ranked duelists Joanna and Bela de Tuscan nicely with a fencing chorus led by Limón to "Look Out for My Heart." The "Raffles" turn designed for Bolger had a Vernon Duke score. Bruce received an ovation for her tap number, "I'll Applaud You with My Feet," as she did with Bolger, Limón, Vane, and Moore with ensemble in "Latin Tune, Manhattan Moon." The whole show was set in Central Park, which furnished the pretext for the title, and included a chorus of six derelicts. At one point they sang "Horse with the Hansom Behind," which was typical of the level of humor in the show. There were a half-dozen sketch writers, two directors, one supervisor, and the Shuberts producing, which ensured that there would be a large number of cooks stirring the broth. Balanchine used his time as economically as he could, since he was also working on *Louisiana Purchase* for that same season and was going to choreograph and direct *Cabin in the Sky* in the fall of the year.

Durante's vitality was the most important element holding the show together, though Bolger helped. Balanchine's dances were not of the same level of previous shows, but then one wonders how they could be with so many people involved in shaping this production. It was a throwback to variety entertainment and exemplified Durante's raspy signature remark "Everybody wants tuh get inta dee act!" There will always be a place for such mixed bills, though they tended to turn up less and less often on Broadway, while the "book" show with integrated music and dance was starting its ascendence.[1]

That rise received a further nudge upward when Balanchine was contracted both to direct and choreograph *Cabin in the Sky*. Previously, direction, that is responsibility for the entire shape of a show, had been kept out of the hands of specialists such as dance arrangers. The newly designated choreographer might be entrusted with overall control, however, and Balanchine was the first to wear both hats.

The show had an all-black cast, including Ethel Waters as Petunia Jackson, Katherine Dunham as Georgia Brown, Dooley Wilson as Little Joe, and Rex Ingram as Lucifer Jr. The plot concerned the profligate life of Little Joe, much given to gambling and fast women, and his good wife Petunia. The first time unrepentant Joe has to face the Pearly Gates it is as a result of a slashing received in a gambling brawl. His loving wife intercedes with the heavenly powers on his behalf and wins him a second chance. Being of a sporting nature, Little Joe, now back on earth, nearly muffs this opportunity as well, by returning to his old ways. With the help of Petunia, who snatches him away from bad companions, he just manages to get across the heavenly threshold and escape the grasp of Lucifer Jr.

In the opera *Aida,* Balanchine had created a sensual ballet based on black dance movement that he recast for his white dancers' abilities. In *Cabin,* however, he had a cast of trained black dancers and approached the task differently. In an interview he explained, "What is the use of inventing a series of movements which are a white man's idea of a Negro's walk or stance or slouch? I only needed to indicate a disposition of dancers on the stage. The rest almost improvised itself. I was careful to give the dancers steps which they could do better than anyone else."[2]

The approach succeeded, as the company was praised for its lack of self-consciousness and its intense projection. The leaping smoothness of the men was singled out, as were the fluent arms of the women. Dunham, in particular, as the wicked Georgia Brown drew praise for her brilliant "somewhat orgiastic" dancing. The "Honey in the Honeycomb" number was cited frequently. While there was little reservation about the dancing, there were some criticisms of the book's black folksiness, which to some suggested a less ingenious approach than *Green Pastures* had demonstrated in dealing with the interaction of heaven and earth. Balanchine's direction was praised and the door was opened for the professional director-choreographer. In the next three decades Jerome Robbins, Agnes de Mille, Michael Kidd, Michael Bennett, Bob Fosse, and Gower Champion would use the position brilliantly.

Hollywood, with its production schedule of hundreds of pictures each year, constantly sought fresh, new talent and beckoned to Balanchine after *On Your Toes* became a hit. Between 1938 and 1942 when he returned to the Broadway stage for good, Balanchine created dance sequences in four movies. For the first, *The Goldwyn Follies,* he brought a nucleus of dancers including Zorina to Hollywood with him. Balanchine wished to exploit the film medium for the possibilities that it and it alone could exercise, but to a great extent he was frustrated by the production-line mentality of the studio system. The best he was able to achieve was demonstration to a mass audience of trained ballet dancers' abilities.

The first dance sequence takes place in the back alley between two facing rows of houses occupied by gorgeous young women who have hung their washing lines with drying clothes. The two sets of houses contain two different types of dancers, one the leggy show girl and the other the trained ballet dancer. As the number proceeds groups of both occupy the stage for a time, demonstrating their respective dance approaches. The competition between them increases until one of the ballet dancers deftly dumps one of the show girls on her well-proportioned derrière.

Zorina and William Dollar appear for a tender duet and are transformed from an everyday pair of lovers into a legendary star-crossed couple. At the conclusion they are seen again in ordinary clothes as the laden washing lines shoot out to reconstitute the scene as it had been at the opening. Choreographically, the duet was simple, but showed off Zorina's long-legged elegance.

The second big sequence was again built around Zorina, who emerges dripping from a pool in the center of a colonnaded clearing. Prior to her appearance, formally dressed young men and women in ball gowns sweep around the area enjoying themselves. Drawn into a circle around the pool, they fall back amazed as Zorina emerges. In a moment she is transformed into one of the gowned beauties and attracts Dollar. Again the choreography shows her off to best advantage as the man evinces more and more his infatuation with her. Chairs are placed in an arc by the other men for their ladies to sit and watch the couple.

Dollar's attempt to embrace Zorina fails as she slips away and leaves him prone. A huge wind makes giant curtains billow and its force pins various of the women alluringly against the fluted columns. Zorina is seen atop a huge stylized horse with her filmy gown fluttering enticingly. The dress is blown away and she is revealed in the water nymph costume in which she emerged from the pool. Gracefully, she slips from the back of the horse and reenters the pool slowly sinking until the water closes over her head. She has appeared mysteriously, enchanted a man, and has just as mysteriously vanished forever.

While Balanchine did not expand the film horizons of dance, he did work with themes that were congenial to him. He humorously presented the case for the trained ballet dancer as opposed to the traditional show dancer in the first number, and displayed the very potent charm of a woman for the hopefully pursuing man who she eludes in the second. He also gave a vast unknowledgeable public a glimpse of classical dance's possibilities.

While MGM first brought him to Hollywood in 1938, the other major studios hopped on the bandwagon; first Warner Brothers with a remake of *On Your Toes* in 1939, then Twentieth Century Fox's *I Was an Adventuress*

1940, and finally, Paramount's *Star Spangled Rhythm* in 1942. Unfortunately, none of them offered him any expanded opportunities. *Slaughter on
Tenth Avenue* was the big dance number in *On Your Toes,* as Eddie Albert
took Bolger's part as the hoofer menaced by a gangster, and Zorina slunk
through as the tough, sexy, club dancer.

The shape of that dance remained essentially the same as it was on
Broadway, and as it appeared nearly three decades later as part of the
repertory of New York City Ballet. The dancer on the stage and ramp at
the left of the stage provoked unabashed adoration from the patrons of the
club. With a brutal shove the owner of the speakeasy dispatched the
unwise fellow who mounted the stage and pumped two well-emphasized
shots into his prostrate form. A general brawl and a police raid emptied the
club for the central duet between Zorina and Albert, during which she was
shot by the manager and Albert finished him. Zorina's habitual pose was
the wilting backbend over Albert's outstretched arm. It worked well
enough, but was essentially a simple transfer of the stage production to a
sound stage.

I Was an Adventuress again featured Zorina, this time as the wife of
Richard Green, and the dance element was minimal. It entered the
melodramatic story only because Zorina happened to be a dancer and not
because of any essential plot linkage. She does a warm-up at the barre in
their bedroom after bringing him breakfast in bed and he looks on
admiringly. What he sees is a brief synopsis of the usual exercises and
Zorina's formidable extention. Later she is shown rehearsing in the theater,
and finally dancing a capsule version of *Swan Lake.*

She appears improbably in a black tutu while the corps women remain
in the customary white. No doubt it was felt that the contrast was needed
so that the public would not lose sight of her. A man in knightly garb sees
a flock of swans moving silently toward the shore where he is standing, and
a castle rises from the middle of the lake. The ballet sets the corps
fluttering prettily as the hero pursues Zorina through clouds of misty
vapor. He manages to embrace her and she leans back as he kneels. The evil
sorcerer triumphs as she dissolves from within his arms, leaving him
holding emptiness. Forlorn, he wades out in the lake and is last seen
embracing the miniature castle.

Star Spangled Rhythm was Balanchine's last film effort and he was
responsible only for Zorina's number. The inane plot featured Eddie
Bracken and a group of sailor buddies on shore leave. His father, Victor
Moore, is an ex-cowboy movie star supporting himself as a studio guard on

the front gate. He has told his son that he is the head of production, and of
course, the young sailors expect to be introduced to beautiful showgirls.
Casually, Moore promises to arrange a benefit show for the crew of their
ship. With the energetic help of Betty Hutton he does just that, and Betty
gets to marry his son.

Before the show is arranged, a sour studio executive has to be circum-
vented, but his boss hears about the all-star show and is so delighted with
its patriotic spirit that he promotes Moore. Among those appearing were
Bing Crosby, Bob Hope, Dorothy Lamour, Veronica Lake, Alan Ladd,
Paulette Goddard, Arthur Treacher, Katherine Dunham and Rochester,
Fred McMurray, Franchot Tone, Ray Milland, Dick Powell, and Mary
Martin, as well as Preston Sturges and Cecil B. De Mille playing them-
selves. In the midst of the skits, Zorina danced a solo dream ballet.

A soldier, Johnny Johnston, lying on his cot stares at a publicity
photograph of Zorina standing on a snow-covered staircase. He sings
"Black Magic" and falls asleep, as Zorina comes alive within the photograph and performs to the music of his song. There is no point work, but
the classical vocabulary of attitudes, arabesques, and chainé turns is
employed extensively. There is a great deal of running through snowy
woods and finally a long dash between a column of trees and a rapid
descent of the staircase. Instead of stopping, however, she steps out of the
frame and begins dancing on the cot next to the soldier who reaches out to
touch her tiny whirling form, upon which she vanishes. His buddy, who
thinks his dreaming friend is reaching for him, gives the soldier a rough,
you've-been-out-here-too-long shove to end the number. It was a slight
piece in which Zorina looked as well as ever, but it hardly showed
Balanchine's talent. The Hollywood interlude was downhill after *The
Goldwyn Follies,* which itself was not all that Balanchine intended. To a
great extent, film was a frustrating experience in a way that the popular
live theater was not.

The first show offered to Balanchine after his return to Broadway was
Lady Comes Across, which was a dullish recounting of a young lady's
involvement with the FBI and German spies. She dreams the incidents
before they actually happen, proving the fact that the dream sequence was
fashionable, if not deftly used. The English music-hall star Jessie Matthews was suffering bouts of severe depression and was hospitalized in
Boston during the tryouts, and her replacement was Evelyn Wyckoff.
Vernon Duke's score was uninspired, and the dances were mixed in
quality, and the book was dreadful. The dream ballets were considered the
best of the dances, and featured Lubov Rostova, Eugenia Delarova, and

Mark Platt, all the of Ballet Russe de Monte Carlo. Singled out for mention also were Jeanne Tyler and Gower Champion.

Balanchine was more fortunate in his next two opportunities. The New Opera Company had undertaken a series of operetta revivals, and *Rosalinda* was the title under which *Die Fledermaus* was presented. Strauss's music gave impetus to Balanchine's imagination and the big waltz staged at the end of Act II was a resounding success, as were all of his dances. To a great extent they dominated the production, which featured José Limón (Humphrey-Weidman Company), and Mary Ellen Moylan, William Dollar, Herbert Bliss, Edward Bigelow, Todd Bolender, and Elise Reiman, all of the American Ballet.

The next year, 1943, followed with even greater success, *The Merry Widow*. Felix Brentano was again the director and the lead singers were Martha Eggerth and Jan Kiepura. The three big waltzes elicited extravagant praise from Louis Kronenberger in *P.M.*, "probably the finest thing Balanchine has done on Broadway." The leading dancers were drawn from the Ballet Russe de Monte Carlo for the most part—Mlada Mladova, Chris Volkov, Lubov Roudenko, and James Starbuck. Their polka and Roudenko's can-can in the last act were also specially praised. The sharp-tongued Wilella Waldorf noted" . . . the audience became so violently excited over the dancers that it was more like the ballet season at the Met than the 'Merry Widow' for quite a while."

Lerner and Lowe's *What's Up* stranded a group of service men escorting a foreign dignitary, in a girls' school after their plane was forced down, and kept them there in quarantine after an outbreak of measles. The dream ballet featured the short Jimmy Savo as the foreign dignitary chasing tall Phyllis Hill around with a chair to equalize the disparity. Notices were mixed.

They definitely were not mixed for *Dream with Music*. Zorina was portrayed as an overworked radio script girl who dreams her way into the world of Aladdin and Sinbad. The score was plundered from the classics by Clay Warnick and did not touch Balanchine at all creatively. Lewis Nichols summed it up: ". . . the dances are not those by which he will be long remembered." Despite the lavishness of the settings and costumes, the result was lackluster and marked Zorina's last appearance in a Balanchine-choreographed show.

Song of Norway featured Grieg's music throughout and offered Balanchine a more sustained base for dancing. He had Danilova, Frederic Franklin, and Natalie Krassovska (all of the Ballet Russe de Monte Carlo) and the *Peer Gynt* ballet for Danilova and Franklin was notable. A vigorous men's dance to The Hall of the Mountain King worked out effectively, as did Franklin's "Freddy and His Fiddle." The production has had a long string of revivals and has engaged a variety of other choreographers, including Eliot Feld in the 1982 production for the New York City Opera.

Mr. Strauss Goes to Boston was an attempt to string together a number of melodies by Johann Strauss and Johann Strauss, Jr., into a musical. It did not get off the ground. Harold Lang (American Ballet Theater) was praised for his dancing, but little else was received with approval. Oscar Strauss's *The Chocolate Soldier* also failed to stimulate Balanchine to any perceptible degree. The ballets were workmanlike but bland, obviously the old operetta format was wearing thin among the public. Mary Ellen Moylan and Francisco Moncion (American Ballet Company) were featured dancers. *Where's Charlie?* had Ray Bolger in top form, which was enough to carry any show, and Balanchine's final show in 1951, *Courtin' Time,* was likable but slight.

Balanchine's career in the popular theater was basically divided into two periods, pre- and post-Hollywood. In the years prior to the outbreak of World War II he seemed to be able to work happily in both ballet and Broadway productions, and between 1938 and 1940 he devoted full energies to Broadway. The Hollywood years with their frustrations stopped the innovative verve Balanchine brought to mass entertainment. In the middle 1940s he became increasingly dissatisfied with the musical theater and for a time returned to be artistic director of the Ballet Russe de Monte Carlo, creating such notable ballets as *Danses Concertantes* and *La Sonnambula* (then *Night Shadow*).

With the end of World War II, Kirstein returned from army service determined to revive the American Ballet, and in 1946 asked Balanchine to be its artistic head. The new group called Ballet Society lasted two years before becoming a constituent of the New York City Center, changing its name to New York City Ballet in 1948. After that Balanchine undertook one final Broadway production.

The halcyon years were 1936–1940, in which he choreographed eight shows, each with innovative approaches. He firmly established the position of choreographer in name as well as fact on Broadway, and broke the dominance of the pretty but limited chorus girl, demonstrating the superior skills of the ballet-trained dancer and establishing a pattern of versatile excellence among succeeding generations of show dancers. Dancing became an integral part of the plot and not just a decorative appendage, and the dream ballet became de rigueur for the following three decades. He also became the first choreographer to be put in charge of direction. At the time it was a radical innovation, but is hardly even remarked on currently. Overall, the thrust of his work raised dance from trivial diversion to an essential ingredient in popular theater, and its creator, the choreographer, enjoyed enhanced prestige.

He left both Broadway and the musical considerably changed, and having done so, returned to his first priority, classical ballet. For him the musical theater was an interlude to which he devoted his immense talents because of necessity. The groundwork for popular acceptance of ballet had been laid in the 1930s by the various Ballet Russe companies, his own American Ballet, Kirstein's Ballet Caravan, American Ballet Theater, Page-Stone Ballet Company, and the Littlefield Ballet. In the confident exuberance that permeated the society after World War II, ballet enjoyed a fresh start, and Balanchine was central to its flowering.

Chapter 6

Tradition and the New

November 1946: in the auditorium of New York's Central High School for Needle Trades, Ballet Society gave its first program. Kirstein had returned from army service determined to present the best of lyric theater (opera and ballet) without the censoring interference of popularity. He conceived the idea of a subscription group of a thousand members whose annual contributions would support distinguished productions without thought to their commercial potential. In addition to attendance at such presentations as would be offered, subscribers would also receive a variety of pertinent publications and recordings. Central to the whole operation was Balanchine. For the first program he staged *L'Enfant et les Sortileges* and *The Four Temperaments*.

His first setting of *L'Enfant* was at the opera house in Monte Carlo for the work's initial appearance, and it had retained its hold on his imagination. He had commissioned the score for *The Four Temperaments* from Hindemith and was anxious to show his conception of it to the public. Aline Berstein's costumes for *L'Enfant* were charming, but Kurt Seligman's designs for *Temperaments* were distracting. The choreography nearly disappeared beneath the swatches and patches of colors that draped the dancers' bodies. Balanchine's habitual suspicion of costume designers was heightened; to his eyes their efforts were always directed toward hiding the dancers rather than revealing the dance. In this case he was decidedly correct. It was only when the original costumes were discarded and replaced by simple leotards and tights that the intricacies of the work were fully appreciated. Subsequently, the women wore plain black leotards and white tights and the men black tights and white tee shirts.

97

Hindemith divided his score into an opening theme with four variations entitled "Melancholic," "Sanguinic," "Phlegmatic," and "Choleric." The overall tone of the piece is somber and the dancers perform it with ritualistic gravity illuminated by gleams of intermittent joy. The three couples who perform the theme present its three different aspects. The first couple is coolly competitive. The man presents his hand without even looking at his partner who is standing beside him. She places her hand in his also without glancing at him. They join both hands in the same manner and he steps forward placing one foot in front of her. She responds by crossing her leg in front of his. There is a small but real competition going on between the two who are feeling one another out in the sparring manner of boxers on their initial encounter. He lifts her and she arcs one leg like a scimitar between his. He sets her down, she opens her arms and legs, and he slides her off in a split with his hands hooked under her arms. They seem united by truce rather than trust.

The second couple is more angular and querulous. She is supported and turned one direction and then another. There is a certain restlessness in their relationship, and to conclude he follows closely behind her as they step to the left side before exiting. As they move, they both hold their arms in a squared-off U shape. She flips hers down and he follows suit but an instant later she flips hers up and he again copies her gesture, a moment behind. The effort to synchronize movement is doomed to failure, and they exit still slightly out of phase with one another.

The third couple displays a modified form of the competitiveness shown by the first two. The woman is once again the object of the man's attention. Their encounter, though, seems less fraught with tension, there is a certain placidity between them. He lifts her and rocks her back and forth. Like the woman in the first variation, she curves one leg back between his but the gesture lacks the emasculating fierceness of the first episode. As she stands on point with one foot drawn up to the knee of the supporting leg and a hand poised on one hip, he holds her other hand above her head and turns her with little pushes on the shoulder. She looks like a bass fiddle being twirled by its player. Closely entwined, they hold hands and it appears as if she is firmly ensnared, but she twists and gracefully steps out of his encircling grasp as if undoing an intricate little puzzle. He extends his arms straight out supporting her as she lifts her feet and points them horizontally forward while he carries her off. The couples have been reserved, restless, and reconciled.

The melancholic theme brings on a solo man who leaps in the center of the stage, stretches upward, and then sinks toward the stage. It is as if

"The Four Temperaments"
[Top] Bart Cook "Melancholic"
[Bottom] Daniel Duell and Merrill Ashley, "Sanguinic"

[Top] Jean-Pierre Bonnefous with Carol Strizak, Nina Fedorova, Linda Homek
and Garielle Whittle "Phlegmatic"
[Bottom] Anthony Blum and Karin vonAroldingen "Choleric"

there is an immense weight that drags him down despite his efforts to remain upright. He reaches out, half twists, and sinks to the stage just breaking his fall with partially outstretched hands. He tries to rise and falls again. He stands and swirls his own arms around his torso as if to reassure himself with such a protective clasp. He reaches out, jumps, and sags, repeatedly dragged down by the unseen weight.

In the midst of his solitary unhappiness two women appear to circle around him moving close enough to touch him as he crouches. He stands and steps forward between them and the three move to the left side of the stage. They turn and face diagonally up to the right as four women enter with menacing high kicks. The quartet stands in a square facing the three who run forward to join them. The man stops in their midst placing their joined hands over his head and behind him then reversing the process. He seems enmeshed and unable to make positive progress.

The large square of four women moves away and he is left, bowed down, with the two original women flanking him. They lightly touch him and are gone. He rises and, bent backward, inches off the stage into the wings with his arms hanging. He seems utterly exhausted by the encounter with the women who have represented some type of threat. He entered alone and exits alone. Something in his character determines his preference for the solitary life weighted down with weariness.

The "Sanguinic" variation is danced by a couple, the only pair to dance any of the four humors. The woman enters and the man approaches her from the opposite side of the stage. She is lively in demeanor and he is attentive. He displays her, twisting her to the right and the left as the couples did in the three-part theme. He lifts her grandly in a large circle around the stage touching her down at the four compass points in a demonstration of her grace. Then at the center of the stage he lifts her again in diminishing circles as four crouched women enter with a slightly hobbled walk. They are like gnats who drive him away. They stand and watch the lead woman do a series of little turns to pose downstage and then exit. The man returns with a leap and is rejoined by her. They dance joyously together and she does a short variation while he watches. The four women move toward them and he lifts her again, reversing the spiral to open outward grandly. At the conclusion he lifts her high over his head and after setting her down they dash off together triumphantly. They have danced harmoniously throughout and have not allowed themselves to be distracted by the circling women with their grotesque walk.

The "Phlegmatic" man walks on and his body collapses like a marionette with its strings cut. He doesn't seem to have the internal fiber to keep himself upright. Bent forward he takes a series of little steps and allows his arms to cross like scissors in front of him. He takes a few big hops and then grasps the heel of one foot quizzically and holds it drawn up, extended in front of him; a child sucking his thumb has the same irresolution. He becomes aware of four women standing around him, two on either side. He retreats upstage, but as the pairs mesh he pushes a tentative hand through their legs as they stand, and then quickly withdraws it. The four link hands with one another in an X and two extend a hand to him. He grasps them and steps into and out of the X shape. He seems intrigued by the novel formation, but again pulls back. The four release hands and return to the sides again.

As they mesh once more he repeats his retreat. He steps forward between them and withdraws. Two pose their hands on his shoulder then all stand side by side with him in the middle. Their arms are stretched out and in succession they draw them back with a mechanical, angular gesture so that their hands hang like animal paws. A spritely tune prompts them into a humorous little sequence of rhythmic steps in which they put their feet forward and pull them back as if they had dipped their toes in cold water. They pose elegantly in attitude to the right and the left swing arms forward and back, stretch upward, and all exit. Characteristic of all of the movements in the variation is a feeling of hesitation, a lack of urgency or conviction. The man would go in any direction following the line of least resistance; his timid reaches outward are inevitably withdrawn.

Totally unlike him is the woman dancing "Choleric," who enters the stage and turns furiously. She pauses downstage where the "Sanguinic" man enters to put his hands on her waist as if to support her. This woman, however, is almost hot to the touch, and he pulls away. The three men from the opening "Theme" duets enter and all four partner her. She stands on point and they turn her like a large weather vane and then leave. She occupies the center of the stage and the "Sanguinic" women and the three women from the duets form a large square around her. Both they and the men seem to arrange themselves to contain her as if she were about to vent her rage.

As the finale begins all of the dancers from the preceeding movements enter. The men from the "Melancholic" and "Phlegmatic" variations lead on the women who surrounded them, and all of the couples are reunited. The solitary humors form a trio at the center as the "Theme" and "Sanguinic" men support their partners for a reverence to the center. The corps women form two horizontal lines into which the three solitary humors blend, and the four men lift their partners serenely across the stage from one side to the other. The final ordering of all of the dancers has a genetic rightness, showing the individual humors harmoniously mixed with the tormenting women in calm parallel lines as the couples sail truimphantly between them, expressing a satisfying male and female joining. The disharmony of weary, indifferent, or furious solitary humors finds a logical resolution as part of the whole system where each will contribute an individual element but not overwhelm the resultant balanced blend.

The presentations of Ballet Society were given a couple of times a year in a variety of locales around New York. Technically, the company was strong, but there was not a sufficient number of performances to constitute extended seasons. Balanchine continued to work off and on in Broadway musicals, and in 1947 was invited to spend six months as the artistic director of the Paris Opera Ballet. A young dancer of flashing brilliance, Maria Tallchief, had become the center of his creative interest and he took her to Paris with him. There he choreographed a new ballet entitled *Palais de Cristal,* which was extravagantly dressed in four different colors, one for each movement of the Bizet symphony. It was an immediate success, and when Balanchine returned to New York he mounted it for his own company with the name *Symphony in C,* the title of the score. Recostumed in white tutus for the women and black body suits for the men, it has become one of the signature pieces for his company.

For the next decade and a half the company was based in the New York City Center for Music and Drama's 55th Street Theater. Balanchine was at the height of his powers and drew on such music standards as *Swan Lake* and *Firebird* as well as commissioned concert jazz *Modern Jazz: Variants* from Gunther Schuller or Westernized Oriental music such as *Bugaku* by Toshiro Myuzumi. He created the first ballet using Ives's music and, commissioned *Agon* from Stravinsky. He collaborated with Martha Graham using the orchestral scores of Anton von Webern and created a ballet to his first electronic score, *Electronics,* by Remi Gassman and Oskar Sala. It was a period of extended experiment combined with sustained invention using scores of the classical repertoire. Compositions by Mozart, Brahms, Gounod, Donizetti, Glazunov, Handel and Vivaldi sat on the music stands with works by Sousa, Gottschalk, and traditional Western folk tunes. For sheer variety and inspiration, no single choreographer had ever demonstrated such high level inventiveness. Supporting the creative drive of the company was the School of American Ballet, which had supplied a new generation of dancers including Maria Tallchief and Tanaquil LeClercq, both of whom were in *Symphony in C.*

The exuberant classicism of this ballet reflected both Balanchine's own mood and the technical skill of the company. The clarity and crispness of the choreography suggested a theatricalized ballet class. Each section was led by a pair of principal dancers backed by two couples and a corps of six to eight women. The tutus suggested the classicism of the traditional school, but the energy of the choreography reflected the keen enthusiasm of the young dancers.

Two diagonal lines of women, each led by a solo female, stand as the curtain rises. Before they even move there is a stunningly ordered clarity to the formation. The lead woman (originally Tallchief) enters through the gap separating them and dances a short variation, after which she stops stock still. She and the two group leaders do a short series of leg beats backed by the corps women, whose more restrained pointing of one leg to the front, side, and back emphasizes the academic base of all that is to follow. Three men enter as if summoned, and each presents his partner and none more grandly than the lead male. After brief variations by the principals they retire, and the corps women reform themselves into a horizontal line as the three men return. They are joined a moment later by the lead woman and the two group leaders, who exit to leave the principal couple framed by the corps women who have realigned themselves into the shallow diagonals that opened the movement. To conclude, they drop back into a line upstage as the principal and other men support their partners in a series of pirouettes. The textbook quality of the movement is like the opening statement of a discourse on classical dancing.

The more romantic mood of the second movement is heightened by atmospheric blue lighting. As the movement begins, two corps women are seen moving out to the center of the stage, followed by four others. All stand in an oblique line that stretches up to the left-hand corner of the stage. Two couples enter from that point with their hands joined above their heads and pass down the standing line of corps women who dip gracefully beneath them. The measured calm of the movement is further emphasized by the walking entrance of the principal couple (originally LeClercq and Francisco Moncion) who stand downstage and form an arch with their hands above their heads for the other couples to pass beneath. As the corps women bowed under these couples, so the latter pass under the arms of the lead couple, formalizing the merit order of their skills. The lead woman's precedence is further emphasized as she is lifted from side to side with her lead foot pointed to pierce the circle of arms formed near the floor by each of the other two couples on both sides of the stage. Two short columns of corps women stand on either side of the principals as the lead woman bends forward with her working leg projected straight upward while the man holds her at the waist. She straightens and leans back to be supported, takes two small steps forward, and is caught again. She leaps upward and is guided to a seated position on his shoulder. He backs upstage and sets her down while the two couples do a brief variation, after which the three men exit.

After a series of lyrical sweeps and turns the women drop to one knee with an arm curved over their heads. Again the men return to their partners and hold them in arabesques. The soloists exit and the corps frames the lead couple in the two shallow diagonals that were first seen in the opening movement. Once more the principal woman is lifted slowly from side to side and placed down. She leans backward the whole length of her body with complete trust, and is caught and returned upright. She takes two steps forward and reclines again as the two secondary couples enter with their arms arched over the heads of the corps women as they did at the opening of the movement. The principal woman is caught once again gently and the lead man half twists her body to lie back across his thigh as he kneels. The ending is like a cradle song visualized.

The third movement is as vigorous as the second was calm. The lead couple dashes on from opposite sides of the stage and leaps repeatedly as the corps of six women form a background almost to contain such energy. Briefly, the principal male supports his partner in a series of turns before they both bound off. When they return it is to repeat their spectacular entrance. They stand side by side and bounce in place, as do the other couples, before executing a series of supported turns.

When the principals leave, the corps and solo couples are in two columns that move to and away from one another almost like the figures one would see in Scottish folk dance. The corps women then form an alley through which the supporting couples exchange partners. The six corps women form a truncated V and the soloists hold hands from either side of the lines and move downstage to the spot where the lead woman is supported in an arabesque, and drop to one knee to conclude the movement.

The sharp clarity of the first movement is followed by the lyrical softness of the second and the unbridled energy of the third. Building on the momentum created, the corps of ten women in the fourth movement performs a series of sharp, stabbing steps on point. They are in a diagonal when the principal woman enters, turning rapidly down the length of the line as each places one foot precisely out to the front, the side, and the back. This tendu step is a leitmotiv underscoring all of the spectacular dancing of the ballet, since it represents the most basic stretching exercise at the beginning of the standard ballet class. It is as if the choreographer is reminding us of the fundamentals even as he shows us the advanced work of the principal and the attendant couples.

The long, exciting finale begins with the entrance of the principals and the corps dancers of each of the preceding movements. The corps women of the last movement have retired to the sides of the stage in two columns of five each, and as the dancers of the opening movement leave, the files are lengthened to nine dancers. The second group enters for its variation and leaves with the lines now containing thirteen women each completely filling the sides of the stage. The closure across the back is completed when the third group leaves. In one of his most brilliantly simple formations, the choreographer now has the four lead women of each of the movements doing rapid fouetté turns in unison in the center, with this large formation of corps women completely surrounding them. Almost as if they were in a huge classroom doing barre exercises, the corps women together sweep legs to the front to the side and to the back repeatedly in rond de jambes à terre that boldly unite all of the dancers in the execution of related basic and advanced steps of the classical vocabulary. The music surges toward its climax as all of the corps women advance in files downstage in a delicate march step joined by the men. The four solo women dramatically lean back on the arms of their partners with one arm curved over their heads. The soloist women are placed on their partners' shoulders and the corps women drop to one knee at the conclusion of the music.

The ballet that began with limited forces, concludes with all of the dancers massed on stage like a formidable army. The sharp attack of the first movement paused for a lyrical interlude in the second and the surge of the third has been amplified by the combined energy of all in the fourth. In each case the focus of the movement has been on a lead couple, supported by two secondary couples backed by a corps of six to eight women. Cumulatively, the individual groups displaying swift, precise feet, lyrical adagio movement, jumps, and whipping turns have demonstrated families of steps that are united in the final movement, which is a compendium of the ballet vocabulary. And underlying it all are those basic tendu steps of initial stretches that all require.

As he did at each new stage of his career, Balanchine turned to Stravinsky. He commissioned *Orpheus* and created a new production of *Firebird,* both of which were notably successful. *Orpheus* was a danced tableau in which the masked poet descended to the underworld to retrieve his beloved Euridice. Their duet in which he strives to avert his gaze from her so that she will not be dragged back to Pluto's kingdom is particularly effective. The poet manages to support and partner the importuning Euridice for an extended time without looking lovingly on her. When she finally forces him to regard her, she is again lost. The brilliant settings by Noguchi contributed substantially to the ballet, and Balanchine's choreography took on some of the weighted movement that was the special contribution of modern dance.

While Balanchine's admiration for Stravinsky never wavered, the composer was enduring a period of eclipse. The music of his middle years was rarely performed and public attention seemed to have concentrated on the early nationalistic scores composed during the Diaghilev years (1909–1929). The commission for *Orpheus* was welcome recognition of his powers and Balanchine made a practical contribution to the composer's security when he decided to mount *Firebird*. The Union of Soviet Socialist Republics had for the first six decades of its existence refused to join the International Copyright Convention. Stravinsky as a Russian national therefore found that his most popular scores were unprotected. Orchestras all over Europe and the United States played *Firebird, The Rite of Spring,* and *Petrouchka* without having to pay the customary performance fees. In mounting *Firebird,* Balanchine selected the later, protected, third orchestral suite the composer, (now an American citizen,) derived from the original, and thereby ensured some royalty income for him during the twenty years that the ballet remained in the New York City Ballet repertory.

Balanchine used the designs created for the production by Chagall after Diaghilev's death. He cast Tallchief in the title role and devised choreography that was mercurially fast, brilliant, and sharp-edged. It highlighted just those qualities she possessed so fully. The ballet was made for her, and despite several subsequent revisions, never fit anyone else quite as comfortably. She gave true magic to the mythical creature who dazzled the young prince and came to his rescue when he was menaced. While Balanchine had created marvelous ballets for talented American dancers, notably *Ballet Imperial* and *Concerto Barocco* for the exceptional Marie-Jeanne, these dancers' fame had not reached the general public. *Firebird,* on the other hand, attracted considerable attention from the weekly national press as well as local daily papers in New York and Tallchief was synonymous with *Firebird.*

While bringing Tallchief to public attention and giving the company a ballet that would invariably ensure full houses, it also created a new problem for Balanchine. He had a box-office star in the traditional sense of a magnetic personality. To his mind, this was a throwback to the Ballet Russe days in which individuals rather than ballets themselves were the central concern of the public. For Balanchine, repertory was the heart and soul of his conception of a performing company, and individual dancers were to be appreciated within that context, not outside or above it. Temporarily bowing to practical need, stars such as Tallchief and the late André Eglevsky were featured and Balanchine devised ballets that drew on their special qualities. *Harlequinade* (pas de deux), *Sylvia* (pas de deux), *Swan Lake* (Act II), and *Scotch Symphony* confirmed their excellence and popular appeal.

Brilliantly attuned to the capabilities of his dancers, Balanchine displayed them with combinations of steps that were suited to them and not necessarily to any other members of his company. Since programming conflicts or indispositions due to illness or injury are facts of performing life, others did have to take over roles that were not designed for their special talents. When this occurred, with the supreme confidence of genius, Balanchine changed the ballets' individual steps without altering their overall effects. Eglevsky's technical brilliance enabled him to perform involved combinations that were, naturally enough, included in *Scotch Symphony*. Others less skilled, however, had to perform the ballet as well. He later commented, "As you know the company really has only one star and that is Balanchine. I remember when I was dancing *Scotch Symphony* there were double sauts de basques at one point and when another dancer was assigned the role I wondered how he would get through it. He didn't have to! The choreography was changed to eliminate them and the new part was made just as beautifully as the role was originally. I realized quite clearly that no dancer was indispensable to the company."

To concentrate public attention on the repertory further, the company took to listing its dancers alphabetically, which was considered quite a departure at the time, though it has become universally accepted now. Tallchief commented succinctly that she didn't mind being listed alphabetically, she just didn't want to be treated alphabetically. Choreographically, she never was. For the duration of its stay at City Center, the company never announced casting of its ballets in advance, the public was encouraged to attend programs that were interesting and not to follow individual dancers.

The devoted, adventurous public that was attracted by the flow of new inventive ballets was not put off by the unusual custom. That public was not even put off by the substitution of another ballet for one that was originally listed. Slowly but surely attention was being fixed on the repertory as the core of the creative enterprise. Probably the most extreme step the company ever undertook in this regard was to suspend company listings in its programs for a period of six years, between 1968 and 1973. Dancers, of course, were credited for those ballets in which they appeared, but not as a group divorced from choreography.

When company listings were restored in 1974 all of the dancers were listed alphabetically, with men and women mixed together without any regard to the traditional clustering of corps, solo, and principal dancers. By 1977 the men and women were divided and grouped according to the three categories.[1] By this time the point had been made that roles they performed were the most important listings dancers could receive, and the company posted advance lists of ballets with their casting in the theater lobby. Public attention had been firmly fixed on the extremely rich and varied repertory, to which with remarkably few exceptions, Balanchine added each year.

Man's infatuation with and pursuit of women as muses, companions, and celebrants of life's joys motivated Balanchine repeatedly to create ballets celebrating those preoccupations. Committed to the inherent, ennobling quality of the classical dance vocabulary, he was able to use it with great humor. He had admired the music of Chabrier since discovering it in France, and he decided to combine all elements in a three-part work he called *Bourrée Fantasque*. The title was that of one of the three compositions he selected for this whimsical celebration of men and women. Part II was set to the prelude of Act II of the opera *Gwendoline,* and concluded with the "Fête Polonaise," which opens the final act of *Le Roi Malgré Lui*.

The jaunty first movement shows a vertical line of dancers wheeling out to the center of the stage to face the audience and then wheeling forward in a vertical line in profile. Their bouncy walk is emphasized with a see-saw swinging of the legs. Smoothly the men and women separate and the women flirtatiously snap open black lace fans that they hold overhead. The lead couple runs on. She is amusingly aloof and his puppy-dog eagerness contrasts with her haughty bearing. He also has a wandering eye and she sharply tugs him back to herself as he strays. When he grasps her waist to partner her, a fastidious shudder greets his forwardness. When they stand side by side he steps over her elegantly pointed leg. She is automatically prompted to step over his in a quiet battle for primacy. They are wittily competitive.

The flip-flop movement of the line of corps couples at the start has been picked up in the stiff-legged swings by the principal couple. As they advance downstage he tips forward and she tips back, humorously out of synchronization. When they separate she strikes a fetching pose as he watches, and then with clownish eagerness pulls himself toward her in a stiff push-up position on the floor. When he stands to support her she whips one leg around him so violently that she catches him lightly in the back of the head. It causes him to turn with a puzzled expression to learn the source of the blow.

Later he boorishly tries to peer down the front of her bodice, which she resists with annoyance. She is an elegant lady, improbably linked to an attentive oaf. Their short variation carries them upstage to face away from the audience, surrounded by the corps couples. Extending first one then the other leg they again find themselves out of synchronization. The elegant line of the leg is broken as he turns with his foot flexed upward rather than pointedly extended. Tenderly he takes her hands and wraps one and then the other arm around her neck which gets them into an amusing tangle. The corps echos their involvement, and to conclude, all do a can-can kick and advance downstage in a flat-footed walk that is charmingly awkward.

The farcical elements of the first section are totally forgotten in the reserved stylishness of the second movement. The six corps women are arranged in two widely spaced files as the lead man enters downstage and the lead woman appears upstage. They walk slowly through the corps obviously looking for someone as the women gently sway in place. In a moment they find one another for a brief sequence of supported turns. When they separate, two of the corps women go to him to be lifted and set down before the lead woman returns to him. He grasps her hands and while holding them extended to the sides, turns her balanced on one leg as he walks in a small circle.

When he releases her he kneels and the corps women form a little arc behind him. Two stand a few paces in front of him and the lead woman walks between them to approach and then back away from him. At the final approach she leaps impetuously and is caught lying across his arms. He sets her down only to lift her again as two of the corps women hold her outstretched hands. Together the two face in the characteristic dance position of the tango with arms joined stiffly to one side as they clasp the others around one another's waists. The passionate intensity of the tango lasts for a brief moment and the two separate to look for one another again through the files of corps women standing quietly. This time their search does not succeed and they exit individually. The corps quietly drifts into the wings accompanied by the calm concluding notes of the music.

The final movement begins in a blaze of celebratory flourishes by individual couples who run on tossing their arms gaily overhead. The men of the two final couples go even a bit further and toss the women outward and upward, supporting them as they do flashing leg beats in the air. The high spirits continue as the women form a large circle and turn like a carousel as the men stand in a large stationary circle about them. The principal couple enters and he lifts her high above his head. All of the gestures are pushed to a joyous extreme by both corps and principals. The lead couple from the first movement enter and again the corps men and women form two large circles. The principal woman is supported in a spritely sequence of turns as the other women circle them, while the stationary men sweep their arms in front of themselves as if impelling the turning circle of women.

The opening notes of the score were trumpet flourishes, and the mood of musical celebration continues as the corps women from the second movement enter to dance with the men of the third. The focus of attention is now the lead dancers from the second movement. The lead woman sits proudly on her partner's shoulders as two rings of women move clockwise and the circle of men remain as a kneeling, stationary contrast. They rise and leap toward one of the circles to sweep the women away.

Three massed groups of corps women led by the principal women of their respective movements leap in a series of diagonals and all then rank themselves with the corps men and principals for the unison finale. All arc their arms in unison above their heads leaping they cross and recross their legs swiftly and give little stiff kicks to the side reminding one of the see-saw look of the opening moments of the ballet as they are united in this joyous blend of classicism and humor.

The ballet has a Gallic thrust and sharpness together with elements of knockabout popular dance. References to the can-can, the ardent tango, and athletic adagio partnering mix easily with the elegance of the classical vocabulary. The first couple was awkwardly amusing, the second moodily romantic, and the third spectacularly exciting. Throughout, the gentlemen pursue their ladies until in the finale they are joined with a flourish of brilliant dancing. In its alternating movements it mirrors a society concerned with stylishness at all levels. In style *Bourée* was French, in balletic vocabulary Russian, and in its verve and energy American. While devoted to the elegance of the classical vocabulary, Balanchine played wittily with its conventions in this ballet and others such as *Tarantella, Harlequinade, Agon, Brahms-Schönberg Quartet* and even the generally somber *Ivesiana*.

That special energy had been put into service in a variety of musical settings, but not until the 1950s, over twenty years since he had first worked with American dancers, was Balanchine able to use them successfully with American music. His older pastiche *Alma Mater* disappeared without a trace shortly after it was presented, and *Bayou,* based on Thomson's "Arcadian Songs," was equally unsuccessful. *Jones Beach,* co-choreographed with Jerome Robbins, featured swimsuits by a noted manufacturer, but little else. But in 1954 he commissioned *Western Symphony,* a collection of American folk music, from Hershey Kay, made a selection of pieces from Charles Ives's compositions, and choreographed *Ivesiana*.

The impulse that led Ives to stretch musical form in uncompromising, experimental ways ensured his lack of popular acceptance. His music rarely turned up on the programs of major symphony orchestras, and he lived an almost reclusive existence outside of musical circles as a successful insurance executive in Hartford, Connecticut. Recordings of his works were few and none of his scores was considered suitable for dance until Balanchine demonstrated their possibilities. The composer was intrigued with Balanchine's interest, but ironically, died a short time before the premiere performance of the first ballet that used his music.

The suite of dances that Balanchine prepared partook of the scores' somber, mysterious qualities. The half-dozen sections were independent of one another, and were uneven choreographically. In subsequent revivals Balanchine eliminated two sections, and the ballet as it presently exists consists of "Central Park," "The Unanswered Question," "In the Inn," and "In the Night." Audiences seeing the ballet for the first time in all likelihood were also hearing the music for the first time. In the late 1940s Leopold Stokowski undertook a series of concerts of new music that were presented by the Museum of Modern Art, and at that time I heard the one and only piece of Ives music that had ever turned up on any concert I attended; it was "The Unanswered Question," Balanchine created one of his most hauntingly eerie duets to it, and subsequently Ives was heard more frequently.

"Central Park in the Dark" begins with an empty stage. There is a dim glow at the back curtain and the men and women of the corps walk on slowly and disperse to occupy the entire stage. They gravely incline to the right as a young girl enters with her hands stretched out in front of her. The group kneels as she gropes her way among them, never making contact until a man approaches her. She melts into his arms, seemingly relieved to have found someone on this dark plain of humanity. The corps has clustered toward the left rear of the stage as the two dance together. She now appears able to see, and the energetic duet is accompanied by snatches of the popular song "Hello My Honey."

The corps has once again spread out. Pairs join hands like jump ropes for the leads to step over, but instead of being supportive or helpful, they create little obstacles in the couple's path as they huddle close to the stage. The man finds the girl and lifts her, only to set her down leaning against the huddled figures of the corps, and leaves. The corps remains immobile for an instant, then begins to disperse, leaving her as they slip noiselessly out through the curtain at the back from where they entered. The woman wanders around totally isolated as the single spotlight following her dims and goes out, leaving the stage in darkness.

"The Unanswered Question" is posed repeatedly by a solo trumpet theme. It draws a skirling confused response from the flute and wood-winds, and both are supported by a sustained theme in the strings that is repeated regularly throughout. A bare-chested solo man backs on stage and is followed by a quartet of men in black who support a barefooted woman in a white leotard. The man repeatedly reaches out toward this mysterious figure who is passed and supported by the members of the group as if they were manipulating a passive object. For one brief moment the man gets to hold her but she is quickly retrieved by the others. The man reacts frantically, but she is placed beyond his reach. He tumbles in an agitated flurry of movement around the men in black. He falls and she is passed over his body as they carry her out. The distraught man rises and follows with his arms stretched outward in a futile gesture.

"In the Inn" places a man and a woman in an energetic, competitive duet. They bounce on and stand side by side in the center of the stage. He looks longingly at her before lifting her and setting her down. In a crouch, he looks at her again while holding both her hands. His variation features lots of rapid little turns and at one point a proffered hand begins a child's game, as they alternate placing one hand on top of the other. She turns in a showy fashion but breaks the line of her leg by deliberately flexing one foot upward. The duet has a coltish quality. He sidesteps stylishly with his hands flipped up under his chin. He goes to touch her but she rebuffs his advances. Their playful exuberance has become athletically eccentric. They both appear tired, approach, shake hands, and leave alone.

Through the dim lighting of the "In the Night" all of the members of the corps shuffle out onto the stage on their knees. They enter from opposite sides and pass one another with their arms hanging listlessly. The promptings of desire are alien to this group. There is not even the questing search of a couple to relieve the prevailing gloom. These people are beyond caring, moving on their restricted little tracks that probably lead nowhere. The light fades on their ceaseless, meaningless passage.

Both musically and technically the ballet was one of the strangest that Balanchine ever made. One has the feeling that the corps is operating in an atmosphere in which the emotional gravity is so powerful that it has pulled them to a grovelling posture. They no longer want anything, but have been reduced to creatures with protective reactions. Ives was fond of using popular and folk themes in his music, but he diluted them with acid dissonances until they became travesties of innocence and sweetness. The couple of the first section seek one another out, but the result is purely sensual encounter. The woman of the second section is kept tantalizingly out of reach, and the third couple look at love as a muscular exercise removed from emotion. The people of the final section don't even look.

The duet of "The Unanswered Question" was unusual from a number of aspects. To begin with, the woman's feet never touched the floor and they were bare. She was totally self-absorbed without any interest in the man who was fiercely determined to attract her attention. It was worse than unrequited love—it was unacknowledged existence. He wasn't important enough to notice; in the most annihilating rejection of all, he wasn't important enough to prompt a reaction.

As much as this narrowly focused, anguished ballet dealt with the sour aspects of contemporary society, *Western Symphony* celebrated the hopeful exuberance of the limitless American prairie. It was as open and joyful as *Ivesiana* was hopelessly resigned. The two ballets were presented within a week of one another, attesting once again to the diversity of Balanchine's creative interests. *Western Symphony* is a pastiche, but a brilliant, witty one. The melodies flow easily and the movements are happy. Originally, the piece was presented in four sections, but was reduced to three when the "Scherzo" was dropped after several years. It has been presented in this shortened form ever since.

The costumes make no attempt to represent the naturalistic look of working cowboy garb. They are colorful, fanciful creations that would fit more easily into one of the singing cowboy films of the 1940s. Heavy boots and bonnets are banished in favor of more danceable shoes and fetching tutus that give the women the look of dance-hall girls. As group upon group of men appear in the first movement, one has the impression that a gang of cowboys are just hitting town and are rarin' to go. They are joined by equally spirited women. The lead couple engage in the friendly competition of people who are sure of themselves and the relatively straightforward roles they are expected to play. The dancing heats up to such a point that the lead man takes off his hat to fan the "hot" feet of the woman he is dancing with.

In the "Adagio" second movement, a laconic man enters with four young women in front of him like pairs of a team of horses. A solo woman enters behind him, delicately stitching her way across stage on point, and catches his attention by tapping him on the shoulder. He is immediately taken with her and their duet is slow and dreamy, enlivened by a couple of diving leaps through the framing arms of the "horse team" in which she is caught just above the surface of the stage. Idly he strums his hat as if it were a guitar. Enjoyable as the interlude has been, though, he has to pack up and move on, and is last seen sending a ripple through the arms of his team as if he were snapping real reins.

The final movement is pure energy, like a technicolor hoedown. The lead couple are again engaged in friendly competition, she wearing an outrageously large hat that matches her flamboyant behavior. At one point she sweeps a scythelike leg across the top of his head so closely that he is obliged to duck. All of the other couples join and the curtain drops on the furiously turning group. It isn't so much a picture of the old West as it is a sentimentalized vision of it. These are the children of fresh air and open spaces, far removed from the circumscribed, slotted existence of the people in *Ivesiana*. Balanchine felt both represented aspects of American life and presented them side by side, like the grinning and grimacing masks of Thalia and Melpomene.

A few years later, in a burst of faux naif jingoism, he decided to celebrate the American character through the music of composer and former United States Marine Corps bandmaster, John Philip Sousa. He might have called it *Sousaiana,* following his custom of identifying the composer of the music from which he drew inspiration, but instead named it *Stars and Stripes* after the march that ends the ballet. If Ives's music was an unusual choice for ballet, Sousa's was no less so. The composer desperately penned varieties of compositions including operettas, but the strictness of march time engaged his deepest musical sensibilities and he is acknowledged as our march king. He lived through the heyday of American imperialism in the late nineteenth and early twentieth centuries and his compositions mirrored the public mood exactly. The mixture of blusterous cadences and engaging melodies proved irresistably attractive to Balanchine. He asked

Hershey Kay, who had arranged the folk tunes for *Western Symphony,* to work with a selection of Sousa's marches, and the result became *Stars and Stripes.*

The ballet is presented in five "campaigns." The first three are danced by "regiments" of corps men or women led by a soloist, the fourth is a pas de deux for principal dancers, and the fifth unites all. In "Corcoran Cadets" a group of twelve corps women demonstrate twirling like eager cheerleaders stirring up a crowd. The soloist gives another use to the baton by "conducting" the young women under her command. The whole has a feeling of adolescent enthusiasm.

The "Rifle Regiment" women are a shade more romantic but equally vigorous in their movement, with a quotation from the can-can suggesting their saucy high spirits. Both "regiments" have the energy of precision dancers such as the famed Rockettes from Radio City Music Hall, but the sequences of steps are carefully drawn from the balletic vocabulary and their show-stopping elan is carefully channeled into the classical mold.

The men make their first appearance in "Thunder and Gladiator." Once again the corps of twelve is led by a soloist who commands his "troops," tossing off snappy salutes while jumping back and forth in front of them. As in the other "campaigns," there is comic irreverence about their movements, which at times demand the most testing combinations of steps. At one point the soloist performs three sets of double tours en l'aire, without preparations, as if the exacting combination were the most routine of feats. At the conclusion, he follows the "troops" off with a crisp salute to the audience.

The pas de deux "Libery Belle" and "El Capitan" present the principals who behave in the exaggerated manner of acrobats performing on a trapeze. Everything is done with a flourish. She is floridly elegant and he swaggers stylishly, at one point performing a series of leg beats with his feet roguishly flexed at a ninety-degree angle rather than pointed. The pas is a cross between popular entertainment and high art, as is the entire ballet.

The finale unites all of the corps "regiments," soloists, and principals in "Stars and Stripes." The stage is a mass of colorful costumes flanked by panels of red, white, and blue. It is quite consciously a production number, and the final touch is the slow unfurling of the flag to Sousa's most stirring march. It is abashedly jingoistic (even the thirteen women and thirteen men of the first three "regiments" have historical precedent in the number of original colonies), but mingles patriotism with laughter.

"Stars and Stripes"—finale

The antics of these outsized people evoke feelings of pride as well as amusement. The balance is finely drawn and consistently maintained as Balanchine grafts obvious show dancing onto a classical base. The aggressiveness of the dancing is lightened by quotations from popular entertainment; the costumes are too gaudy to be real; the music, for all its martial air, has a heart-on-its-sleeve lyricism. The ballet received mixed notices abroad, but has remained a delight to home audiences.

When *Stars and Stripes* was first presented in 1958, one of the most popular television programs was the "Ed Sullivan Show." As host of the hour, Sullivan was always on the lookout for new acts, and he sought out Balanchine backstage after a performance. "Georgie, wunnerful, wunnerful, we gotta have it on the show!" Balanchine tactfully explained that there were a lot of dancers involved—forty-one, in fact. At the time the limited scan of the video camera could comfortably present six dancers. "Don't worry about a thing," he was reassured. A few days later a subdued Sullivan called. "Georgie, why don't we put it on with six of the prettiest girls." Balanchine explained that it didn't work that way, and so *Stars and Stripes* with its forty-one corps, soloist, and principal dancers never made it to network television.[2] Sullivan's enthusiasm, though, did indicate just how popular elements of the ballet were.

For the next twenty years Balanchine received various offers to present his ballets on television, all of which he resisted. He didn't like the way that the camera made dancers' noses and feet long and their legs short, but when an opportunity to work with Stravinsky was presented in 1962, he relented. *Noah and the Flood* was the result, and Balanchine hated it. To make a commercial package, the twenty-minute ballet had to be surrounded with enough material to fill up an hour. The additional material included historical information about Stravinsky's life and an anthropological discussion of ancient cultures and ceremonial masks. The chat was either specious or irrelevant. What bothered Balanchine most, however, was the manner in which the ballet was presented. It did not represent the best that the dancers could do because the time-pressured director accepted flawed takes as being good enough, rather than holding out for the best possible presentation of the choreography. Balanchine had ideas for ways to use the new medium innovatively as well, but was overruled at almost every turn. In a way it was a repeat of his frustration in Hollywood thirty years previously. He avoided American television for the next decade and a half, and his company appeared on telecasts of the Canadian Broadcasting Corporation or German television. It was only in the late 1970s when National Educational Television offered him the opportunity and the time to restage his ballets properly for the two-dimensional image that he began a comfortable relationship with the medium in America.

A man who has always worked with a long-range plan, Balanchine wanted to round out *Apollo* (1928) and *Orpheus* (1948) with a third ballet based on Greek mythology. Accordingly, he proposed the idea to Stravinsky and commissioned a new score. At the time Stravinsky had begun to incorporate techniques of serial composition in his work, and the score for *Agon* (*The Contest*) was sparse and wittily dry. The ballet did not celebrate any individual mythological character, as had the previous two in the trilogy, but concentrated on presenting old dance forms reworked in terms of twentieth-century rhythms. The dancers didn't compete with one another, but with the demands of their craft, and Balanchine made those demands the most complex he had ever devised. It was decided that since Stravinsky was composing with a twelve-tone row of notes, there would be twelve dancers who were presented in as many diverse varieties of trios and quartets as the composer and choreographer could devise in dances based on seventeenth-century dance forms. Twelve old French melodies provided the base for the composition and there were a baker's dozen of dances, since the opening number is repeated for the conclusion. The creative challenge was immense, and so was the performing challenge.

The work is divided into three sections with a pas de deux made to conclude section II. There is tension and excitement in the lean music that is precise and economical. Despite the large orchestra, augmented with a sparely used mandolin, the music itself is transmitted in bursts of esthetic Morse code rather than lushly unfurled in tapestries of sound. The full resources of the orchestra are used surgically, never broadly. The choreography doesn't include an excess gesture or throwaway motion, and is more densely packed than any other ballet Balanchine ever did.

In part I, trumpets introduce the four men who are standing at the rear of the stage with their backs to the audience. The ballet begins with a musical flourish as well as a gestural one, as the four turn swiftly and stride proudly downstage to face the audience. At first they seem to be marking time. In turn each steps, kicks forward, stretches in an arabesque (uncharacteristically balanced on the heel), jumps beating legs, and pirouettes while remaining in place. They switch places with their neighbors and then return upstage. In one minute they have run through an entire desiccated ballet class, touching the stretches, balances, leaps, and turns that comprise the basic equipment of any dancer. Seeing the four men performing the exact same sequence of steps slightly after one another stirs up a memory of one of the greatest male quartet set pieces in the classical

"Agon" Part I triple pas de quatre

[Top] Final pose Part I Jean Pierre Frolich, Peter Martins, Tracy Bennett (partially obscured) Daniel Duell, Suzanne Farrell and Colleen Neary

[Bottom] Part II First pas de Trois Renee Estopinal, Bart Cook and Kyra Nichols

[Top] Second Pas de Trois Victor Castelli, Karin vonAroldingen and Tracy Bennett.
[Bottom] Pas de Deux Adam Lüders and Heather Watts

repertory, that of the cavaliers in *Raymonda*. Their style was smoothly elegant; the male dancers of *Agon* are athletically elegant.

The double pas de quatre of eight women enter as the men leave. Strings and woodwinds accompany them, as opposed to the martial blare of trumpets to which the men danced. Their urgent high kicks to the front and subsequent fingersnaps suggests a group of classical chorines launching into a fast routine, after which they all droop fetchingly and disperse in two squares. The triple pas de quatre brings the men dashing on in their own square to circle the formation before occupying the empty central space between the two sets of women. The two horizontal lines are comprised of four women, four men, and four women. Pairs of men and women exchange places until the quartets of women are side by side and the four men are reunited but located at the right end of the two horizontal lines. The momentum slows momentarily for adagio duets framed by four of the women, after which all stop and pose with one hand posed insouciantly on the hip and the other held aristocratically across the heart. The appearance is flip, but the four minutes of this introductory section have been classically balanced by opposing masses—pairs of men facing, quartets of women anchoring opposing ends of horizontal lines—and by gestures repeated to the right and to the left in the duets. The energy is contemporary but the ordering symmetry is traditional, as throughout the ballet we encounter formal conventions given a contemporary twist. This duality is stressed; old-new, male-female, hard attack-soft recoil, formality-informality, earnest execution-deadpan wit. It is almost as if Balanchine and Stravinsky decided to test the biblical proverb that warns against putting new wine in old bottles lest they burst. For them, the old was to be stretched to its limits without bursting.

While part I concentrates on quartets of dancers, part II works with two trios. The first pas de trois is announced with an urgent 40 second percussion introduction. Two women and a man arch arms above their heads and gracefully interlock them to promenade in a tight little formation. The women exit abruptly for the male variation, which is in the form of a sarabande. He leaps forward and then unfolds one leg upward flourishing it like an aristocratic greeting. While he keeps his feet pointed for the most part, occasionally he breaks the line of the leg by flexing the foot at a ninety-degree angle. For all his mannered gesture, he is not a nobleman but a trained twentieth-century dancer employing the gestures of another age in a new way. As with all of the sections of the ballet, there is a tongue-in-cheek relish of old-fashioned forms distilled to their essential gestures. With a final leap he bows forward to the audience sweeping his arm down formally but exageratedly so that it almost brushes the floor. Having completed his formal dance he exits.

The women's variation is a galliard, and the strumming mandolin in the orchestra gives a pastoral flavor to their duet. They move in unison, often doing mirror images of one another in turns. Together they stand on point, leap for rapid crossing beats of the legs, and clap hands as they circle upstage to strike an attitude. A rapid exchange of hand gestures gives an informal conversational accent to their movements before they drop to one knee side by side to conclude.

Their cavalier returns for the coda and starts with a leap on the diagonal, which they follow. While the variations have old forms, this section is very much in twentieth-century style. The man is no longer the faintly creaky aristocrat, but a bold young male with two slinky and competitive women on his hands. He alternates rapidly between them, hastily supporting each in turns on point and barely able to reach the other before she begins her sequence. It suggests the proverbial haste of the one-armed paperhanger. Then smoothly they all bow to the audience and depart.

A variant of the 40 second percussion theme heard previously brings on the second trio for their pas de trois. The first trio consisted of two women and a man and the second is reversed, with two men flanking a single woman. Among female dancers, the element of balance is highly stressed, as is the quality of the leap among men. In this pas, Balanchine instantly puts the female into a sustained demonstration of balance. She rises to point with her arms held out to the sides. Each of the men supports one of her hands and turn her in place in a traditional promenade. When they return to their original places they uncharacteristically remove their supporting hands and walk around her to switch places, and offer their supporting hands again. She has held rock steady during the exchange, and now bends forward with her free leg extended almost straight up as they kneel. Returning to an upright position she walks proudly off. There has been no gradual build-up to this climactic pose, as one would expect in the traditional manner, but an abrupt assumption of it. Once the feat has been accomplished she leaves with the point economically made.

The men proceed to their variation the bransle simple. One stands slightly behind and to the side of the other, and their variation again uses the canon form used by the four men in the opening formation. In a subtle reversal of the usual order, the man behind begins and the one in front picks the step up a moment afterward. They prance festively. Musically, they are supported by the brass and are quite vigorous until they abruptly halt balanced on one leg, with their arms hooked together, and the other leg cocked archly in the air.

They retire to the sides of the stage as the woman enters for her solo. They clap rhythmically as Spanish dancers might to accompany one of their number. This is a bransle gay, which she performs with an amusingly sensuous look as she wiggles a shoulder. Standing on point with legs spread, she lowers herself into a demiplié that has a slightly peek-a-boo quality to it. Standing in place, her arms snake up and down and then suddenly stop. Even a siren call has to obey the strict metrical time of the score in which nothing is allowed to go to excess.

In the coda, which is a bransle double, the two men join to lift her as she does a split in midair. Her first big "trick" in the opening sequence of the trio was the unsupported balance, and now it is a midair split with untraditional support. She is tossed from one man to the other who catch her, and together the three do a backbend. They repeat the midair split and then the men stand behind her in a line making a large X with their arms as if marking the spot where attention should be focused. The coda ends with another big toss and the woman being caught and held in an attitude.

Both of the trios follow the traditional form of a pas de deux, that is, they have an opening adagio followed by the male variation and the female variation, and conclude with all dancing together for the coda; however, nothing else about them is traditional, including their length. The first requires four minutes and twenty-five seconds, and the second, three minutes and forty-five seconds. The dance patterns, while built on conventional figures, are stretched well beyond their original limits and the naturalistic hand clapping and finger snapping are novel introductions. Obviously, there is nothing conventional about the development of *Agon,* and the pas de deux that follows is no exception.

It begins with a variation of the same insistent percussion theme that starts the two trios. The couple enters and each turns furiously as they move downstage where he grasps both her hands while standing behind her, and she whips one leg behind his back to lock her heel behind his neck. It almost gives the impression of two protagonists meeting in a ring. In this case, however, the enclosure that pens them in will be variations on the classic ballet steps.

They walk slowly and she leans against his back, then regains her balance, and the two stand side by side. He supports her again in an arabesque in which she again locks her foot behind him. Throughout the adagio they remain linked to one another so that all of their movements have to be done within the restructed space of two arm-lengths. He gently lifts her forward. Sliding to the floor, he offers her support with two upstretched hands as she extends one leg behind her while balancing on point. While she does this, he makes rapid little scurrying steps with his feet, placing his own balance on his shoulders beneath her hands. It is a decidedly odd way to offer support, but has its logic in this intricate pas, which has to find movement possibilities for the cavalier within its restricted format.

They separate for the brief variations, of which each does two. The man's stress the jump, and he performs leaps with the feet classically pointed and also humorously flexed. The traditional arm configurations are also stretched as he appears to be hauling himself hand over hand up a rope at one point, and during one of the leaps hits the palms of his hands on the toes of his flexed feet. Her variations emphasize balance. To conclude, he grasps her hand and brings her downstage where they are again linked closely. They repeat the opening sequence in which her legs whip around his back, and then he kneels and she softly folds herself over him.

The spirit of the traditional pas de deux is honored throughout, but the laws of partnering have been stretched almost beyond the point of credibility. Unexpected but logical movement is the rule that governs their relationship. Gallantry and ardor exist but are expressed with athletic tension. There is no attempt to hide virtuoso movement. Everything is on display, and when one expects the traditional outward blaze of fireworks at the conclusion, one is offered soft, inwardly enfolding intimacy.

The two retain their position for a moment and then stand to walk to the center of the stage. A single man enters to stand downstage at the left side and a woman enters alone on the opposite side upstage. With the appearance of two other men and women, part III begins with the danse des quatre duos. The four couples move in unison with the men displaying the women most effectively in supported pirouettes. The classical line is again tested as knees and hips jut out daringly. The dance is brief and the remaining four women join the couples for the danse des quatre trios. The men partner each of the pair women in turn, then leap away to leave the four pairs of women doing high kicks like chorines, as they had in the opening double pas de quatre. The men rejoin them and all let their hands droop like paws in front of themselves at chest height. The two horizontal lines of women sandwich the men between them. All drop to one knee as the opening trumpet theme is faintly heard. The women rise and exit, leaving the men alone, and the opening trumpet theme is heard clearly and commandingly. The men sweep upstage where they face one another in the same horizontal line that opened the ballet; the two on the right push the palm of one hand forward to the pair on the left who freeze in a similar pose as the music ends.

The contest played out in *Agon* is a game of great intensity in which there is hardly any time to dawdle over emotional entaglements. Both men and women perform in a perpetual game demonstrating maleness and femaleness, but little individuality. Even in the intimacy of the pas de deux, one has the feeling of two people linked in a competition against the exceptional demands of the classical vocabulary rather than in a personal contest. Overriding and governing all of their actions is the rhythmic insistence of the score in which the musical pulse dominates. Orchestral color is used sparingly. One has the feeling that the essence of behavior is stressed, and not personal idiosyncratic expression. In its brief twenty-minute length it is packed with as many permutations and combinations of individuals as one would encounter in a full-evening ballet. Time is measured out as if it were a precious commodity in limited supply. This economical use of time stands in contrast to the flowing discursiveness of traditional full-evening productions in which plots, subplots, diversions, and digressions are all given full development. By contrast, *Agon* is a highly compact compendium of gesture that is poetic in its conciseness.

Underlying Balanchine's frequently stated admiration for Stravinsky was his admiration of the composer's rhythmic inventiveness. Prior to the twentieth century, the ballet composer was locked into small set forms of marches, galops, waltzes, mazurkas, and the like. These were devised by varieties of composers, and in Tchaikovsky's case, one of special rhythmic genius. He stood apart from all others in this respect in the way that Stravinsky does in the more fragmented twentieth century. *Agon* used the materials of the past with contemporary urgency, almost as if Balanchine and Stravinsky were realigning the atoms of experience with the necessity of packing them into a space-age ark of limited capacity. The required adjustments were made, tradition was served, and the shape of the new was presented as a continuation of, not a break with, the old. In their long and profitable artistic association, *Agon* holds a central position.

Although the experimental high-water mark of the New York City Center years (1948–1964) was the wry, bare-bones *Agon,* Balanchine continued his output of mainstream works in a variety of forms. He presented forty-seven new ballets and seven revivals, some of which were extensively re-choreographed, such as *Firebird, Swan Lake* (Act II), and *Pas de Dix.* Among the new productions were full-evening ballets such as *The*

Nutcracker and *A Midsummer Night's Dream,* and intimate duets including *Pas de Deux Romantique* and the Tchaikovsky *Pas de Deux.* Danced tableaus *The Seven Deadly Sins, Tyl Eulenspiegel,* and *Opus 34* were presented, as well as the haunting *Liebeslieder Waltzer.* Amid this enormous variety, Balanchine always kept an ear attuned to Stravinsky's regular output and continued the experimental line of ballets using concise movement that now included *Monumentum pro Gesualdo* and *Movements for Piano and Orchestra.* The latter was the first ballet made for the young Suzanne Farrell, and was followed quickly by *Meditation* and a host of others.

The seventeen-year span during which New York City Ballet was resident at City Center saw an enormous expansion in the performing seasons. The performing weeks, which numbered two at the beginning, expanded to ten times that amount, as a loyal, discriminating audience steadily developed and the School of American Ballet steadily graduated young dancers of exceptional talent into the company. These included Farrell, Allegra Kent, Patricia McBride, Patricia Neary, Mimi Paul, Jacques d'Amboise, Arthur Mitchell, and Edward Villella. The company made two extensive tours of Europe, which established its international reputation. The smooth succession of Robert Irving as musical director following Leon Barzin ensured the excellence of the orchestra.

The advantages of having a home base far outweighed the disadvantages of City Center, however, it was obvious to both the company and to patrons that the theater had severe limitations. The most conspicuous flaw to audiences was the peculiar design of the orchestra. The floor dipped in the middle so that the dancers' feet were invisible to patrons sitting in the first dozen rows. The pitch of the second balcony was exceptionally steep and was remote from the stage, so viewers found themselves looking down almost on the tops of the dancers' heads, an angle that foreshortened their bodies to an extreme degree.

Behind the proscenium, dressingroom space was minimal and there was virtually no place to store productions. The latter limitation would have been an almost impossible barrier to a company that relied on elaborate scenery and decor, but New York City Ballet had few such productions and used simple costuming and distinguished, imaginative lighting. Still, physical limitations had to be considered an inhibiting factor that would keep future planning of elaborate settings at a minimum. Then there were limits imposed by the size of the stage itself and the extremely shallow wing space where dancers made their exits; they were hardly out of public view on the left side when they were confronted by a brick wall. Rehearsal studios in the building were broken by support pillars that could not be removed. The flaws of the house were irritants, but not debilitating conditions, so the company was able to move ahead by making the necessary accommodations; however, it was an open secret that a more spacious, better designed house would be needed if the company were to grow.

Chapter 7

Opera House Scale

As a child of the Maryinsky Theater and its traditions, Balanchine believed that opera house scale was proper for presentation of ballet. His first experience with the Metropolitan Opera House shortly after he arrived in the United States had been a bitter disappointment to him. At the time (1937), ballet simply was not taken seriously by the administration, and he terminated his association. The board of New York City Center of Music and Drama under the direction of Morton Baum was far more hospitable, and Balanchine's seventeen years at the City Center 55th Street Theater proved to be the most creatively diverse ones in his career. In 1964 the company was offered the opportunity to move to the New York State Theater at Lincoln Center, which was then being constructed.

The architect, Philip Johnson, was an old friend and supporter of Balanchine and Kirstein, as was Nelson Rockefeller, then governor. The theater was built as a house designed for dance, and offered the company a chance to mount productions on a large scale. Balanchine had already presented two full-evening ballets at City Center, *The Nutcracker* and *A Midsummer Night's Dream*. In addition to redesigning them for the new house, he created four more; *Jewels, Coppélia, Harlequinade,* and *Don Quixote.* While he continued to design lean, stripped-down ballets, the new, large-scale house encouraged him to work on a number of shorter ballets that were as lushly conceived as the full-evening works. Among these were *L'enfant et les Sortileges* (*The Spellbound Child,* as it was known in this, his third staging), *Glinkiana, Pulcinella, Union Jack* (logistically, the most complicated ballet the company has ever presented), *Tricolore, Davidsbündlertänze, Symphony no. 6, Pathetique,* and *PAMTGG (PanAm*

131

Makes the Going Great). Not all were successful but they were all physically sumptuous. *PAMTGG* was an advertising jingle that attracted Balanchine, but its music did not offer him the creative impetus to devise a good ballet. The need to undergo heart surgery prevented him from working on *Tricolore,* which was completed by Jerome Robbins, Peter Martins, and Jean-Pierre Bonnefous.

Along with the changes in emphasis in repertory there was a corresponding change in the company class that Balanchine gave. Where detail and finish had previously been emphasized, now amplitude in gesture was stressed.[1] Extensive center-floor work concentrated on jumping to achieve the look Balanchine felt was proper for the new house. Among members of the company it had been a long-standing joke that one ought to take class before taking class with Balanchine. The opening warm-up and stretch exercises at the barre were always the shortest part of any Balanchine class, and the dancy, center-floor work the longest and most exhausting. With the remarkable resilience that characterized these professionals, they accommodated to this new emphasis and began to give Balanchine the look he was striving for.

While the newly reworked productions of *The Nutcracker* and *A Midsummer Night's Dream* proved durably popular, the reception of *Jewels* was particularly warm. It was called "the first evening-length abstract ballet" and consisted of three separate and independent sections. The first, "Emeralds," was set to music of Fauré selected by Balanchine, the second, "Rubies," was Stravinsky's Capriccio For Piano and Orchestra, and "Diamonds," set to four movements of Tchaikovsky's Symphony no. 3 in D Major, concluded the ballet. Each section had its own principal dancers and soloists who did not appear in any other part of the work.

During his lifetime Balanchine had known three homes—Russia, France, and the United States. In the three sections of *Jewels* he offered a homage to each of them. The social refinement of France ordered the relationships of the principals in "Emeralds"; playfulness dominated the happy, eager dancers of "Rubies"; and classically shaped composure bespoke the imperial tradition as Balanchine experienced it in the theater and school of the Maryinsky.

The green-costumed corps women of "Emeralds" form circles and an arc around the principals looking like a lacy necklace. The first principals perform a romantic duet including a hand kiss by the man. For much of the time the woman seems to be pulling or leaning away from him as he courteously attends her. Their behavior is measured and not given to emotional excess. The extremely active corps makes a social frame for them, at one point forming a long diagonal like the corridor of a mansion, down which the couple decorously proceed. The man and the corps women leave. The principal woman's solo is meditative and also expansively joyful as if celebrating the approved order of her partnership.

The second principal woman appears, younger and more vulnerable, in her solo that is haunting with a hint of playful melancholy. Again one has the impression of a woman acting out her life within the confines of a society with a strong sense of proportion. She is followed by a trio of two women and a man who have not yet crossed the line at which they will have to choose one partner. They romp happily together never losing the voluptuous elegance that is the special quality of this movement.

The first two principal dancers reappear, approaching one another until they meet at the center, where each arabesques before working closely together. At one point he kneels and she balances on his shoulder; a moment later they both kneel and he assists her to rise for their exit together. Appearing from the opposite side, the second principals enter. Their relationship appears more stately and correct and it always seems that there is a dignified arm's length between them. One has the impression that they are on public view and will show outsiders the bearing of correctness, but not personal intimacy.

We have been introduced to the individual members of this measured society and now they are all brought on together. The first principal male dances a brief solo and is joined by the other two men, then the two principal women, and the corps of ten women who again frame the action. They move to the back of the stage with the trio of two women and a man as the couples occupy the front of the stage. The men appear to be like energetic racehorses in a sea of floating green costumes. Suddenly all stop and arc their arms overhead, with the three men and the four women principals and soloist at the front. The light dims as the corps women drift off.

The seven join hands for a formal dance that involves them in intricate linked swirls of movement. The men kneel, still holding the women's hands, and the latter tilt forward on one leg extending the other up behind them. They separate momentarily, then closely entwine themselves once again. As they unwind the women continue off as the men gravely drop on one knee in a diagonal with an arm curved upward in an eloquent gesture of farewell.

"Rubies" opens with all of the corps men and women on ball of the foot or on point in a huge arc. The formation has a poised look of readiness. A solo woman steps forward from the group for a brief variation before the entrance of the playful principals. Their duet has the suggestion of a tango, and the image of old-time ballroom dancers is never far from their encounters.

The corps succeeds them, forming the same arc that opened the section. The solo woman steps forward and four corps men rush out to grasp an ankle or a wrist. They surround her and as she stands on one point they deftly and energetically maneuver her around in a way that suggests the four cavaliers' attentiveness in the "Rose adagio" from Act I of *The Sleeping Beauty.* This young woman, however, is far removed from the privileged world of the court, and is closer to the sound stage of a movie musical. When they release her she exits alone, doing grand pliés in second position that have a pratfall coarseness contrasted with the straight-faced elegance she has just displayed.

Repeatedly, slapstick episodes follow more serious moments as the ballet's tongue-in-cheek course unfolds. The principal couple returns for another duet, as before, replete with humorous touches. He bounds around, jutting his elbows out from his sides like a cartoon rooster as she sashays and prances. There is a mock heroic element in the dancing that is capped as he kisses her hand at the end of the duet, when one might more reasonably expect a friendly, informal hug.

The men's variation takes the form of a chase, as the principal man jogs on and circles the stage, glancing occasionally over his shoulder to see whether the four men in a square formation are gaining on him. All the corps men and women form up behind the principals in the finale. The language of classic dancing has been mixed with a vernacular informality almost as if someone were saying, "Look Ma! I'm doing ballet!"

"Rubies" is a sportive romp following on the silky smooth heels of the measured order of "Emeralds," and "Diamonds" is a restrained, distilled presentation of elegance. The numbers of dancers involved are larger; two principals, four secondary couples, and two dozen corps men and women. All are dressed in white, with the women in short tutus and elbow-length white gloves. The movement begins slowly with the corps women backing two secondary soloists in a slow sustained variation that sets the scene for the entrance of the two principals who approach one another on a long diagonal. The entire movement is built around their pas de deux with its double number of individual variations, with interludes for the corps in between. The tone is refined and restrained, with touches of Russian character gesture for the corps. The finale begins with a grand polonaise that has the entire corps, led by the principal couple, end in a stunning tableau.

"Jewels" Suzanne Farrell and Peter Martins in the final section "Diamonds"

Luxurious solemnity characterizes the first movement as the dancers move in a world invisibly governed by balanced order. The raucous adult-children of the second movement fairly burst with energy as their lives are presented as a saucy game, and the third set of dancers present life as an elegant ceremony.

While there was no formal linkage between the various sections there was some musical relationship between the first and third, which suggested elements of shared experience. In the years following its premiere performance Balanchine added the closing sequence (as described) to "Emeralds," which gave it a somewhat more somber conclusion than it had when first seen. Other portions of the ballet were unchanged, and "Rubies" has been presented as an independent ballet. Theoretically, each portion can stand alone, but once seen together, some sense of context is lost from separate presentations.

While this ballet and the three other new evening-length works created for the stage of New York State Theater, (*Coppélia, Harlequinade,* and *Don Quixote*) all enjoyed success, nothing in the history of New York City Ballet ever was received as rapturously on such a sustained basis as Balanchine's *The Nutcracker.* The ballet was recostumed and redesigned for the new house on a lavish scale and has solidly occupied a sold-out block of five weeks during the Christmas season, and it looks as if it will continue to do so in perpetuity. Not only is it the most durable money-making production that the company has ever had, it functions as an irresistible magnet drawing students to the School of American Ballet. Each season it uses the talents of dozens of younger students from the school, and has spawned innumerable related stagings throughout the country. Almost unnoticed in the furor is the fact that it is a very good ballet.

Balanchine has noted that in Russia the celebration of Christmas follows the German custom, and so he set his ballet in a comfortable German home. It is divided into two acts, following the traditional practise of a "naturalistic" Act I and a supernatural Act II set in the legendary Land of Sweets. (The decor for the latter used to feature diet-busting turrets, battlements and staircases of cakes, puddings, chocolate candy, and other sugared wickedness, but has been replaced by organic clusters of fruit and nuts more in keeping with our national obsession with excess weight.)

It is Christmas Eve in the Stahlbaum household and the adults are putting the last touches on the tree. Their eager children wait outside the door of the living room and from time to time run up to peer through the keyhole. The guests, children and parents, begin to arrive, and everyone enters the darkened living room delightedly. The children jump up and down, illuminated by the lights of the tree. Somewhat mysteriously, all raise their hands and approach the tree as if making an obeisance in the presence of some magical object. The room is lit and a series of games is begun. Parents dance with their children and Fritz, the Stahlbaum's son, teasingly pulls his sister Marie's hair. An old friend of the family, Drosselmeier, arrives with his nephew, carrying two large beribboned boxes that he places by the tree.

From the first box he draws two life-sized wind-up dolls, Harlequin and Columbine, who dance an innocently romantic duet before being returned to their box. A Soldier follows, and is comically belligerent, whirling his arms and leaping to peer in all directions as if trying to sight an enemy. When he finishes, party favors are distributed and Marie gets a special treat, a large nutcracker in the form of a soldier, with a moveable jaw for cracking shells. She puts him in a toy crib around which she and the other little girls settle. The boys with their toys instruments and paper hats march through the group, disrupting it, and are hauled away by the parents. Later, Fritz snatches the nutcracker and stamps on it angrily, breaking it. The party is drawing to a close and the parents collect their

"The Nutcracker" Shaun O'Brien presenting the toy nutcracker

children, who of course, are reluctant to go, especially Drosselmeier's nephew. He and Marie have developed an instant affection for one another.

Marie doesn't want to retire upstairs and later sneaks down to snuggle on a sofa near the tree, with the nutcracker in her arms. Her mother finds her asleep and carefully drapes a shawl over her before retiring. Drosselmeier stealthily returns to the house, retrieves the nutcracker, and fixes it before returning it to its crib and leaving. Marie awakens (or is she dreaming?), and the magic of her imagination begins to work. The lights on the tree brighten and dim several times, and the tree itself begins to grow as Marie imagines herself a member of the toy world beneath it. To complete the illusion, everything else expands to the size it would be if seen from the vantage point of a toy. Huge windows replace the normal-sized ones and a toy guard house becomes full-sized. A cackling Drosselmeier takes the place of the carved owl on the grandfather clock. Tiny mice, now the size of humans, scurry back and forth as the soldiers prepare to fight them off. Finally, a life-sized replica of the toy crib rolls in with the Nutcracker in it. He leaps out to lead the troops against the mice and their evil, seven-headed King. The battle begins to go badly and the Nutcracker is losing his duel with the Mouse King until Marie hits the latter with her thrown slipper, distracting him enough for the Nutcracker to run him through. The battle is over and the mice tearfully carry their King off, but not before the Nutcracker retrieves his crown.

The sofa, to which Marie has returned, is now outside amid the snow-covered pine trees. The Nutcracker approaches her with the crown; and with a twist of his body his costume falls away and he is revealed as a handsome young Prince who looks just like Drosselmeier's nephew. He places the crown on Marie's head and the "Waltz of the Snowflakes" accompanies them to the Land of Sweets. The dance features sixteen corps women carrying snow-covered branches, who whirl intricately and beguilingly as Marie and her nutcracker Prince end the act walking in the direction of a large star that indicates the way.

In Act II little Angels with tiny Christmas trees in one hand line the stage and circle and cross before stopping and holding up the trees as if invoking a benign spell. It recalls a similar moment in Act I where the tree is treated as if it has some mysterious power. The Angels retire to the sides of the stage and the Sugar Plum Fairy enters with a magic wand. She is gracious to the little Angels, and her proud bearing during the solo announces clearly that she is the mistress of this wonderful kingdom. She then summons up all of her subjects and leads her squad of Angels off.

Dramatically, a boat with a hull of half a walnut shell and propelled by a lollypop sail glides in carrying the Prince and Marie.

Sugar Plum Fairy has returned with her Angels who carry an assortment of musical instruments. Unlike the harsh trumpets and drums of Fritz and his friends, these play sweetly. The Prince and Marie dash excitedly from one Angel to another and look at the court of the Sugar Plum Fairy with wonder. The Fairy then asks the Prince to tell them all who they are and how they arrived. In a lovely passage of mime the young Prince describes the battle, the thrown shoe, and the conquest of the Mouse King. Everyone is very impressed at the daring of the two young people, and bring them a throne from which they watch the divertissements that are offered for their pleasure.

"Hot Chocolate" is a lively dance for five couples with the high, arched carriage of Spanish dancers. "Coffee" suggests Arabia and is a sensuous solo for a woman in harem costume who evocatively clangs finger cymbals. "Tea" is a trio featuring two women in Chinese robes who wheel out a tea chest, and when they open it, a lively man with a coolie hat and queue bounds out for a short variation. The women follow him with fluttering fans and retreat when he chases them. After a series of leaps in which his outstretched legs kick his palms, he retires to the chest. They close the lid and hop on it to pose prettily.

The "Candy Canes" are a group of eight young women in striped costumes covered with tiny bells, led by a similarly garbed man with a hoop. He leaps and turns furiously and periodically leaps through the hoop as if it were a whipping jump-rope. The variation is bouncy and exciting, and is substantially the same as the one for which Balanchine himself won praise in Russia as a young dancer. The leader of the Marzipan Shepherdesses carries pan pipes on which she mimes playing as she leads the others through their pastoral dance. They in turn follow her direction, posing archly with their own pipes.

"Mother Ginger and her Polichinelles" brings on a large bustled figure with an enormous skirt beneath which crouch eight little Polichinelles. One by one they emerge from a little tentlike flap in the skirt front and dance a social round that is reminiscent of the adults' dance in Act I. Mother Ginger primps and looks on approvingly before they scurry back under the skirt and they all leave.

As a balance to the cool whirling snowflakes at the end of Act I, Dew Drop leads her group in the warm "Waltz of the Flowers." The dance is one of the loveliest in the ballet, and one of the finest waltzes that

Balanchine ever created. It is full of lyric invention and includes brief quotations from the dance of the four cygnets in *Swan Lake*. Dew Drop is fetchingly impetuous and the dance sets the scene for the climactic pas de deux of the Sugar Plum Fairy and her Cavalier. Set in the classical adagio form of male variation, female variation, and coda, it incorporates spectacular leaps to shoulder-sit catches, and the Sugar Plum Fairy posed in attitude gliding smoothly along on a hidden slide. It is a little bit of extra stage magic added to a production that is already full of charming devices. Just as the Christmas Eve party had to end, however, so does this lovely visit in the Land of Sweets.

Sugar Plum Fairy summons up all of the sweets for one farewell reprise of their variations. As they finish, they line the sides of the stage and make the characteristic arm gestures of the "Tea" and "Candy Canes" dances. The Prince and Marie climb into a reindeer-drawn sleigh and rise up as all of the inhabitants of the Land of Sweets wave goodbye to them.

The colorful happy atmosphere of Act II ideally completes the promise of Act I. The Nutcracker has become a charming prince and the essence of a child's Christmas has been spread out before all. The staging is spectacular, especially the growth of the room-sized tree to occupy the full height of the ninety-foot proscenium of New York State Theater. The two big waltzes are among the best that Balanchine ever created in their evocation of the Maryinsky style, and the pas de deux capsulizes the romantic vision that underlies the whole of the ballet.

As a child, Balanchine danced in the Ivanov production and obviously has tried to re-present its special flavor. As a teenager just out of the Maryinsky School, he had a particular success with the "Candy Canes" variation, which was known as the "Dance of the Buffoons," and has incorporated it faithfully in the divertissements. The production suffers somewhat from its enormous appeal to children in that it is not looked at as attentively as some of his other works. As if to correct this attitude, however, he included "The Waltz of the Flowers" in a compendium called *Tempi di Valse,* presented during the 1981 Tchaikovsky Festival given by New York City Ballet. In that context it revealed its beautiful, flowing balance without any question.

The second evening-length ballet that Balanchine choreographed in his career was *A Midsummer Night's Dream,* following Shakespeare's play fairly closely but basically inspired by Mendelssohn's incidental music. He had long been familiar with the play, as the author is one of the most popular foreign writers in Russia and his plays receive frequent stagings. Balanchine even appeared in a minor role as a child in *Dream.*

For this production he decided to put all of the plot development in Act I the enchanted wood on midsummer eve, and reserve the pure danced divertissements for Act II. Essentially, the ballet is a succession of duets between members of the enchanted fairy world, various human couples, and in one special instance, a transformed human and Titania.

Puck, while acting as a faithful servant of his master Oberon, cannot help but be an amused spectator at the foolishness of love-entangled mortals. He further compounds the tangle in which the four lovers have enmeshed themselves, but finally settles each down with the right companion. In so doing he makes it quite clear that there is little that he sees in any of them that would cause one to be preferred to another. He cheerfully fetches the magic flower that permits Oberon to cause the proud Titania to fall in love with Bottom, whose humble state has been made even more humble by his being transformed into a donkey. As haughty Titania seeks to involve him in a love duet, he scratches fleas or dives after a specially succulent bunch of grass. Their duet is one of the wittiest Balanchine ever created. The noble Theseus is united with Hippolyta and Oberon and Titania settle their differences over the changeling servant and are reconciled.

The action of Act I slips back and forth smoothly between the real and fairy worlds. Act II starts with the weddings of all of the humans, followed by the divertissements and a beautiful pas de deux, which is a resumé of all of the tenderness that exists between lovers warmly dependent on one another. The concluding tableau shows the members of the enchanted world again in possession of the stage. Puck insouciantly sweeps up with a besom, and tossing it aside, begins to ascend as the lights of butterflies and fairies wink below him.

During the company's first four years of residence at State Theater (1964–1967) Balanchine created four new full-evening productions; more than the number he had done during the whole of his previous career. As a special project he commissioned a score from Nicholas Nabokov, whom he had known from his Diaghilev years. The ballet was based on Cervantes's novel *Don Quixote,* and Balanchine treated the character as a tragic hero doomed to be misunderstood and villified by the rest of society that does not share his special vision. Central to the development of the story is the figure of a young woman who turns up in a variety of guises in the course of the three acts to inspire and comfort the Don in his crusade to liberate people from shackles of servitude and ignorance.

He is first seen in his study at night examining books from his library. He sees a vision of a young maiden, Dulcinea, menaced by warriors, and fights a duel to save her. He is tormented by nightmare images and falls asleep exhausted in his chair. The next morning his serving girl opens the curtains to his room, washes his feet, and helps him on with his shoes. Sancho Panza arrives, buckles on the Don's armor, and touches his shoulders with a sword, dubbing him a knight. The statue of a roadside madonna inspires him further in his quest for justice. He frees a young man who is being whipped and loosens the chains binding some prisoners, only to have all turn on him and go back to their cruel masters. Undaunted, he travels to La Mancha where he saves a young shepherdess from a vengeful family, and in a moment of madness charges a traveling puppet show to "free" a young maiden being threatened by a wrathful Sultan. In all cases, the women seem to him to represent aspects of Dulcinea. The puppeteers flee as his sword swipes bring the whole stage apparatus tumbling down around him. Local nobility passing by take him and Sancho Panza back to their castle, away from the disarray caused by his impetuousness.

Act II is set in the castle ballroom where the two are entertained by a series of divertissements and then invited to participate in the aristocrats' stately social dance. During it, various of the courtiers jostle or make sword jabs at the Don. The purpose of the invitation becomes clear; he is meant to be the butt of their cruel humor. The nightmare atmosphere is heightened, as the women appear to have grown beards and the two of them are hoisted on the back of a wooden horse that emits a loud explosive crash. The "fun" is not over. As the Don stands confused and in need of aid, a vision of Dulcinea comes to him, but one of the noble women approaches him softly only to thrust a handfull of gooey cream in his face. He ignores the indignity and stumbles after the fading vision.

Act III finds him in a net outside the castle walls, and in his dream he again sees Dulcinea in a tranquil setting that is broken as she is menaced by a woman in black and an evil magician. The Don struggles to his feet to defend his ideal woman, but all vanish. Beaten and confused, he charges a huge knight waving a mace. The knight vanishes, and as Don Quixote continues his assault with his lance, he is hooked by the vanes of a turning windmill, which lift and then drop him heavily. In this weakened condition he attempts to fight a duel with a knight in glittering armor, and loses. As Sancho Panza binds up his injured head, a herd of swine trample them. The Don now crawls on all fours like a wounded animal, but is trapped in a cage-like litter and carried back to his home.

The final scene has him in bed surrounded by his servants and a priest. They depart and the halucinating Don sees his foes in a line of passing hooded clerics and high church dignitaries. The old man rises in his bed as he imagines a file of crusaders garbed in chain mail who enter and drop to one knee by his bed to acknowledge him as one of their company. This is the group with which he identifies, not the persecutors in places of position and power. He collapses, surrounded by his friends, and the serving girl makes a cross of two sticks and places it on his bed. The crusade is over.

Don Quixote's impassioned campaign for his vision could be read as that of the artist pursuing his ideal spurred on by the unattainable female muse, a recurring theme in Balanchine's work, or it could be the quest of every individual for a sense of justice in an unjust world. What is not in doubt is that the finest of Balanchine's dances were created for Dulcinea in all of her manifestations. The court dance was aristocratically menacing, and among the divertissements the duet pas mauresque was truly effective, as was the dream ballet of the third act. The Don's role, eloquently mimed in isolated performances by Balanchine himself, was touching, but the production as a whole was not animated by the choreographic invention that was characteristic of Balanchine at his finest. It remained in repertory for ten years, but one always had the feeling that the grab-bag nature of Nabokov's score contributed materially to the ballet's unevenness. Balanchine reworked it almost every season, adding and subtracting elements, particularly in Act I, but these changes never lifted the ballet substantially from the level of a flawed masterpiece. It was magnificent in its reach, but its grasp was somewhat short.

Harlequinade was known as *Les Millions d'Arlequin* when first presented at the Maryinsky Theater in 1900, created according to a formula devised by Petipa in his fifty-year reign over the Russian ballet stage. Balanchine attempted to reproduce the spirit of that time with settings that were fetchingly artless in their childlike imitation of Pollack's toy theaters, and bright costumes that contributed much to the happy quality of the ballet. Ricardo Drigo conducted the ballet orchestra in Saint Petersburg, and also composed the score that Balanchine admired.

The socially aspiring Cassandre wishes to contract an advantageous marriage for his daughter, Columbine. In Act I he is about to leave his house and gives the key to his lovably witless servant Pierrot, whom he summons by banging his cane on the ground. Pierrot understands that he is to conceal the key and protect the house until Cassandre returns. He tucks the key inside his voluminous pullover with its extra-long sleeves, and curls up on the doorstep like a guard dog. His romantic wife Pierrette appears, easily extracts the key from him, and ties his sleeves together, imprisoning him. He works loose and implores her to return the key but she kicks playfully at him, driving him off with a series of unfolding leg movements.

Harlequin arrives in his patchwork suit to serenade Colombine, who joins him after throwing down the key, which Pierrette has given her, to unlock the door. He moves as if he were dancing on hot coals or had springs in his shoes. She is flattered but draws her hand away when he attempts to kiss it. Looking out at the audience for its opinion, she seems to sense approval of his suit, so she nods assent and returns to the delighted Harlequin who clutches his heart and wiggles with ecstasy. In the midst of their delight, Cassandre returns and is furious. He sets Pierrot on Harlequin, who escapes into the house after kicking Pierrot. (Throughout the ballet everyone takes turns kicking Pierrot; he seems to invite it.) Some evil Sbires (local cops) summoned by Cassandre chase after Harlequin and emerge on the balcony to toss down the colorful bits and pieces of the dismembered lover. Cassandre then sends Pierrot to keep watch for the soldiers' patrol. Pierrot returns to report their approach and kneels humbly. After the customary kick, he and the Sbires conceal the pieces of Harlequin beneath a convenient cloth at the front of the house and then all hide.

The patrol arrives stamping and lurching in a rough semblance of military order. Their officer drinks from a canteen and it is obvious that all of the patrol have been nipping. They hold lanterns up and give a half-hearted look around before stumbling humorously off. La Bonne Fée arrives and restores Harlequin, who dances joyously. Léandre, a fat, doddering, wealthy suitor of Columbine arrives and primps before starting his own serenade. During the playing he strums wrong notes repeatedly, and is additionally deviled by eight little Harlequin figures. Cassandre, who approves of Léandre's wealth, emerges with Pierrot to bring the fat fellow into the house. He is so fat and his hat so broad that he has to turn sideways to enter. Colombine and Pierette, her mischievous friend, stand on the balcony as Harlequin prances on with the magic wand given to him by La Bonne Fée. He reaches up with it and touches the balcony, which descends like an elevator. While his rival is inside the house, he, Colombine, and Pierrette steal away. They are missed almost immediately by Cassandre, Pierrot, and Léandre, who give chase together with the knout-wielding Sbires as Act I ends.

Act II takes place in a park where a group of adult and child revelers perform. The adult corps dancers from Act I are joined by thirty-two children dressed as miniature Harlequins, Policinelles, Pierrots, and

"Harlequinade" Act II "Danse des Invités" (front) children (back) company

Pierrettes. When they have finished, the pursuing party arrives and Cassandre demands a dowry from Harlequin, who of course has no money. Suddenly, a black-robed figure stands on a bench revealing herself to be La Bonne Fée. She pours gold coins from a full cornucopia and Harlequin presents the treasure to Cassandre, who demands to see whether Léandre can match it. When he cannot, Cassandre sends him off with a kick and the celebratory divertissement of the Alouettes begins.

Two little Harlequins set up a glittery cutout resembling a splashy fountain around which the Swallows flutter delightedly as it spins. The climactic pas de deux of the lovers concludes the ballet, with the Alouettes in the background. Throughout, the leitmotiv of authoritarian gesture has been stamping and kicking, and that of the lovers the lighthearted bounce or prance. When Balanchine first presented *Harlequinade* it appeared to many as an imitation of an "old" ballet, but the physical demands on the dancers were very much in the contemporary range of technical ability. Subsequently, he added the balabile of the revelers in the first and second acts and dramatically increased the number of children to what it contains today.

Looking back at his own valuable and happy experience on the Maryinsky stage, Balanchine had included as many children in previous New York City Ballet productions as he could, and the practice has continued and expanded in the large performing space of State Theater. There were children's roles in *The Nutcracker, A Midsummer Night's Dream, Harlequinade,* and *Don Quixote,* and so naturally, when he decided to stage a revival of *Coppélia* he included a corps of twenty-four little girls.

Coppélia belongs to the hardy breed of a half-dozen ballets that have survived among the hundreds produced during the nineteenth century. Balanchine was aided by Danilova in mounting the work, which followed the Petipa version with which they both had been familiar in Russia. Danilova danced the role hundreds of times during her long career and was considered its finest interpreter. The production as it emerged followed the traditional version in the first two acts for which Danilova was mainly responsible. Balanchine interpolated a new male solo for Frantz in Act I and reshaped some of the ensembles, but otherwise concentrated his energies on the new Act III. He had long been an admirer of Delibes, who composed the score and was the first composer to introduce character dances in the form of the czardas and mazurka to the ballet stage. Being Balanchine, he decided to restore all of the music that had been cut from the score in Petipa's staging.

Since 1964 New York City Ballet had had a summer home at the Saratoga Performing Arts Center in Saratoga Springs. The huge open-sided theater was almost twice the size of State Theater, although its stage had exactly the same dimensions. During its annual month-long season in July 1974, the company unveiled the new production to a delighted audience. It brought to five the number of full evening ballets that were included in the company's repertory.

The setting is a village square in a small Balkan town. A vivacious young girl, Swanilda, emerges from her home and sees an aloof girl, Coppélia reading on the balcony of Dr. Coppélius's home. Swanilda dances a lovely variation in which she tries unsuccessfully to catch the attention of the absored Coppélia. Petulently, she stamps her foot and shakes her fist and hides as Frantz, her fiancé, appears. She watches him bowing and scraping to the remote Coppélia, and seeing her throw him a kiss, is furious. Dr. Coppélius appears and draws Coppélia back into the house. Suddenly, Frantz sees Swanilda chasing a butterfly, helps her capture it, and quite casually pins it to his lapel. Swanilda sees the action as a cruel demonstration of his heartlessness, bursts into tears, and vows to have nothing to do with him.

The young people of the village now appear and dance a vigorous mazurka, which concludes as the Burgomaster enters. He announces that the next day they will celebrate a festival of bells in honor of new ones being donated to the church by a wealthy landowner. In addition, any couples married on the day will receive a purse of gold as a present. Various couples happily anticipate the unexpected gift, but Swanilda is unhappy. There is an old belief that if a young girl shakes a wheat stalk and hears the faint tinkling of bells, she is about to marry. Swanilda shakes the stalk presented to her by the Burgomaster and hears nothing. She goes to each of her friends shaking it and they hear nothing as well. She throws the stalk to the ground and joins her friends as if she didn't care. The young men and women launch into a czardas, which concludes the afternoon's activities.

The twilight finds the square deserted except for Frantz and a few of his friends, who surprise Dr. Coppélius emerging from his house after care-fully locking the door. The young men tease him and suggest that they all go to a tavern together. He refuses and they jostle him loutishly. He swings his cane at them and they disperse, but in mopping the perspira-tion from his brow, Dr. Coppélius inadvertently pulls the key from his pocket along with his handkerchief. It drops to the ground but he leaves without being aware of the loss. Swanilda now returns with her friends and finds the key. Intensely curious about and jealous of Coppélia, she drags her friends to the house to find out the truth about this mysterious young woman. Dr. Coppélius returns looking for his key and notices the door of his house ajar. He enters angrily and closes the door just as Frantz returns and places a ladder against the balcony and begins to climb it. The curtain falls.

Act II opens as Swanilda leads her trembling friends upstairs to Dr. Coppélius's workshop. They see that it is filled with wonderful life-sized dolls. One young woman accidently brushes one and it begins to move. They are frightened, but then delight in animating all of the rest. Swanilda finds Coppélia still seated in her chair and politely bows to her, but still getting no response, daringly tugs at her dress only to discover that she too is one of the marvelous puppets. At this point Dr. Coppélius bursts in on them and chases them all from the house, except Swanilda, who has hidden herself in Coppélia's alcove.

He restores order and conceals himself as the ardent Frantz climbs in through the window. The older man seizes the intruder painfully by the ear and demands to know what he is doing in the house. Frantz explains his love for Coppélia and Dr. Coppélius asks whether he has enough money to consider marriage. Frantz turns out his empty pockets in response. The doctor has another idea, however, and invites the young man to join him in a drink. He fills their tankards but surreptitiously disposes of his own while the guileless Frantz drains his. After a second round Frantz drops into a drunken slumber, and Dr. Coppélius spreads out his book of spells.

He draws the seated Coppélia into the center of the studio and begins the ritual that will transfer life from the unconscious Frantz to his creation. In his excitement, he fails to notice that Swanilda has assumed the costume of Coppélia. She plays along with his magic-making and begins to become more and more animated as one incantation follows another, finally coming fully to "life." She is charmingly doll-like up to this point, but now she blossoms into womanhood. Dr. Coppélius is beside himself with joy and has her dance "Spanish" and "Scotch" variations to show her newly acquired grace. Frantz slumbers on even as the wily Swanilda tries to rouse him. Finally, Dr. Coppélius, exhausted after chasing her around, bundles her back into her alcove and settles down for a rest.

Frantz now awakens and the gleefully vengeful Swanilda in her own clothes pushes out the stripped doll Coppélia to show him that the austerely beautiful creature he was infatuated with is a lifeless puppet. Dr. Coppélius wakens and is distraught, Frantz is chastened, and Swanilda is triumphant as she leaves with her newly enlightened fiancé to end Act II.

"Coppélia" with Patricia McBride

In Act III the shards of the plot are briskly dispatched with the celebration of the various couples' weddings and presentation of the promised marriage purses. The complaining Dr. Coppélius is heartlessly paid off with his own purse, and the divertissements begin. These are cast in the form of solos and ensembles that recount the day in a typical peasant's life, beginning with "Dawn" (awakening), "Prayer" (acknowledgment of God's order), and "Spinner" (daily work). A pseudo-Wagnerian episode, "Discord and War," temporarily clouds over the happy day and is followed by Frantz's and Swanilda's delirious pas de deux. To conclude, all return, including a high-stepping curve of twenty-four little girls to cap the celebration.

Balanchine's mastery of mime and dance was superb, and the climactic final scene is a triumph of effect piled on effect until the stage is alive with animated dancers of all ages. His Act I czardas and mazurka are prime examples of intricate character dance, and the demands made upon the children are exceptional. In Act III they form increasingly complicated formations around the solo dancers and add the final filip of color to the finale. The production celebrates young love, but does not shy away from the tragedy of the deceived old inventor Dr. Coppélius, whose dream bursts when challenged by the jealous love of Swanilda.

Balanchine did not begin to create evening-length ballets until his fiftieth[2] year and was seventy when he produced *Coppélia*. Having come to the form later in life, he showed himself completely comfortable with its demands. Whether he would have produced more of them in other circumstances is open to conjecture. What can be said is that given the resources of the State Theater, he used them to the fullest.

Chapter 8

Mature Master and Recurrent Themes

Secure in his creative maturity, Balanchine continued to show his mastery of traditional forms and his personal esthetic concerns with a flurry of new ballets. From the beginning of his career he had been interested in the creative and artistic challenges posed by superbly trained female dancers and by the twentieth-century rhythms of Stravinsky. He had worked with the passionately romantic waltz and always took special care to "animate the masses" throughout ensemble passages. For him the corps was not a passive frame, but a living entity, and in *Le Tombeau de Couperin* he decided to devise a ballet for sixteen corps dancers exclusively without roles for soloists or principal dancers.

The occasion arose during the Hommage à Ravel Festival presented by New York City Ballet in 1975. Balanchine had long been an admirer of the composer, and for this ballet selected a commemorative score written after the First World War. Ravel had lost six friends during the hostilities and composed a suite of as many pieces to their memory. For his ballet Balanchine selected the four of these pieces that Ravel orchestrated. He divided his dancers in two quadrilles of four couples each (in France, quadrille is the customary term applied to the corps de ballet).

In the first movement the groups line up in a square and stand side by side. Throughout, the men and women move in unison with very little jumping. The ballet is almost all à terre, like a renaissance court dance. The couples each stand at one corner of their quadrille and the women of each group go to the center to meet and then return to their own partners. Now the men walk to the center, leaving the women behind, and return to them. Greetings have been exchanged in a quiet, courtly fashion. It is like a square dance between aristocrats, only these dancers wear practice costumes of white tunics with little skirts for the women and black tights

"Tombeau de Couperin"

and white tee shirts for the men. Couples rather than individuals now move together and exchange corners. Couples, not individuals, move to the center of the formations and circle. Now brief exchanges of partners are effected at the center. To conclude, all of the women execute a tiny series of whirling châiné turns to the center and return to their partners. All is as it was when the ballet began, except that the individuals and the couples of each individual quadrille have met and greeted one another in a restrained manner through a complex series of crossings and exchanges. Each quadrille performs the same steps in the same patterns at the same time, but they remain totally isolated from one another despite the fact that they are standing side by side.

The second movement finds the two groups aligned like a shallow flattened M. As before, all of the men from both quadrilles move together, as do all of the women. From the two short diagonal lines of men slanted toward the left, the men step forward, and when they resume their places, the women from the two short diagonals slanted to the right move forward and back. They move very carefully and do not exchange greetings, but return to their places. There is, however, a greater feeling of openness to their movement because they are not facing inward as they were in the tidy squares of the first section. One feels that their little closed societies are expanding, which is reenforced as each group later forms two long diagonal lines that pivot around one another in a large, wheeling arc. Hands and arms that have been held in formal patterns are now allowed to sweep in more expressionistic curves overhead. Men from each group place their arms around one another's shoulders as the women of the group, with arms around their waists, meet them, and couples again emerge to conclude in the formal square.

Four diagonal rows of women and men alternately open up even further the tidy little closed formation with which the ballet began. In this third movement couples exchange places between the quadrilles, which until this time had been kept strictly separate. Groups of eight men and women link hands in long lines and break into couples to walk in planetary orbits. The couples make arches with their arms and at the conclusion step back into their opening diagonal rows. The socializing has been easy and more informal than in the other two movements, suggesting a less rigid but still ordered society.

The dancing of the fourth movement is the most vigorous, even though it starts in the enclosed squares that opened the ballet. Men and women hook arms as they exchange places. They adopt the face-to-face social dance posture, jutting hips out provocatively while rocking back on heels. Then both groups melt into two long diagonal lines, with the men and women kneeling and facing one another. A man and a woman rise and move to the center between the two lines and begin to dance as one would expect in square dancing. It is as if boisterous twentieth-century ballroom dance has joined forces with the folk forms that predated the dances of the previous three movements. They retire to their places and are succeeded by two other couples. The movement picks up briskly as couples arch hands over the heads of the others who duck under them. The grave formality has totally disappeared as the men of both quadrilles dash over to shake hands with one another. It is a far cry from the lofty polite behavior that governed the start of the ballet. They dash back to the square formations that have been considerably animated in this movement. To conclude, the women all kneel with one arm raised and the men stand behind them echoing their formal gesture.

The ballet is like a resumé of social dance from the restraint of court measures through the increasingly less and less reined-in dances that characterized successive centuries. Finally, we are presented with a jazz age set of variations that breathes the atmosphere of Paris in the 1920s. They conclude the ballet with the earthy vivacity that the final "Gypsy" movement caps the more stately preceding movements of the *Brahms-*

Schönberg Quartet that was a resumé of the Austro-Hungarian culture it depicted. The dominant movement is the walk with dozens of interesting variants on it. There is no doubt that we are faced with a whole society in which there are only the most minimal variations for couples alone. The entire ballet is like a small intricate mechanism that moves at its own happy pace. Despite the somewhat sobering title (*Couperin's Tomb*), the ballet has a joyous lightness and gaiety throughout. If there are dark shadows somewhere, they cloud another horizon. The ballet is a perfect miniature in which there are no individual stars, only the group moving through ingenious choreographic patterns. It is a tour de force of inventiveness that rests on the essentially anonymous mass, and is a masterful demonstration of economy. It represents the high water mark in Balanchine's efforts to make a "character" out of the corps de ballet. The more spectacular lifts, leaps, and poses that are incorporated in most ballets are almost totally absent from this one. It relies on pattern, precision, and unison execution to make its point using only those qualities that characterize corps dancing. The lovely finish of Ravel's orchestration, so subtle and delicate, is the suitable festal garland on the dancing. We are presented with successive societies as they speak for themselves in their characteristic dance forms, brilliantly animated by Balanchine.

No dance form has more romantic and passionate connotations than the waltz, and throughout his career Balanchine has been fascinated with three-quarter time. One of his earliest ballets was set to a waltz of his own. At the same period he selected one of Ravel's "Valses Nobles et Sentimentales" for a ballet, and six decades later redid "The Garland Dance" from *The Sleeping Beauty,* Act I. He has created waltzes as needed in various ballets; one thinks of the "Scherzo Waltz" of *Cotillon,* the waltz in *Serenade,* the miniature "Valse Fantaisie" and "Waltz-Scherzo," which were designed as showpieces in themselves, and of course the two big waltzes in *The Nutcracker.* Periodically he has created ballets consisting of nothing but waltzes, such as *Waltz Academy, Trois Valses Romantiques,* and *Liebeslieder Waltzer.* These dances have consistently appeared throughout his career and reveal a strong romantic element in his sensibility.

The waltz made its appearance in Austria as a recognized dance form in the middle of the eighteenth century, and by the end of the nineteenth century it was associated imperishably with Vienna. The great masters of the form were Johann Strauss, Jr., his father, and Josef Lanner, and their melodies swept other dances off society ballrooms. Forgotten were the days in which the waltz was condemned as being a lascivious dance, threatening the social order. Far from a threat, it had become the embodiment of social order as the dance of kings and noblemen. It was the first social dance in which men and women openly embraced in public. Prior to its appearance, contact was restrained to hand-clasps and partners were confined to large groups decorously following the intricate measures of more stately dances. The waltz banished all of that and brought men and women face to face in their own little whirling world, quite openly celebrating the embrace. Variations on the form could be made for groups of women, as Balanchine did for the waltzes in *The Nutcracker,* but the emotional heart of the waltz was in the relationship of individual couples. It was this aspect of the form that exercised primary facination for Balanchine, though he also quite clearly saw a mirror of society in its cadences.

Coupling this feeling for the waltz with his admiration of Ravel's music, he choreographed one of his most lyric yet chilling ballets, *La Valse.* As might be expected, the work takes its name from the major piece of music selected. In itself, the composition was not long enough to offer Balanchine the developmental time he needed to delineate an over-refined society on the brink of dissolution. Accordingly, he selected another composition, the suite "Valses Nobles et Sentimentales," and made it the introduction to the ballet. The first of the eight waltzes in the suite is used as the overture.

Almost concealed at the back half of the stage by a transparent grey curtain are three chandeliers draped with black. As the curtain rises we see three formally dressed women with elbow-length gloves and midcalf-length tutus. The basic tutu color is a passionate red but a transparent overlay of dark grey chiffon mutes the color's intensity. It is a faintly disquieting combination.

The three women dance together unhurriedly, and one is struck by the gossipy eloquence of their arms as they pass and lean toward one another inclining their heads to whispering distance while flicking their hands palm forward and then reversed. Their number suggests the three Fates of classical myth who spin, measure, and cut the thread of life. There is something distrubing about their sophisticated banter.

They are succeeded by an ardent but restless couple who dance together but cannot make total commitment to one another in this world of fugitive encounters. To conclude, they part at opposite sides of the stage. The next couple are like the first, but more animated in their leaps and turns. Seemingly, everyone in this society is doomed to brief encounters. The man of the third couple pursues his partner with great ardor, but she is flirtatious and not interested in a binding union. When he kneels to kiss her hand she coquettishly whips it away.

When she leaves to dance alone the man finds himself confronted with the three women of the opening waltz, and they dance together, but the trio retains stronger links to one another and he finds himself continuously isolated. Abandoned by them, he drops to one knee and sways his arms from one side to the other overhead as the other couples pass and repass by him as if driven by some unknown wind that urges them relentlessly on. Finally, even these fleetingly bound couples break apart and the individuals pass the man who is still desperately chasing after some phantom of stability. At the conclusion of this waltz the stage is bare.

Cautiously, the principal couple enters. The man is dressed in the dark formal clothes that all the other men wear, but she wears a white ball gown in complete contrast to the costumes of the other women. The two are slightly furtive, and conceal their faces as if afraid that they will be recognized. Even in their cautious approach, her torso surges forward as though she is impelled to attend an event that perhaps she ought not to. As they dance, a man dressed in black is briefly seen to observe them from behind the translucent curtain that separates the chandeliered portion of the stage from the front half. The introduction is over, and her partner lifts her off.

The stage is darkened as the veiling curtain is lifted. Spotlights momentarily pick out one or another of the dancers from the first half. The trio of women looks more menacing than ever as each conceals her face with a gloved arm. One of the men approaches them but flees, terrified after a brief convulsive embrace with one who has uncovered her face. The meetings and partings of individuals take on an even more harried tone as fragmented bits of melody struggle to coalesce into a waltz.

The sputtering musical theme finally catches fire as the stage brightens and is occupied by a large group of dancers who wave friendly greetings to one another. The whole throng wheels together in the center in a furiously energetic dance that suggests unconcerned gaiety. The principals enter, the young girl clearly standing out from the crowd. The two join in the festivities showing a careless rapture that is in complete contrast to the furtive uncertainty with which they approached the ball.

Suddenly, a stranger enters attended by a servant. His was the face that was dimly seen looking out at the young girl and her escort as they made their tentative way to the affair. Although the music continues, all of the others stand frozen in position. The young girl alone is free to move, but she does so hesitatingly as if she were both repelled and attracted by the strange authoritative man. He presents her with a black necklace that contrasts sharply with her white dress, and holds up a mirror for her, but she turns away frightened at the image in the black, cracked glass. He presents her with black elbow-length gloves and a light black crinoline wrap to cover her white gown. He then offers her a bouquet, also black and menacing, but by this time she has been totally caught up in the rapture of the moment and dances with him. Moments later he releases her from his embrace and she falls lifeless to the stage. He exits quickly and the rest are freed from their frozen state. They are horrified at the sight of her body, which is an accusation of their revel. Her partner picks her up as the group goes into the large wheeling formation that characterized the first burst of the full waltz melody. Now the girl's body is held sacrificially aloft at the center as her partner helplessly circles around the outside of the group. Three couples enter and the men lift their partners straight up and down in orgasmic bursts, and then all circle the wheeling cluster as the curtain drops.

One is left with the feeling that the young girl has served as an innocent offering from a corrupt society to stave off impending destruction for one more day. The usually alluring waltz has been raggedly lyrical, interrupted by dark rumblings in the orchestra, and as flawed as the society that danced to its cadences. Social ties were in tatters, but the group still exuded a deadly glamor that drew the young woman into its fatal grasp. The beautiful phosphorescence of decay was its beacon and its mood suggested the glittery menace of *Cotillon* taken to its logical conclusion.

If *La Valse* was the dark side of the waltz, then *Vienna Waltzes* represented the brighter aspect. In its consideration of all levels of society from mansion dwellers to the denizens of gaudy dance halls, *Vienna Waltzes* presents a portrait of an entire social order. "Tales from the Vienna Woods" takes place in the famous Viennese park. A military man is escorting his lady and they walk slowly through the trees. She ducks away flirtatiously and he chases her. Together they waltz, and are joined by four other couples who dance for a moment and exit. The principal couple remains in the center as ten couples surround them. The women circle clockwise, and slightly outside of them. The men circle counterclockwise, and are almost absurdly gallant with formal clicking of the heels and roguish gestures stroking their moustaches.

The men leave and the women dance together, and the men return to find their partners. The lead man is not to be seen, and there is a hint of anxiety in the principal woman's eager glances. When he does appear, she

greets him with a grave curtsey to show her relief. Again all are caught up
in the sweep of the dance. The principals exit but the lead woman returns
to dance with the other women and they are joined by the men who form a
large circle. The women curtsey to the men, but none so profoundly and
graciously as the principal woman, who knows that matters of great
import between the sexes can be settled in the course of a formal waltz.
Couples leave and the principals are the last, walking slowly in the
twilight.

"Voices of Spring" is set in an unidentified glade and is the only section
in which the women wear toe shoes, which gives an ethereal air to the
movement. The lead woman whirls on in a flurry of dazzling turns like a
woodland sprite. Her cavalier prances on to the heavy oompah of the brass
and then comically leaps backward as eight corps women suddenly emerge
to startle him as if they had materialized from nowhere. As in the first
movement, the woman makes a reverence to the man, but it is decidedly
lighthearted. There is a "hiding" sequence during which she looks around
to see where he has gone. He quickly emerges to join her. The festive air is
heightened by the decorous group of eight women who pass under the
arched hands of the lead couple and then form an arc behind them for the
final pose when they all kneel and he stands.

The "Explosions Polka" brings us back to the city to a popular dance
hall. The women wear Minnie Mouse shoes and abbreviated dancing
dresses, and the men high-collared jackets that come up to their ears with
their hair combed into ridiculous pompadours. Together they are carica-
tures of fashion, having exaggerated their appearance to the point of
parody. Their dancing is a loutish reflection of the dances that have
preceded. Delicacy and refinement in the contact between the sexes have
been replaced by obvious displays of prowess. The subtle hide-and-seek
between couples has been supplanted by an oafish element of peek-a-boo
as the men duck-walk to the four standing women peering through their
cupped hands as though through binoculars. The women turn suddenly to
face the men at the last bass drum "explosion," startling them into
bufoonish backward tumbles.

The "Gold and Silver Waltz" brings the two principals together in an
elaborate café. Decorous women are attended by an assortment of men in
civilian and military dress. A glamorous woman in black enters and is
greeted by those already there. The lead man in cream-colored military
tunic and dark red trousers enters alone. He is immediately attracted to the
woman and loses his somewhat distracted air. When he attempts to kiss
her hand she draws it lightly away. He persists and they waltz together, the

"Vienna Waltzes" final movement Adam Lüders and Suzanne Farrell

obvious center of this cosmopolitan gathering. The dance is interrupted for a champagne toast and then the couples resume dancing. It is obvious that romantic flirtation has been brought to a fine art in this worldly circle, and it is equally obvious that the two are drawn to one another. At the end of the waltz they stand upstage silhouetted in an embrace.

The final movement takes place at the pinnacle of society, in a grand ballroom with a huge mirror. The music is the first waltz sequence from *Der Rosenkavalier*. One by one couples enter from the corners near the audience and walk diagonally to the opposite corner to exit. They cross the stage forming a large X. The women wear shell-white floor-length ball gowns and the men black swallow-tail jackets. They walk slowly and with calm dignity in the dim light. The moment suggests the end of an era as well as the opening of a formal ball. After nine couples have crossed, a single woman enters and walks to the center where she curtseys dreamily to an invisible partner. Gathering the hem of her skirt she begins to waltz as if she had a partner. From time to time her real partner emerges from the wings and is with her briefly, but then leaves. Almost as if she were grieving at his real presence as opposed to the dream, she keeps her face averted and covered with her hand, giving small shudders to coincide with a sobbing sound from the strings. The understated anxiety that touched all of the other movements is here fully expressed in her solo. When she exits, the dim room is brilliantly illuminated and couples emerge from both sides to fill the stage.

All of the principal dancers of the other movements are brought together with twenty couples to re-create the lush spectacle of a full ballroom floor. It is a beautiful climax to all that has gone before. The elegance of a formal waltz pervades the scene as the women's dresses flare becomingly about them in the swirling patterns that accelerate then diminish, only to conclude with a rush as all turn to face the audience and make a unison reverence.

In the course of the ballet Balanchine has presented all elements of the society from the clownish to the most refined, and has linked them with threads that run through each movement. Men are gallant pursuers operating within the conventions of the formal dance, and women place themselves tantalizingly but not really out of reach. At moments the women's flirtatiousness turns to anxiety, but that is almost immediately swept away by the lilting impulse of the music. Their lives are not totally carefree and there is a seriousness that underlies their dancing, but rituals performed on the dance floor enable them to resolve romantic tangles in a socially sanctioned manner. Coming after a long line of waltzes, it stands as one of Balanchine's most developed expressions of his feelings about the form and its place in commenting on social order.

A theme of special personal interest to him all through his career has been the search of a man looking for his Muse cum beloved. In *La Sonnambula* the poet's death is caused by this ardent quest, and in *Meditation* the man's journey from nowhere to nowhere is illuminated briefly by the presence of his beloved who leaves him. During *Don Quixote's* dramatic quest he is constantly drawn onward by the vision of his Muse, finally to death with mystical visions of triumph and vindication. The "guided" man of *Serenade* follows her promptings without question and moves on when she compels him to. The man and woman in "Divertimento" from *Baiser de la Fée* are also separated by "fate." Connected with this search for the ideal woman and/or artistic Muse is an air of fatal resignation. The ardent pursuit should be sufficient unto itself. Man should never stop his quest, but neither should he expect it to be conclusively successful. He must search out, seize, enjoy, and release the moment without expecting permanence.

For Balanchine, musically ordered time has consistently stimulated his finest choreographic efforts, and in *Duo Concertant* he united Muse and choreographer, male and female, creation and presentation with imaginative directness. The ballet is designed for two dancers, and the music is provided by two musicians on stage. The dancers stand behind the piano as the curtain rises, and the violinist stands in front of it with the music spread out on a stand. The movements of the two dancers relate directly to the individual instruments.

As the music begins, the dancers listen to it attentively without moving. When the playing of the first section is finished they step out to stand side by side. They push one then the other leg outward and return to the standing position. Just as the choreographer himself never designs any movement patterns until he has understood the shape of the music, the dancers have been absorbed in it before expressing their physical understanding of it. At first they seem very tentative, trying out varieties of gesture. As they begin to move more freely, he responds to the percussive piano, and standing behind her, describes large clockwise, staccato arcs. She simultaneously arranges her arms as though they were the hands of some invisible clock face. Together they suggest both the pulse and melodic line of the score.

At the start of the third movement, they are again listening together as the music begins. The interruptions for attentive listening quite firmly suggest the choreographic process as it transpires in a rehearsal studio.

They step away slowly and calmly. She leans back confidently in his arms and he supports her elegantly. The shape of a traditional pas de deux emerges, the entree followed by a slow adagio, capped by male and female variations, and concluded with a coda.

The fourth movement also begins with attentive listening, and he prances out holding his arms down by his sides for a moment, suggesting the quiet upper body dancers maintain in a Scottish jig or reel. (Musically, the movement is marked gigue.) After his lively variation, which concludes with large circling movements of the leg and then a balance, she executes a series of little jumps, châiné turns, and a small galloping steps. He presents his hand to her and she declines to take it with a prankish shake of the head. She relents and they dance off together with his arm around her waist. Deliberately, the two separate, and each goes to look intently at the music, he at the piano score and she at the violin portion. Both dancers and musicians accept guidance from the musical notation: the players express it through their instruments and the dancers interpret it with the steps of the classical ballet vocabulary. She begins to spin off movement, dancing the score as the violinist plays it. A large lift brings the partners back together again to stand side by side as the music concludes.

The fifth movement presents the man as a suppliant and the woman as an aloof presence. The stage is darkened except for a spotlight on the woman and another on the musicians. She slowly raises a hand to her lips and blows a kiss out on the air as the spotlight tightens to a small circle illuminating her hand, which is now withdrawn. There is a certain impersonality in the gesture that is not directed to any individual but is broadcast to whomever may be receptive. The man extends his arm into the spotlight and she returns. He takes her hand and gently turns it upward. The spotlight widens and he leaps to her side cupping his hands about her face, after which they embrace. There is a suggestion of violence in the encounter as he drops to one knee and she throws one leg across his before slipping away from his eager arms.

He looks about, bewildered and anxious. The stage is again darkened for her return to repeat the blown kiss. Her drooped hand as before is illuminated by the tight spotlight and her head is averted. He gently kisses the back of her hand, turns it upward, and renders his homage by dropping to one knee. This time he does not attempt to embrace her, but remains humbly at her feet as the light dims.

With the reduced forces of two dancers and two musicians, Balanchine has shaped a ballet that honors both choreography and music profoundly

"Duo Concertant" Peter Martins and Kay Mazzo

and economically. The dancers clearly listen to and respond to music, and the pauses between danced passages suggest the actual progress of choreographic shaping that comes in response to the musical order. The final adagio passage refers both to the dependence that exists between partners in the pas de deux and the special relationship of the attentive male to the inspiring female. It is he who supports her in the opening of the second movement after they listen to the music together, but it is also he who manhandles her, causing her to flee his embrace. The lesson of the latter has been learned; he continues to be attentive and responsive but humbly acknowledges her elusively reserved Muse quality. In the pas de deux she playfully refuses his hand, but then accepts his partnering support. As Muse she must remain unpossessed, but she will accept his adoration.

The Stravinsky Festival presented by New York City Ballet in 1972 marked the occasion of the composer's death the previous year. The event was an enormous undertaking and produced three of Balanchine's finest ballets; *Symphony in Three Movements, Duo Concertant,* and *Violin Concerto.* It was obviously a very personal tribute by Balanchine, and his brilliant response makes one wish that the composer had as many lives as a cat.

Stravinsky composed the violin concerto in 1931 and Balanchine created a short-lived ballet to it, called *Balustrade,* in 1941 for the Original Ballet Russe. The ballet was dropped after two performances but the music obviously held Balanchine's interest. Three decades later he created a ballet for two principal couples and sixteen corps men and women. The tough, edgy character of Aria I dictates the athletic, outward energy of the first couple much as the softer inward Aria II governs the dancing of the second principal couple. While their duets exist independently of one another, together they show two aspects of men's and women's relationship, with the female dominant in Aria I and the male prevailing in Aria II. Both are seen together in the finale.

The ballet has enormous energy, which is evident from the entrance of the principal woman from Aria II. She is in black leotards and tights with a short skirt, and is accompanied by four men in black tights and white tee shirts. Four other men accompany the Aria I woman's entrance. This first toccata section of the score introduces all of the principals in turn, and the ensembles who move on and exit like the quartets of men and women in *Agon.* The lead man from Aria I enters and is accompanied by four women wearing black leotards with short skirts and white tights. Almost before they have a chance to exit, the lead man of Aria II dashes on with four additional women. Then entrances and exits are repeated by each of the four principals, except that the second time around they are accompanied by corps dancers of the same sex. The final entrance by the lead man in Aria II is the most spectacular, as he runs on alone for a brief variation before his accompanying quartet gallop in a wide square around him, going from corner to corner while maintaining their tight square.

Aria I begins after their exit. The woman has discarded her skirt as if stripping for action. Each of the principals stands in a spotlight as they begin a long side-stepping progression toward one another. It is sensually suggestive and they quickly become athletically entwined. Their spot-lights merge as they do, and separate as they step apart. They move as if in a confined space and he pushes his palms out as though feeling invisible walls. She does a backbend and "walks" her feet in a half-circle as she supports her weight on her palms. He circles her and she takes tiny steps as one might see toddling children. He embraces her and she does the tiny steps within the frame of his arms. He kneels and she places one leg provocatively over his shoulder, and as he rises to face her she deftly and gracefully flips over backward to escape from his embrace. She leans back a second time, arching her body upward, and he lies on his back seemingly exhausted from the encounter.

The couple in Aria II come on stage together. The woman, like the other principal female, has discarded her skirt for this more intimate duet. Their movement is more tender, and indicates dependence. The woman leans against the man and in turn is supported. Responding to a sharp chord in the music, she flings her arms and legs out to form a large X. He kneels in front of her as her inwardly bent knees touch. He is attentive and tender, and while standing behind her later, softly covers her eyes with his hand to conclude their duet. She remains passively trusting in this position.

The capriccio that ends the ballet starts with the Aria I couple leading on four women and four men for their brief, bouncy ensemble dance. The principal woman is once again wearing her short skirt. The couple from Aria II (she, too, wears a skirt again) return with similar groups following them. He supports her in a turn to the right and left with the corps members stretched out in lines on either side turning their linked arms like a giant crankshaft. The Aria I couple return with their group. The principals line up in front and the two men fold arms across their chests as in folk-dance style for their joggy variation. The two female leads pursue as if they were dutiful peasant women. All join hands and stomp around then change partners. As a backdrop to their happy pas de quatre, the corps runs through an angular sequence of movement turning a knee inward or outward and bringing one arm across the torso, suggesting the flip/formal

"Stravinsky Violin Concerto"

gesture seen in *Agon*. They thrust arms stiffly on the diagonal or straight out, and then corps and principals are united in a flashing folk-tinged finale, but it is a folk dance that has been computerized.

Balanchine's creative vigor in this ballet, done over five decades after his first choreographic effort, was undiminished. He showed the same command over animating the masses, devising fresh duets for the two principal couples, and revealing his still passionate interest in the female dancer. He combined character dance elements with the supercharged energy of the classical dance vocabulary as he had modified it throughout his career. He was also working happily with the music of Stravinsky, whose supple and varied rhythms had provided him with the foundations for many of his most successful ballets dealing with distilled human passions.

Essentially, the basis for Balanchine's mature development was laid down in the imperial ballet school and theater system in Russia. Technically, he developed the classical vocabulary of Petipa as he learned it, and thematically, he explored the relationships of men with woman as beloved, the Muse, and unattainable object of affection and need.

In each role, woman was the stimulant. Among his youthful works, the early adagios such as *Night* and *Enigma,* the image of the beloved predominated, while the dancing girl of *Orientalia* had a muselike function. During the Diaghilev years, *Apollo* concentrated on this aspect of woman, while in *Prodigal Son* the unattainable Siren was the clearest example of woman's power to stimulate desire and also disappointment. Later, *La Sonnambula* touchingly examined the same disappointed enchantment.

Most of the earliest ballets where done without the support of a libretto, indicating his preference for plotless structure; they were all one-act ballets as opposed to evening-length spectacles. Without question, the opposition of the directors of the Maryinsky Theater forced Balanchine into alternate spaces where full-evening productions were difficult to achieve, but his subsequent career with its predominance of one-act ballets confirmed his basic inclination. The difficulties of the revolutionary days also precluded elaborate costumes, but his desire for simplicity in stage dress continued even when the necessity for it was removed.

Following Fokine's preference for danced gesture over mime, Balanchine dispensed almost totally with traditional mime in framing his new ballets and later in life removed such passages of it that he had incorporated into *Apollo* and *Tchaikovsky's Piano Concerto no. 2*. Again as an admirer of Fokine's innovative use of the corps de ballet as a character in and of itself, in *Chopiniana* (known in the West as *Les Sylphides*) he began his own approach to animating this large mass of dancers. His work with the more experimental Maly Opera and Alexandrinsky drama company enabled him to experiment with group choreography in Rimskykorsakov's *Coq d'Or* and Shaw's *Caesar and Cleopatra*. These efforts were praised by other young experimenters but condemned by traditionalists. Balanchine's continued interest in animating the corps became one of the central marks of his work, as shown again and again in landmark pieces such as *Serenade, Agon,* and *Symphony in C*. Pushing the idea to the utmost he created *Le Tombeau de Couperin* entirely for group dancing. As a dedicated admirer of Fokine's innovations he remounted a production of *Chopiniana* (under its original name) for New York City Ballet in 1972, and again for the workshop performances of the School Of American Ballet in 1982.[3]

As much as Balanchine has contributed to the artistic developments of twentieth-century ballet, he has always reaffirmed his connection with the nineteenth-century tradition of Petipa. The technique that had been developed in the imperial system remained the bedrock vocabulary for Balanchine, though he rejected or modified some of its conventions. What is more important than his use of bare feet or the introduction of acrobatic gesture into the vocabulary was his expansion of the points of contact between the male and the female, permitting greater expressiveness and visual richness.

The male and female of Petipa's theater touched at the wrist, hand, waist, or shoulder, and all partnering could be accomplished within these restrictions. For more spectacular lifts, Balanchine pushed the partner straight overhead with locked elbows, placing the man's hands in the small of the female's back. In *Apollo* the man kneels and bends his back so that the woman can rest on it with her whole torso and seem to float. In *Prodigal Son* the Siren slithers down his back on her chest like a snake. Also, she wraps her body around his like a provocative circlet to indicate her conquest. The gestures were found startling at first, but they were used for expressive purposes and not capriciously. Women are lifted under the arms or show intimacy by entwining arms with the man's while standing back to back. The partner may scoop a woman up by lifting from under one thigh or supporting her under the elbows. The tension and beauty of poses can be accentuated by the element of off-balance partnering, in which the male allows a partner to swing out beyond her natural point of balance before concluding the sequence by returning her to her natural balance. In supported pirouettes, the man allows the woman to start the turn by herself before stepping to her to assist the balance and maintain the momentum of the turn. The movement is more complex in its timing, but this adds to the excitement of the sequence.

Governing all of his changes in technique have been the time demands of music. Balanchine added quickness to the execution of all the steps of the classical vocabulary to approximate more closely the rhythmic demands of music. Basic to this change was a redeployment of the weight of the dancer's body. For Balanchine, that weight had to be placed forward on the balls of the feet rather than on the heels, to make rapid changes of direction easier. With this basic change in speed and weight distribution came the elimination of preparations, those momentary anticipatory stances assumed before virtuoso steps, which of necessity slowed down the flow of the music.

Some of the most unusual partnering support is found in *Agon,* where the male and female stay within an arm's length of one another and he supports her in an arabesques while lying on his back and stretching his arms up to her. The configuration is unusual, but responds directly to the intricate development of the score's serial composition. To emphasize the diminution of hope in *Ivesiana,* the corps listlessly walks on its knees. The deformed line of the body is shocking but the reduced expectations of the characters is expressed clearly and powerfully. While the female partner customarily places her hand on a man's arm or shoulder, could anything more clearly express the untamed vigor of the young god in *Apollo* than to have the women swing from his biceps? It certainly isn't traditional, but it is expressively direct.

While rejecting traditional, formal mime, Balanchine has retained a fondness for everyday gesture, which has found its way into a number of ballets. In the final movement of *Le Tombeau de Couperin,* the men of the two isolated quadrilles, who have gradually become more involved with one another, openly lean over and shake hands as do the "Inn" couple of *Ivesiana.* The gesture is one of conventional greeting and also characteristic of our own time rather than of the courtliness of the preceeding generations. In *La Valse,* newcomers to the ball happily wave to those already arrived. The woman of the second movement in *Western Symphony* openly demands the attention of a distracted man by tapping him vigorously on the shoulder. In the military worlds of *Union Jack* and *Stars and Stripes,* the salute is employed quite naturally, as it is in the lovely *The Steadfast Tin Soldier.* A disappointed lover slaps his chest and points to his beloved in *A Midsummer Night's Dream* bluntly to assert, "She's mine!" In each case there is a man-in-the-street naturalness that was not to be found in the more formal mime of the nineteenth century. In this choice as in others, Balanchine inclined to the conventions of the present century rather than to the rituals of another.

Even while pressing ahead to address his own times in the terms he felt most appropriate, Balanchine has proclaimed his affiliation with the past. Tchaikovsky wrote only three scores—*The Nutcracker, Swan Lake,* and *Sleeping Beauty*—directly for ballet presentation and Balanchine has staged all of them in whole or in part, as well as remounting productions of *Coppélia* and *Harlequinade.* In Russia Balanchine danced in *Don Quixote* and the Fokine/Meyerhold *Orpheus,* appeared in a dramatic production of *A Midsummer Night's Dream,* and has prepared his own versions of all three. In all cases he has brought his own creative insight to the ballets, and has not attempted to present carbon-copy versions but to blend the best of the old with the new. As a choreographer who initially fought tradition, he has emerged as its foremost exponent.

The essence of balletic tradition for him is the expressiveness of disciplined movement to challenging music. He has made over two dozen ballets with librettos, but finds his greatest interest aroused by the dramatic structure suggested by music. He is stimulated creatively by an existing score such as "The Four Temperaments," conceives an idea and looks for appropriate music, as he did for *Jewels* or *Cotillon,* or he works with a composer, as he has done successfully with Stravinsky in *Orpheus* and *Agon.* In each instance, however, he favors musical rather than verbal plotting. In Russia he worked with existing scores for the most part, and with Diaghilev, he had new music commissioned for the occasion. For the bulk of his career he has used both sources.

The greatest shift in his musical taste occurred after leaving Russia. While there, he favored romantic music and selected pieces by Rubinstein, Rachmaninoff, Sibelius, Mussorgsky, Chopin, Arensky, Cui, and Rimskykorsakov. Diaghilev presented him with scores by Stravinsky, Auric, Sauguet, Rieti, Ravel, Satie, and Lord Berners. On his own he selected scores by Webern, Schönberg, Hindemith, Ives, and Weill, as well as dipping into the past with Schumann, Brahms, Mendelssohn, Bizet, Gounod, Verdi, Bach, Mozart, Vivaldi, and Handel. His aversion to Wagner was intensified when he was forced to play selections for his first wife's father, and he has never designed a ballet using this music, except under duress. Contemporary Soviet composers have not interested him outside of Prokofiev, nor have Bartok, Debussy, or Berlioz engaged him. Aleatory music, musique concrète, and electronic scores have been of little interest to him except in rare experimental instances. For him, music is time and dancers are squeezed into time. Music without such a rhythmic impulse cannot provide him with the basis for dancing.

His strictness with the individual steps in ballets has two sides. "I don't tell them what to express which could cause them to stray from the way in which their role has been conceived. I show each dancer exactly what he is to do and demand that he obeys me down to the smallest detail." This rather doctrinaire approach indicates more his mistrust of words and belief in the innate expressivity of danced gesture than it does a dictatorial rigidity. He regularly changes steps in his ballets to accommodate individual dancers, while retaining the mood of the ballet overall. This flexibility extends most particularly to epaulement, the carriage of the head shoulders and arms. Both in the School of American Ballet and in his company, Balanchine has tended to let dancers find their own suitable epaulement. In this he again follows the tradition of the imperial system. Russian style was a combination of French finish and Italian virtuosity, and the native temperament was allowed to find its expression in epaulement. In the same way, Balanchine is letting American dancers find the epaulement that is most natural to themselves.

In the course of his long career he has brought music and dance closer together by developing ballets according to the structures of their scores. The relationship of dance to music exists without the curtain of a story to separate them. Dramatic elements such as mime were abandoned in favor of danced gesture. Fokine had felt that the traditional mime gestures were outmoded, and that rather than express meaning through hand gesture, dancers ought to express meaning through danced gesture. He himself very rarely abandoned dramatic pretexts for his ballets, so it was left to Balanchine to take this innovation to its logical end. By bringing music and dance closer together, Balanchine emphasized the expressiveness of classical dancing. Dancers were not required to show acting talents in his ballets, they were to wield the classical vocabulary with greater speed and fluency than had ever been seen before. They would communicate directly with audiences through this, and not through impersonation of literary characters. They were free to be themselves within the ingenious choreographic designs that are Balanchine's ballets, and audiences could relate to those ballets with the imaginative freedom they might bring to a performance of concert level music without an overt program.

Notes

Chapter 1

1. Referring to *Movements for Piano and Orchestra,* Stravinsky commented, "was like a tour of a building for which I had drawn the plans but never explored the result." Remarks quoted in *Themes and Episodes,* by Igor Stravinsky and Robert Craft (New York: Alfred A. Knopf, 1968).

2. *New York Times,* January 19, 1968.

3. *Dance Index,* Vol. 6 (New York: Arno Press, 1947), pp. 254–55.

4. This occurs during the final pas de quatre in the original version described in the text. In the version revised by Balanchine in the 1970s, the opening birth scene was cut and the sunburst pose was moved to conclude the ballet.

5. Tamara Geva, *Split Seconds* (New York: Harper & Row, 1972), p. 289.

Chapter 2

1. For all facts regarding Balanchine's life up to the time he entered the Imperial Ballet and Theater School, I have drawn on *Balanchine,* Bernard Taper (New York: Harper & Row, 1963).

2. Mikhail Mikhailov, "My Classmate George Balanchine," *Dance News,* March 1967.

3. Ibid.

4. Yuri Slonimsky, "Balanchine—The Early Years," *Ballet Review* 5, no. 3 (1976):37.

5. *Dance News,* March 1967.

6. Geva, *Split Seconds,* p. 308.

7. Ibid., p. 309.

Chapter 3

1. Geva, *Split Seconds,* p. 329.
2. Richard Buckle, *Diaghilev* (New York: Atheneum, 1979), pp. 89–157.
3. S. L. Grigoriev, *The Diaghilev Ballet 1909–1929* (London: Constable & Co., 1953), pp. 270–71.
4. Ibid., pp. 256–57.
5. Interview by Pierre Tugal, *Dancing Times,* September 1947.
6. *La Nouvelle Revue Française,* July 1, 1926, p. 116.
7. *Dancing Times,* December 1929, p. 254.

Chapter 4

1. *Dance Magazine,* December 1937, p. 14.
2. By Vittorio Rieti whose *Barabau* and *Le Bal* Balanchine had choreographed previously for Diaghilev. Subsequently, Balanchine choreographed Rieti's *La Sonnambula, Waltz Academy,* and his Fifth Symphony under the title *Native Dancers,* in the United States.
3. Edwin Denby, *Looking At the Dance.* Selected and arranged by B. H. Haggin. (New York: Horizon Press, 1949), p. 225.
4. Lincoln Kirstein, *Thirty Years: The New York City Ballet* (New York: Alfred A. Knopf, 1978), pp. 29–37.
5. In a version staged for the Ballet Russe de Monte Carlo in 1940, guest artist Marie-Jeanne danced all of the female solo roles.
6. *New York Times,* April 13, 1938.
7. In South America it was decided that the company needed closing ballets, and Balanchine devised *Divertimento* and *Fantasia Brasiliera.* Neither was presented in the United States.

Chapter 5

1. The durability of the revue format was demonstrated in television's fledgling decades of the 1940s and 1950s. The period was dominated by variety entertainment "Texaco Star Theater" (Milton Berle), "Your Show of Shows" (Sid Caesar and Imogene Coca), and "The Ed Sullivan 'Toast of the Town' Show" (Ed Sullivan introducing a variety bill.)
2. *Dance Magazine,* November 1940, p. 10.

Chapter 6

1. Performance programs 1948–1977.
2. Author's interview with the choreographer in 1979.

Chapter 7

1. Author's interview with Melissa Hayden in 1975.

2. In 1946 Serge Denham, director of the original Ballet Russe, decided that he needed a full-evening production, and Danilova and Balanchine put together an abbreviated *Raymonda*. Bits and pieces of it as *Pas de Dix* or *Raymonda Variations* or *Cortege Hongrois* cropped up in New York City Ballet's repertory subsequently.

3. Staged by Alexandra Danilova.

Selected Bibliography

Books

Balanchine, George, and Mason, Francis. *Balanchine's Complete Stories of the Great Ballets,* Garden City, N.Y.: Doubleday & Co., 1977.

Beaumont, Cyril. *Complete Book of Ballets.* London: Putnam, 1937.

————. *Supplement to the Complete Book of Ballets.* London: Putnam, 1942.

————. *Ballets of Today.* London: Putnam, 1954.

————. *Ballets Past and Present.* London: Putnam, 1955.

Buckle, Richard. *Diaghilev.* New York: Atheneum, 1979.

Denby, Edwin. *Looking at the Dance.* Selected and arranged by B. H. Haggin. New York: Horizon Press, 1949.

Eakins Press Foundation *Choreography by George Balanchine,* A Catalogue of Works. New York: Eakins Press, 1983.

Geva, Tamara. *Split Seconds.* New York: Harper & Row, 1972.

Goldner, Nancy. *The Stravinsky Festival.* New York: Eakins Press, 1973.

Grigoriev, S. L. *The Diaghilev Ballet 1909–1929.* London: Constable, 1953.

Kirstein, Lincoln. *Movement and Metaphor.* New York: Praeger, 1970.

————*Thirty Years: The New York City Ballet.* New York: Alfred A. Knopf, 1978.

Reynolds, Nancy. *Repertory in Review.* New York: Dial Press, 1977.

Taper, Bernard. *Balanchine.* New York: Harper & Row, 1963.

Periodicals

Lederman, Minna, ed. "Stravinsky in the Theater." *Dance Index* 6 (1947).

Mikhailov, Mikhail. "My Classmate George Balanchine." *Dance News* (March, April, May 1967).

Slonimsky, Yuri. "Balanchine, the Early Years." *Ballet Review* 5, no. 3 (1976).

Appendix

Performance Credits for Selected Ballets

Chapter 1

Apollon Musagète (1928), *Apollo, Leader of the Muses* (1951), *Apollo* (1957)
Choreography: Balanchine (substantially revised 1979)
Music: Stravinsky, "Apollon Musagète" 1927–28
Costumes and decor: André Beauchant, "Coco" Chanel (1928), Stewart Chaney (1937), Tomas Santa Rosa (1941), Pavel Tchelitchev (1942), Karinska (1951-costumes only), Balanchine (1957-costumes only; 1979-decor only)
Lighting: Diaghilev (1928), Jean Rosenthal (1951), David Hays (1964), Ronald Bates (1979)
Premiere: June 12, 1928, Theatre Sarah-Bernhardt, Les Ballets Russes de Serge Diaghilev
Revival: April 27, 1937, Metropolitan Opera House, American Ballet
Revival: November 15, 1951, New York City Center for Music and Drama, New York City Ballet

Cast:	(1928)	(1937)	(1951)
Apollo	Serge Lifar	Lew Christensen	André Eglevsky
Terpsichore	Alexandra Danilova	Elise Reiman	Maria Tallchief
Calliope	Liubov Tchernicheva	Daphne Vane	Diana Adams
Polyhymnia	Felia Doubrovska	Holly Howard	Tanaquil LeClercq

The ballet's numerous recostumings and stagings always suggested the godlike Apollo, until 1957 when Jacques d'Amboise assumed the title role wearing black tights and a small triangular white shirt. The final demythologizing occurred in 1979 when Mikhail Baryshnikov joined New York City Ballet. All of Scene I (the birth) was eliminated, as was the ascent to Parnassus at the conclusion. The "sunburst" from the final pas de quatre was switched from its usual position and became the closing pose. Behind the dancers, a sunrise in golden orange was projected. Balanchine maintained that Stravinsky had been asked by Diaghilev to add the birth scene, it was not part of his original conception, and that the 1979 revision went back to the original conception.

Chapter 2

Marche Funebre
Choreography: Balanchine
Music: Chopin, Sonata No. 1 in B Flat minor, second movement
Costumes: Unknown, most likely a member of the company
Lighting: Unknown, most likely a member of the company
Premiere: 1923, City Council Hall, Petrograd, Young Ballet

Cast:

Solo Woman	Alexandra Danilova
Secondary Solo Woman	Olga Mungalova
Three men	Unknown
Six women	H. Stoulkine, V. Kostrovitskaya, unknown

This piece was presented on the first evening of the Young Ballet. As was to be habitual with Balanchine, he named the ballet after the piece of music he had selected. The work was never publicly performed after its first showing in Petrograd, though Balanchine did set it for the Diaghilev company when he first joined them, but it was never offered on any Diaghilev program. A newspaper review of the work written by Tatiana Bruni discerned qualities in it that were not present in works previously seen (Balanchine had made his first ballet in 1920): "With this work one can begin to speak seriously about Balanchivadze as a ballet master."

Chapter 3

Le Fils Prodigue (1929), *The Prodigal Son* (1950)
Choreography: Balanchine
Libretto: Boris Kochno
Music: Prokoviev
Costumes and Decor: Georges Rouault
Lighting: Serge Diaghilev (1929), Jean Rosenthal (1950)
Premiere: May 21, 1929, Theatre Sarah-Bernhardt, Les Ballets Russes de Serge
    Diaghilev
Revival: February 23, 1950, New York City Center For Music and Drama, New
    York City Ballet

Cast:	(1929)	(1950)
Prodigal	Serge Lifar	Jerome Robbins
Siren	Felia Doubrovska	Maria Tallchief
Father	Michael Fedorov	Michael Arshansky
Servants	Anton Dolin	Frank Hobi
	Leon Woizikowsky	Herbert Bliss

Nine drinking companions

This was the last ballet that Balanchine made for the Diaghilev company. Three months after its premier, Diaghilev died and the company dissolved. It was the first ballet to be revived by New York City Ballet and has proved to be very durable. Edward Villella made a splendid Prodigal, and the role also suited Mikhail Baryshnikov who performed it on the "Dance in America" television series.

Chapter 4

Cotillon
Choreography: Balanchine
Libretto: Boris Kochno
Music: Chabrier ("Menuet Pompeux," "Tourbillon," "Mauresque," "Scherzo-Valse," "Idylle," "Danse Rustique" from "Dix Scenes Pittoresques," and the third of the "Trois Valses Romantiques," "the Danse Rustique" was repeated at the end)
Costumes and decor: Christian Bérard
Lighting: Unknown
Premiere: April 12, 1932, Theatre de Monte Carlo, Ballet Russe de Monte Carlo

Cast:

Young girl	Tamara Toumanova
Young man	David Lichine
Conductor of the Ball	Leon Woizikovsky
His assistant	Valentina Blinova
Guests	Roman Jasinsky and others

There has never been a serious attempt to revive this ballet although the late A. V. Coton believed that it was the finest ballet that Balanchine had ever done. This comment must be taken in the context in which it was made. At the time Coton could only have been familiar with the ballets of the Diaghilev years and those done prior to Balanchine's departure for the United States. The assertion is a strong one, however, when we consider it against the background of *Apollo* and *The Prodigal Son*. The ballet was a vehicle for Toumanova. At present only a snippet of choreography exists—that of the "Hand of Fate" duet, which Roman Jasinsky mounted for the Tulsa Civic Ballet.

Serenade
Choreography: Balanchine, substantially revised in 1941
Music: Tchaikovsky, Serenade in C for String Orchestra, 1880, arranged and
    orchestrated by George Antheil
Costumes: Jean Lurçat (1935), Candido Portinari (1941), Balanchine (1948),
    Karinska (1952), Uncredited (men's costumes only 1982)
Decor: Gaston Longchamp (abandoned after 1936)
Lighting: Jean Rosenthal (1948), Ronald Bates (1964)
Premiere: March 1, 1935, Adelphi Theater, New York

Cast:

Sonatina	Leda Anchutina, Holly Howard, Elise Reiman, Elena de Rivas, and thirteen corps women
Waltz	Anchutina, Gisella Caccialanza, Howard, Helen Leitch, Annabelle Lyon, and ten corps women
Russian Dance (1941)	Marie-Jeanne, William Dollar, and sixteen corps women
Elegy	Howard, Kathryn Mullowny, Heidi Vossler, Charles Lasky, eight corps women, and four corps men.

The ballet is romantic in mood and in its gestural styling. It is very much a
dance about dancing, as is *Symphony in C*. The latter is sharp-edged in its attack,
while *Serenade* has a more rounded softness to it suggesting the flowing style that
was very much a characteristic of Fokine's choreography, especially in *Les
Sylphides*. Balanchine expressed his admiration for Fokine's ballet on several
occasions and Danilova has remounted it for both New York City Ballet (1972)
and workshop performances of the School of American Ballet (1982) under its
original title, *Chopiniana*.

Ballet Imperial (1941), *Concerto no. 2* (1973), *Tchaikovsky Piano Concerto no. 2*
    (1973)
Music: Tchaikovsky, Piano Concerto in G Major, 1879
Choreography: Balanchine, revised 1973
Costumes and decor: Mstislav Doboujinsky, Rouben Ter-Arutunian (1964),
    Karinska (costumes only, 1973, decor eliminated)
Premiere: June 25, 1941, Teatro Municipal, Rio De Janeiro, American Ballet
    Caravan
Revival: October 15, 1964, New York State Theater, New York City Ballet
Revival: January 12, 1973, New York State Theater, New York City Ballet

Cast:	(1941)	(1964)	(1973)
Principals	Marie-Jeanne	Suzanne Farrell	Patricia McBride
	William Dollar	Jacques d'Amboise	Peter Martins
Soloists	Gisella Caccialanza	Patricia Neary	Colleen Neary
	Fred Danieli	Frank Ohman	Tracy Bennett
	Nicholas Magallanes	Earle Sieveling	Victor Castelli

In addition to the principals and soloists, there were two female secondary soloists, sixteen corps women, and eight corps men. The choreography was fast, brilliant, and very demanding. Marie-Jeanne put her special stamp on the role. Before leaving on its South American tour the company presented the work in an open rehearsal in the Concert Hall of Hunter College.

Concerto Barocco
Choreography: Balanchine
Music: J. S. Bach, Double Violin Concerto in D Minor
Costumes and decor: Eugene Berman, Balanchine (costumes only, 1951, decor dropped)
Premiere: June 27, 1941, Teatro Municipal, Rio De Janeiro, American Ballet Caravan

Cast
Principals	Marie-Jeanne, William Dollar
Soloist	Mary Jane Shea
Corps	eight women

The ballet was on the opening program of New York City Ballet in 1948 and has been seen regularly since. The simple black tunics of 1951 subsequently were changed to white for the women.

Chapter 6

The Four Temperaments
Choreography: Balanchine
Music: Hindemith, "Theme with Four Variations"
Costumes: Kurt Seligman, Balanchine (1951)
Lighting: Unknown
Premiere: November 20, 1946, Central High School of Needle Trades, Ballet Society

Cast:
Theme
    1. Beatrice Tompkins and Jose Martinez
    2. Elise Reiman and Lew Christensen
    3. Gisella Caccialanza and Francisco Moncion

First Variation: "Melancholic"	William Dollar and six women
Second Variation: "Sanguinic"	Mary Ellen Moylan and Fred Danieli and four women
Third Variation: "Phlegmatic"	Todd Bolender and four women
Fourth Variation: "Choleric"	Tanaquil LeClercq and entire cast

The elaborate allegorical costumes prepared by the surrealist painter Kurt Seligman were to a great extent ungainly and concealed the line of the body. In Balanchine's eyes "less is more" with regard to costuming, and the simple black and white practice costume as worn in the current production has become something of a uniform for New York City Ballet. The ballet has seen many cast changes since its premiere performance, but no one has replaced Todd Bolender's slinky wit in "Phlegmatic," though Mel Tomlinson, who joined the company in 1981, comes very close. Balanchine commissioned the score.

Le Palais de Cristal (1947), *Symphony in C* (1948)
Choreography: Balanchine
Music: Bizet, Symphony no. 1 in C Major 1855
Costumes and decor: Leonore Fini (1947), Balanchine (1948 costumes only), Karinska (1950 costumes only)
Lighting:
Premiere: July 28, 1947, Opera, Paris Opera Ballet
Revival: March 22, 1948, New York City Center of Music and Drama, New York City Ballet

Cast	(1947)	(1948)
First Movement	Lycette Darsonval, Alexandre Kalioujny	Maria Tallchief, Nicholas Magallanes
Second Movement	Tamara Toumanova, Roger Ritz	Tanaquil LeClercq, Francisco Moncion
Third Movement	Micheline Bardin, Michel Renault	Beatrice Tompkins, Herbert Bliss
Fourth Movement	Madeleine Lafon, Max Bozzoni	Elise Reiman, Lew Christensen

In each movement the principals are joined by two secondary soloist couples and six or eight corps women. The entire cast, usually numbering fifty, joins for the finale. Fini's design theme of jewels, rubies, sapphires, emeralds, and diamonds—was later reflected in Balanchine's own ballet incorporating three of the gems. Nearly every principal dancer in the history of the company has danced in this ballet. Tallchief of the original cast was particularly memorable in the First Movement, and Suzanne Farrell brought the most commanding ease to the Second Movement. Robert Barnett's springiness was not to be forgotten in the Third Movement.

Bourrée Fantasque
Choreography: Balanchine
Music: Chabrier, "Marche Joyeuse," "Bourée Fantasque," prelude to the second act of "Gwendoline," and "Fete Polonaise" from the third act of "Le Roi Malgre Lui."
Costumes and decor: Karinska
Lighting:
Premiere: December 1, 1949, New York City Center for Music and Drama, New York City Ballet.

Cast:

Bourrée Fantasque	Tanaquil LeClercq, Jerome Robbins, eight corps women, four corps men
Prelude	Maria Tallchief, Nicholas Magallanes, two secondary soloist women, eight corps women
Fête Polonaise	Janet Reed, Herbert Bliss, two secondary solo couples, six corps women, four corps men, joined by entire cast.

Tanaquil LeClercq and Jerome Robbins were superb as the mismatched couple of the *Bourrée Fantasque*. They "sold" every witty gesture in the movement but never broadened the movement to caricature. The ballet slipped from repertoire in the middle 1960s and was never revived by New York City Ballet. In 1981 American Ballet Theater revived it with the same costumes but slightly different decor, and it proved durably amusing. It shows Balanchine in a playful mood commenting both on eccentricities of ballet technique, and also the relations between men and women.

Ivesiana

Choreography: Balanchine

Music: Ives, "Central Park in the Dark," 1906; "The Unanswered Question," 1906; "In the Inn," 1904; and "In the Night" 1906

Costumes: Balanchine

Lighting: Jean Rosenthal

Premiere: September 14, 1954, New York City Center for Music and Drama, New York City Ballet

Revival: March 16, 1961, New York City Center for Music and Drama, New York City Ballet

Revival: April 30, 1975, New York State Theater, New York City Ballet

Cast	(1954)	(1961)	(1975)
Central Park	Janet Reed, Francisco Moncion, twenty women	Patricia McBride, Francisco Moncion, twenty women	Sara Leland, Francisco Moncion, twenty women
Unanswered	Allegra Kent, Todd Bolender, four men	Allegra Kent, Deni Lamont, four men	Elise Flagg, Deni Lamont, four men
Inn	Tanaquil LeClercq, Todd Bolender	Diana Adams, Arthur Mitchell	Suzanne Farrell, Victor Castelli
Night	Ensemble	Ensemble	Ensemble

In the original ballet there were two additional sections, "Hallowe'en," with Patricia Wilde, Jacques d'Amboise, and four women; and "Over the Pavements" with Diana Adams, Herbert Bliss, and four men. The year after the premier Balanchine substituted "Arguments" for "Hallowe'en," and a few months later replaced it with "Barn Dance." When he revived the ballet in 1961 these sections were dropped and remained absent from the 1975 revival.

Western Symphony
Choreography: Balanchine
Music: Hershey Kay (traditional, arranged and orchestrated)
Costumes: Karinska (renewed in 1968)
Decor: John Boyt
Lighting: Jean Rosenthal
Premiere: September 7, 1954, New York City Center for Music and Drama, New York City Ballet

Cast:

Allegro	Diana Adams, Herbert Bliss, eight corps women, and four corps men
Adagio	Janet Reed, Nicholas Magallanes, and four corps women
Scherzo	Patricia Wilde, André Eglevsky, four corps women
Rondo	Tanaquil LeClercq, Jacques d'Amboise, and four corps couples

The open, expansive nature of the ballet with its display of high energy has made it very popular with audiences. As the curtain falls the whole cast is on stage furiously turning, and they continue as the curtain cuts them off from view. The Scherzo, was dropped before the company moved to State Theater in 1964, and the ballet has been presented without the movement ever since. Jacques d'Amboise was memorable in the Rondo.

Stars and Stripes
Choreography: Balanchine
Music: Sousa, "Corcoran Cadets," "Thunder and Gladiator," "Rifle Regiment," "Liberty Belle," and "El Capitan." "Stars and Stripes" adapted and orchestated by Hershey Kay
Costumes: Karinska
Decor: David Hays
Lighting: Nananne Porcher, David Hays (1964)
Premiere: January 17, 1958, New York City Center For Music and Drama, New York City Ballet

Cast:

First Campaign	Allegra Kent and twelve corps women
Second Campaign	Robert Barnett and twelve corps men
Third Campaign	Diana Adams and twelve corps women
Fourth Campaign	Melissa Hayden and Jacques d'Amboise
Fifth Campaign	Entire cast

The ballet is brash and exuberant, like Sousa's music, which celebrated American imperialism of the turn of the century. Balanchine did not look away from that aspect of the music, but added humor to his presentation of it. He also decided to move the men's campaign from the second to the third spot shortly after the premiere performance. Deni Lamont was unforgettable as the leader of the men.

Chapter 7

Jewels
Choreography: Balanchine
Music: Fauré, "Emeralds" from "Peléas et Melisande" and "Shylock"
      Stravinsky, "Rubies"; Capriccio for Piano and Orchestra
      Tchaikovsky, "Diamonds"; final four movements from Symphony no. 3
      in D Major
Costumes: Karinska
Decor: Peter Harvey
Premiere: April 13, 1967, New York State Theater, New York City Ballet

Cast:
  Emeralds — Violette Verdy and Conrad Ludow, Mimi Paul and Francisco
          Moncion; Sara Leland, Suki Schorer, John Prinz, and ten corps
          women
  Rubies   — Patricia McBride and Edward Villella; Patricia Neary, eight
          corps women, and four corps men.
  Diamonds — Suzanne Farrell and Jacques d'Amboise, four secondary solo
          couples, twelve corps women, and twelve corps men

It was the unquestioned assumption of most of the ballet audience that the plotless ballet was a one-act form since it had been traditionally. The advent of a three-act plotless ballet was a stunning surprise. Portions of the work have been given separately on occasion, showing that the sections are not tied by narrative threads, but their collage-like affinity makes them most satisfactory when presented as a group.

Agon
Choreography: Balanchine
Music: Stravinsky
Costumes: Balanchine
Lighting: Nananne Porcher
Premiere: December 1, 1957, New York City Center for Music and Drama,
    New York City Ballet

Cast:

Part I	Ensemble	Eight principals and four corps women
Part II	First pas de trois	Todd Bolender, Barbara Milberg,
		Barbara Walczak
	Second pas de trois	Roy Tobias, Jonathan Watts,
		Melissa Hayden
	Pas de deux	Diana Adams, Arthur Mitchell
Part III	Ensemble	

No one ever doubted that this was a definitive statement of twentieth-century classicism. It took a while before its humor was fully appreciated. Adams and Mitchell were stunning.

The Nutcracker
Choreography: Balanchine (Mouse King, Jerome Robbins)
Music: Tchaikovsky
Costumes: Karinska
Masks: Vlady
Decor: Horace Armistead, Rouben Ter-Arutunian (1964)
Lighting: Jean Rosenthal, Rouben Ter-Arutunian (1964)
Premiere: February 2, 1954, New York City Center of Music and Drama, New
    York City Ballet

Cast:
Act I

Dr. and Frau Stahlbaum	Frank Hobi and Irene Larsson
Clara and Fritz	Alberta Grant and Susan Kaufman
Herr Drosselmeyer	Michael Arshansky
His nephew (the Nutcracker)	Paul Nickel
Toys: Harlequin and Columbine	Gloria Vauges and Kaye Sargent
Soldier	Roy Tobias
Maid, Guests, eight parents, eleven children, and two grandparents	
Mouse King	Edward Bigelow
Mice	Eight corps men
Soldiers	Nineteen children
Snowflakes	Sixteen corps women

Act II

Sugar Plum Fairy	Maria Tallchief
Her Cavalier	Nicholas Magallanes
Angels	Eight girl students
Hot Chocolate	Yvonne Mounsey, Herbert Bliss, and four corps couples
Coffee	Francisco Moncion and four children
Tea	George Li and two corps women
Candy Canes	Robert Barnett and six teen-age girls
Marzipan Shepherdesses	Janet Reed and four corps women
Bonbonnière	Edward Bigelow and eight children
Dewdrop	Tanaquil LeClercq
Flowers	Two female secondary soloists and twelve corps women

One of the most memorable features of the production has been the growing Christmas tree. At first it was made of huge accordian-cut paper, but in New

York State Theater it was one solid piece, the tip of which appeared to be the whole in the Stahlbaum's living room. The production followed E. T. A. Hoffmann's story "The Nutcracker and the Mouse King," and evoked two contrasting responses. The public was enchanted and critics were divided on whether or not Balanchine was betraying the avant-garde audience, which had come to cherish the lean, spare, practice costume ballets. The truth was that he was creating a repertoire for a total audience. Three years later he choreographed *Agon!*

During the life of the ballet, Balanchine has constantly altered details of the staging, especially in the first act. There the number of mice have bounced up and down, bits of stage business have been altered, and the caps were slowly but surely removed from the little "boy" guests at the party. At the time they were played by little girls since there were insufficient numbers of male students in the school. It is a small barometer of the growing popularity of ballet that these roles are all now filled by real little boys.

Bonbonnière was retitled "Mother Ginger and Her Polichinelles" and she stomps happily on stilts under her huge panniered skirt. Coffee was rechoreographed as a solo for a harem dancer, and no one who ever saw the voluptuous Gloria Govrin has ever been able to forget her impact.

A Midsummer Night's Dream
Choreography: Balanchine
Music: Mendelssohn, overture and incidental music to "A Midsummer Night's Dream," overtures to "Athalie," "The Fair Melusine," "The First Walpurgis Night," and "Son and Stranger," and Symphony no. 9 for Strings.
Costumes: Karinska
Decor and lighting: David Hays assisted by Peter Harvey
Premiere: January 17, 1962, New York City Center of Music and Drama, New York City Ballet
Cast:
Act I

Butterflies	Suki Schorer, four corps women, eight children
Puck	Arthur Mitchell
Helena	Jillana
Oberon	Edward Villella
Titania	Melissa Hayden
Her Cavalier	Conrad Ludlow
Bottom	Roland Vazquez
His companions	Six corps men
Theseus	Francisco Moncion
His courtiers	Four corps men
Hermia	Patricia McBride
Lysander	Nicholas Magallanes

Demetrius	Bill Carter
Titania's retinue	Twelve corps women
Oberon's retinue	Thirteen children
Hippolyta	Gloria Govrin
Her hounds	Six corps women
Act II	
Courtiers	Eighteen corps women and eight men
Divertissement	Violette Verdy, Conrad Ludlow, and six corps couples

The famous "Wedding March" opens the second act and correctly pairs off all the lovers. With that the last few ends of the plot are tidied up to clear the stage for dancing without plot entanglements. The humor of Act I is nowhere seen in Act II, which is serene since all conflicts have been resolved. After the ballet was restaged for New York Stage Theater, a filmed version of it was made in 1966. The role of Puck was one of the finest created by Arthur Mitchell during his years as a principal dancer with the company.

Don Quixote
Choreography: Balanchine
Music: Nicholas Nabokov
Costumes, decor, lighting: Esteban Francés, assisted by Peter Harvey
Premiere: May 28, 1965, New York State Theater, New York City Ballet

Cast:

Don Quixote	Richard Rapp
Dulcinea	Suzanne Farrell
Sancho Panza	Deni Lamont
Duke	Nicholas Magallanes
Dutchess	Jillana
Merlin	Francisco Moncion
Divertissements	
Danza Della Caccia	Patricia Neary, Conrad Ludlow, Kent Stowell
Pas de deux Mauresque	Suki Shorer, John Prinz
Courante Sicilienne	Sara Leland, Kay Mazzo, Carol Sumner, Earle Sieveling
Rigaudon Flamenco	Gloria Govrin, Arthur Mitchell
Ritornel	Patricia McBride and female child
Pas d'Action	
Knight of the Silver Moon	Conrad Ludlow
Maidens	Mimi Paul, Marnee Morris, and sixteen corps women
Cavaliers	Anthony Blum, Frank Ohman
Night Spirit	Gloria Govrin
Slaves, guards, townspeople, palace guards, ladies and gentlemen in waiting	

The most convincing portrayal of the Don was made by Balanchine on selected occasions. In these performances the ballet hung together through the intensity of his presence. At other times there were longeurs. He himself never seemed satisfied with the ballet, and each season that it was presented for a decade, he made changes, principally in Act. I.

Harlequinade
Choreography: Balanchine
Music: Ricardo Drigo, "Les Millions d'Arlequin"
Costumes, decor, lighting: Rouben Ter-Arutunian
Premiere: February 4, 1965, New York State Theater, New York City Ballet
Cast:

Harlequin	Edward Villella
Columbine	Patricia McBride
Pierrot	Deni Lamont
Pierette	Suki Schorer
Cassandre	Michael Arshansky
Léandre	Shaun O'Brien
Les Scaramouches	Four corps couples
Les Sbires	Three corps men
La Patrouille	Five corps men
Alouettes	Carol Sumner and eight corps women
Les Petits Harlequins	Eight children

The New York City Opera had commissioned sets for a production of La Cenerentola, which it was suggested would be suitable for a ballet. The sets were borrowed and adapted, costumes designed, and the company had its first new full evening ballet suitable for its new home. It wasn't quite a full evening until 1973, when Balanchine added a tarantella in Act I, a polonaise in Act II, and lengthened various other sequences to use the entire Drigo score. Twenty-four additional children were added to the cast as well as a dozen corps couples. McBride and Villella were unforgettable.

Coppélia
Choreography: Balanchine and Alexandra Danilova after Marius Petipa
Music: Delibes
Libretto: Charles Nuitter and Arthur Saint-Leon, based on E. T. A. Hoffmann's story "Der Sandmann."
Costumes and decor: Rouben Ter-Arutunian
Lighting: Ronald Bates
Premiere: July 17, 1974, Saratoga Performing Arts Center, Saratoga Springs, N.Y., New York City Ballet

Cast:

Swanilda	Patricia McBride
Frantz	Helgi Tomasson
Dr. Coppelius	Shaun O'Brien
Swanilda's friends	Eight corps women
Villagers	Eight corps couples
Mayor	Michael Arshansky
Waltz of the Golden Hours	Marnee Morris and twenty-four female children
Dawn	Merrill Ashley
Prayer	Christine Redpath
Spinner	Susan Hendl
Discord and War	Colleen Neary, Robert Weiss, and eight corps couples

In the "Peace" pas de deux that concludes the ballet, Balanchine retained elements of his Sylvia pas de deux done years earlier for Maria Tallchief and André Eglevsky. The ballet as originally performed had fish-scale gold costumes for the corps of twenty-four little girls, but was changed to pink satin for presentation at New York State Theater; the title of the variation wasn't changed to the "Waltz of the Pink Hours." The ballet was later telecast as part of Channel Thirteen's "Live from Lincoln Center" series.

Chapter 8.

Le Tombeau de Couperin
Choreography: Balanchine
Music: Ravel, "Le Tombeau de Couperin," prelude, forlane, rigaudon, and minuet
Costumes: Balanchine
Lighting: Ronald Bates
Premiere: May 29, 1975, New York State Theater, New York City Ballet

Cast:

Left Quadrille	Judith Fugate, Jean-Pierre Frolich, Wilhelmina Frankfurt, Victor Castelli, Mueiel Aasen, Francis Sackett, Susan Hendl, David Richardson
Right Quadrille	Marjorie Spohn, Hermes Conde, Delia Peters, Richard Hoskinson, Susan Pilarre, Richard Dryden, Carol Sumner, Laurence Matthews

Of all the ballets presented throughout the course of the Hommage à Ravel Festival, this one quite clearly stood apart for its structural unity and fresh design. It remains a crowning testimony to Balanchine's interest in animating the corps. Even though there were three solo-level dancers included in the original casting, they were not singled out for special variations.

La Valse
Choreography: Balanchine
Music: Ravel, "Valses Nobles et Sentimentales" and "La Valse"
Costumes: Karinska
Lighting: Jean Rosenthal
Premiere: February 20, 1951, New York City Center of Music and Drama, New York City Ballet

Cast:
First Waltz	Overture
Second Waltz	Vida Brown, Edwina Fontaine, Jillana
Third Waltz	Patricia Wilde, Frank Hobi
Fourth Waltz	Yvonne Mounsey, Michael Maule
Fifth Waltz	Diana Adams, Herbert Bliss
Sixth Waltz	Diana Adams
Seventh Waltz	Herbert Bliss, Vida Brown, Edwina Fontaine, Jillana
Eighth Waltz	Tanaquil LeClercq, Nicholas Magallanes
La Valse	Tanaquil LeClercq, Nicholas Magallanes, Francisco Moncion, sixteen corps women, and nine corps men.

The brooding undercurrent of Ravel's music in *La Valse* could almost be taken for a lament over post-World War I Europe. That war shattered the longest peace that Europe had ever experienced, 1870–1914, and in the process destroyed the web of social values that had held it together. The dissolution of the waltz, the dance most characteristic of the period, was a fitting epitaph for the era.

Vienna Waltzes
Choreography: Balanchine
Music: Johann Strauss, Jr., "Tales from the Vienna Woods," "Voices of Spring," "Explosions Polka"; Franz Lehar, "Gold and Silver Waltz"; Richard Strauss, First waltz sequence from "Der Rosenkavalier"
Costumes: Karinska
Decor: Rouben Ter-Arutunian
Lighting: Ronald Bates
Premiere: June 23, 1977, New York State Theater, New York City Ballet

Cast:
Woods	Karin von Aroldingen, Sean Lavery, ten corps couples
Spring	Patricia McBride, Helgi Tomasson, eight corps women
Polka	Sara Leland, Bart Cook, three corps couples
Silver	Kay Mazzo, Peter Martins, eight corps couples
Rosenkavalier	Suzanne Farrell, Jorge Donn, and ensemble

The popularity of the ballet took the company by surprise, but merely demonstrated once again the incredible range of Balanchine.

Duo Concertant
Choreography: Balanchine
Music: Stravinsky, Duo concertant for violin and piano
Costumes: Balanchine
Lighting: Ronald Bates
Premiere: June 22, 1972, New York State Theater, New York City Ballet

Cast:

Dancers	Kay Mazzo, Peter Martins
Musicians	Lamar Alsop, violin; Gordon Boelzner, piano

The utter economy of the production proclaimed the work of a mature master in complete control of every facet of his craft. Mazzo's reserve and chaste modesty remain indelibly in memory.

Stravinsky Violin Concerto
Choreography: Balanchine
Music: Stravinsky
Costumes: Balanchine
Lighting: Ronald Bates
Premiere: June 18, 1972, New York State Theater, New York City Ballet

Cast:

Karin von Aroldingen and Jean-Pierre Bonnefous, Kay Mazzo and Peter Martins, eight corps women and eight corps men

Seeing the *Symphony in Three Movements* and this ballet on the same evening back to back was almost too much to comprehend. The coupling, though demanding on both viewers and performers alike, certainly set the triumphant tone for the entire festival.

Index

About the Author

Don McDonagh has written five books on dance, including *How To Enjoy Ballet, The Complete Guide to Modern Dance,* and *Martha Graham: A Biography.*

He is the dance critic of *Commonweal* and a contributor to *Les Saisons de la Danse.* He has written criticism and articles for the *New Republic,* the *Hudson Review, Film Culture, Dance and Dancers,* and *Ballet Review.* For eleven years he was a dance critic for the *New York Times,* and is the editor of Twayne's Dance Series.